August 11. 1777

while your Country is engaged

tract your Attention, more

Time, and as the Future Cir

cumstry, may require other Wars,

and Negotiations, Similar to

Agitations, I wish to turn

Such Studies, as will afford

Instruction and Improvement

be allotted you to act

The Founding Fathers

Engraving after an 1815 portrait by Gilbert Stuart
in the collection of the National Gallery of Art, Washington, D.C.

The Founding Fathers

JOHN ADAMS

A Biography in His Own Words

VOLUME 1

Edited by

JAMES BISHOP PEABODY

With an introduction by

L. H. BUTTERFIELD

Editor in Chief, *The Adams Papers*

JOAN PATERSON KERR

Picture Editor

NEWSWEEK

New York

John Adams, A Biography in His Own Words,
has been produced by the Newsweek Book Division:

Joseph L. Gardner, Editor

Janet Czarnetzki, Art Director

Thomas Froncek, Assistant Editor

Susan Storer, Picture Researcher

S. Arthur Dembner, Publisher

This book is based on *The Adams Papers*—
principally the *Diary and Autobiography of John Adams* (4 volumes, 1961)
and *Adams Family Correspondence* (4 volumes published as of 1973)—
edited by L. H. Butterfield and others,
published by The Belknap Press of Harvard University Press,
and copyright by the Massachusetts Historical Society.
The texts of all documents in this edition from the Adams Papers
have been supplied by Mr. Butterfield.
Permission to reproduce excerpts has been granted through the courtesy
of The Belknap Press of Harvard University Press and
of the owner of the Adams Papers, the Massachusetts Historical Society.
Other sources are acknowledged on page 409.

ISBN: Clothbound Edition 0-88225-039-6; ISBN: Deluxe Edition 0-88225-040-X
Library of Congress Catalog Card Number 72-92141
Copyright © 1973 by Newsweek, Inc.
All rights reserved. Printed and bound in the United States of America.
Endpapers: John Adams to John Quincy Adams, August 11, 1777; THE ADAMS PAPERS

Contents

Introduction

by L. H. Butterfield
Editor in Chief, The Adams Papers
Massachusetts Historical Society

Among all the founders of the American Republic in the first rank of importance, John Adams enjoyed the fewest moments of popularity during his lifetime and, until recently, has had the least public attention and acclaim. Except by sufferance of being second on the roll of Presidents, his has never been a household name in the United States. A tally would show far fewer towns, counties, schools, mountains, and the like named for him than for Franklin, Washington, Jefferson, or perhaps some others. Almost any page of the present biography of John Adams in his own words will show that he is one of the most irresistibly quotable of writers; and yet for a century and more after his death, the standard books of quotations either left him out or gave him the scantiest sort of treatment. They do only a little better today, but the trend is upward.

The twenty-five years that followed Adams's retirement from public office by the American electorate in 1801 salved his wounded feelings and reconciled him, if not to obscurity, at least to a subordinate pinnacle of fame. "Mausoleums, statues, monuments will never be erected to me," Adams wrote in 1809 to a friend who also had been reading John Marshall's massive and pietistic *Life of Washington.* "I wish them not. Panegyrical romances will never be written, nor flattering orations spoken to transmit me to posterity in brilliant colors." So it would surprise Adams to find that in the 1970s his reputation never stood higher. One could wish for his comments upon learning that a definitive edition of his papers is in progress, that biographers and students of all aspects of his career and thought are busier and more numerous than ever, and that he is the leading character—and a highly attractive one—in a musical play, *1776,* that ran for years on Broadway, has been performed with great success elsewhere, and is now a popular film.

This contrast between underestimation and long neglect on the one hand and present heightened interest, esteem, and even affection on the other, surely needs explanation, but only some hints toward it can be offered here.

In somewhat overcharged language, Benjamin Franklin—a patient man whose patience Adams often tried—gave an important hint when he said of his colleague: "I am persuaded . . . that [Mr. Adams] means well for his country, is always an honest man, often a wise one, but sometimes and in some things absolutely out of his senses." To Franklin there were two John Adamses, and so it seemed to many others at the time. Adams's personal probity, his devotion to his country, his learning, his industry, and his courage were beyond dispute. But so were his independence, his insistence on acting on his own judgment, no matter what the cost to his associates as well as to his adversaries. "He was *terribly* open, earnest, and direct," said Theodore Parker in one of the few warm tributes paid to Adams during the nineteenth century, "and could not keep his mouth shut." These are qualities quite opposite to those essential to diplomatic finesse, and they can easily destroy social harmony. They led Adams into indiscretions and sometimes serious quarrels, and they caused many of his contemporaries to distrust and dislike him more than they esteemed and respected him. But it is noteworthy that those who knew him most intimately liked and trusted him most unreservedly. Jefferson wrote of him to Madison in 1787: "He is as disinterested as the Being who made him.... He is so amiable that I pronounce you will love him if you ever become acquainted with him." Madison, however, was among those in the Continental Congress during Adams's foreign missions who felt least confidence in his judgment. Fifty years after the crisis in Congress over Adams's exclusive peace mission, which Madison had voted to revoke, Madison furnished an estimate that conceded Adams's patriotism but condemned "the fervors and flights originating in his moral temperament." He meant, of course, his impulsiveness, stubbornness, vanity, and self-righteousness — all traits that Adams admitted he possessed, though he did not think they were all, or always, faults.

If, then, those who knew him best esteemed him most during his lifetime, it is natural to suppose that those who knew, or know, his writings best would think most highly of him. This was true once and is again true today. But just as there were two sides of John Adams the man, and many then knew only one of them, so there was John Adams the writer known by the general public and a very different writer known to his family and friendly correspondents. As a general proposition, we may say that the more we have been able to read of what Adams wrote for private rather than public consumption, the more he has won our hearts and minds. So that the story of his reputation is in good part the story of the availability of his papers and especially of those he did not write for publication.

Allowing for some exceptions — for example, his early newspaper tracts, "A Dissertation on the Canon and the Feudal Law" of 1765, and some brilliant but dispersed passages in his late letters to the *Boston Patriot* — Adams's public writings are marked by an uninviting dryness that only the student of old political disputes will willingly labor through. Though the commander, as Benjamin Rush once said, of the very "artillery of style," Adams seemed to feel, when he held high national office, that he had to get up on stilts to address his countrymen. The result is that scarcely a one of his presidential papers, invariably composed in pompous Ciceronian periods, is memorable or — one is almost inclined to say — even characteristic. Still another serious fault is displayed by the most elaborate literary work that Adams ever undertook, his *A Defence of the Constitutions of Government of the United States of America,* the writing of which occupied much of his last several years abroad and which was issued in three ponderous volumes in 1787–88. The *Defence* contains redeeming flashes of wit and eloquence that make one think of the *other* John Adams, but it is entirely formless. Once described as "a morbid anatomy of a hundred dead republics," it consists mostly of great indigestible chunks from earlier political commentators' and historians' books to prove Adams's thesis that "There is danger from all men" who enjoy power, and the greatest danger from those who enjoy the greatest power. Not an original idea to be sure, but one worth keeping in mind today as well as yesterday.

Thus, in sketchiest outline, the record stood at the death of John Adams. His son John Quincy Adams was too absorbed in politics until he died at his post of duty in Congress to undertake a proper edition of his father's writings, and the task devolved on John Quincy's son, Charles Francis Adams, who found in historical editing his earliest and most congenial vocation. Charles Francis spent years in sorting and copying the great accumulation of his grandparents' papers. His first publication was a small collection of Abigail Adams's letters (1840). This he followed with a matching collection of John Adams's letters to Abigail (1841). In spite of the editor's trepidation about invading the privacy of a remarkable marital relationship, these editions were successful beyond all his hopes. (They were, after all, the very first of their kind dating from the Revolution.) Abigail's letters were reprinted again and again, quite overshadowing her husband's, but Adams's letters did at least show a man in the round, not a mere engraved image of a self-important statesman who had succeeded George Washington for a single term. Though but a taste, it was a taste of the real John Adams in all his moods, from humorous to heroic, sometimes within the bounds of a single letter.

The family editor knew his task was but just begun. He was to devote a decade or more to selecting and annotating *The Works of John Adams,* preceded by a volume-length biography, the whole appearing in ten volumes from 1850 to 1856. By all odds the best-edited documentary work of its period, the *Works* nevertheless had serious shortcomings. Bound in black "as if for mourning" (as Zoltán Haraszti has said), it has something of the air of the mausoleum that John Adams neither expected nor wanted. Charles Francis had the good sense and courage to draw largely on his grandfather's diary, but he interwove it confusingly with the much later *Autobiography,* and by placing them in the second and third volumes without specific spine titles hid them from all but the most pertinacious seekers. Nor would any seekers find any language or matter offensive to Victorian taste, which was a good deal blander than that of John Adams's own generation. The rest of the edition is organized by classes of material, running through numerous chronologies and almost guaranteeing that the reader will not find what he is looking for without a diligent search. The elephantine *Defence* occupies the better part of three volumes. Official letters and dispatches, messages, and addresses fill nearly three more, with the result that Adams's magnificent "general correspondence" is crowded into the last volume and a half of text and constitutes, as the editor apologetically admitted, a mere tithe of what deserved publication.

That, however, was that. John Adams's manuscripts were bundled away and seldom examined again even by members of the family in the century that followed. Though occasional groups of his letters turned up from other sources and were published in the journals of historical societies or privately issued in small editions, little further scholarly work was done on John Adams for want of fresh materials. Essays and appraisals of course appeared, but no biography of permanent value was published between that of Charles Francis Adams and Gilbert Chinard's *Honest John Adams* (1933). Chinard's work, by drawing on both the old materials and such new sources as had by then come to light, presented a strikingly sympathetic and incisive portrait. The first anthology of its kind, doubly welcome because judiciously selected and annotated, was Adrienne Koch's and William Peden's *Selected Writings of John and John Quincy Adams* (1946). John Adams first reached the best-seller lists in 1950 with Catherine Drinker Bowen's *John Adams and the American Revolution.* This beguiling book, which actually ends on the night of July 4, 1776, according to one reviewer, brings the reader "to know, comprehend, and like John Adams as probably nobody has since Abigail." This is a pardonable exaggeration. The point is that Mrs. Bowen's book, though it draws freely on the author's imagination in episodes for which documentation does not exist or was not accessible to her, signaled a striking upturn in John Adams's reputation as an American patriot and in his standing in the hearts of his countrymen.

Soon afterward a work of a very different and more durable sort appeared in Zoltán Haraszti's *John Adams and the Prophets of Progress* (1952). No other book quite like this one exists, but that is because no other man was quite like John Adams. The large remains (some 3,000 volumes) of his personal library are held by the Boston Public Library. When interested in a book—and his interest tended to be keenest when he disagreed with the author—Adams habitually and copiously answered back in the margins and the flyleaves of the volume he was reading. *John Adams and the Prophets of Progress* is a collection of what amount to lively dialogues between author and reader, drawn from books relating primarily to political history and theory during the Age of Enlightenment. In this form of intellectual cut-and-thrust, Adams excelled. His ripostes, written for nobody but himself, sparkle with wit, sarcasm, and insights into the behavior of men as individuals and social beings that we would be ever so much poorer without. Thus this volume too helped upgrade a President usually thought of as simply the one who came between Washington and Jefferson.

The great body of John Adams's papers had meanwhile slumbered on, almost undisturbed. They had been well cared for by successive family custodians and in 1905, along with the papers of the other Adams statesmen, were placed beyond risk of plundering, sale, or dispersal by a formal transfer of their ownership to the Adams Manuscript Trust. A typical Boston expedient, the Trust was established to run for fifty years, and it designedly deferred the thorny question of the ultimate disposition of the family archives for at least another generation. (For their physical protection the papers had already been placed in a double-locked room in the new building of the Massachusetts Historical Society.) There were several trustees, who had the power to fill vacancies, but in 1951, when Henry Adams of Concord (nephew and namesake of the historian) died, only one trustee survived. This was Charles Francis Adams, banker, yachtsman, and sometime Secretary of the Navy, who promptly appointed as trustees two much younger men who bore the historic names of Thomas Boylston Adams and John Quincy Adams.

Unlike most of their predecessors, neither of the two new trustees nursed expectations of working with the papers as editors or historians, and now that the Trust was soon due to expire, they called on representatives of the historical profession for advice. The advice given, and promptly accepted, was to arrange and issue the entire corpus on microfilm for purchase by research libraries for the use of scholars everywhere. The *Adams Papers Microfilms* were published in four installments (608 reels) by the Massachusetts Historical Society between 1954 and 1959. By unrestricted gift of the trustees, the papers themselves passed into the ownership of the Society forever in 1956.

The opening of the Adams manuscripts was news of such consequence in the learned world that it caused a stir among scholarly publishers and in the world of journalism as well. In 1954 a simple tripartite agreement was worked out among the Society, as prospective owner and as editorial sponsor; Harvard University Press, as prospective publisher over its Belknap Press imprint; and Time Inc., on behalf of *Life* magazine, which supported the costs of editorial work for ten years by purchase of advance serial rights to the edition.

After the manner of Adamses, the family had discharged its trust well. It then became the responsibility of the Editor in Chief to see that the expectations of all the parties were fulfilled. He arrived in Boston at the end of 1954, and the work has been going on continuously ever since. The first published fruits of the enterprise were the *Diary and Autobiography of John Adams* (4 vols., 1961), which had the distinctions, first, of being accepted as a gift at a *Washington Post* book luncheon by President Kennedy, who was not unmindful in his remarks of the contrasts and parallels between the Adams and the Kennedy families, and second, of being reviewed by Mr. Kennedy in the *American Historical Review.* Through early 1973 eighteen volumes of *The Adams Papers* will have been published, and others are in the press. Not all of these are devoted to John Adams, but they include three volumes of his *Legal Papers*; his *Earliest Diary*, which had been lost from sight for two centuries; four volumes of *Adams Family Correspondence, 1761–1782*, in which John Adams plays a leading role; and a volume devoted to *Portraits of John and Abigail Adams.* In preparation are the earliest volumes of his *General Correspondence and Other Papers*, the first amplification and revision of his *Works* as issued almost a century and a quarter ago.

The publication and circulation of the family manuscripts on film and the appearance of annotated texts in the Belknap Press edition (followed at intervals by paperback reprints issued by Atheneum Publishers) have, as was to be expected, stimulated investigation of every aspect of John Adams's life and mind. Not since he was President has Adams been so lively a subject for debate; never before has the sprawling mass of his tracts and treatises and the thousands of personal letters and diplomatic dispatches been so scrutinized to disclose and assess his contributions to politics and to political thought in its widest reaches. For him, these reaches were very wide indeed. The "divine science of politics" he called it; and all his life he wondered why more of the best minds in the past and currently did not devote themselves to the study of men in society in the same scientific spirit that so many studied, say, anatomy or the phenomena of nature. For did not men's happiness depend basically on how to organize themselves so that they could pursue their own ends with the least exploitation of other men? And did not this divine science accordingly embrace not just political philosophy, law in all its branches, history, and economics, but also psychology, sociology, and anthropology? These latter terms had not yet even been coined, and as fields of study they scarcely existed. Yet Adams was fascinated by them, annotating furiously as he read forgotten treatises and the latest controversial pamphlets, drawing something from all of them in his endless effort to find answers to the searching questions he was always asking, from youth to his last days as a nonagenarian.

Yet in the end Adams's greatness as a thinker and as a writer owes more to his own powers of observation than to what he read in others' books. He was, above all, a relentlessly keen and candid observer of himself. Beginning with the merest jottings in his earliest diary entries and in his youthful correspondence with friends, he shows how strongly impelled he was to excel in some field of worthy endeavor. He chose the law because the good lawyer, especially if he moves into public service, must concern himself with "the preservation of the health and properties, lives and tranquility, morals and liberties of millions of the human species." But, he kept asking himself, did he possess the "genius" to fill so elevated a role? Not according to the signs he frequently saw and faithfully recorded of backsliding from his appointed regimen of study. He spent far too much time, too many whole days, "gaping and gazing," "wandering in the woods," "dreaming away" the afternoon, reading Ovid to a neighbor's wife, gathering wood for a fire so that he could study comfortably, or just "smoaking." Yet he progressed in his studies and was soon being spoken of as one of the most learned young barristers in Boston. This brought him well-to-do clients, got him elected to town offices, then to the Great and General Court, and in 1774 to the Massachusetts delegation to the First Continental Congress.

At this stage he could well conclude that ambition pays, though he remained deeply diffident of his powers among such an assembly of men from the whole "Continent." Earlier, then, and throughout his long career, he was to find that ambition, "this passion for superiority," "vanity"—call it by whatever name one liked—was the strongest motive force in human behavior, ever present but infinitely ambiguous in its good or evil effects. He knew this because he was forever analyzing its effects upon himself and his own behavior—and constantly recording them in the wonderfully unselfconscious way that is the greatest gift of a diarist or letter-writer. From none of his great colleagues in the Revolutionary era do we have anything to match this revelation of a man's inner self. Franklin in his *Autobiography* wrote charmingly about his early life and portions of his later life, but he wrote from memory and selectively and with all the detachment, it usually seems, that a novelist writes about a character he has created. Washington, the least introspective of men, kept a diary valuable exclusively for information on people, places, and events ("Where & how my time is Spent," he often heads a new year's entries). Jefferson, most self-disciplined of men, kept no diary, wrote only a fragmentary set of memoranda instead of a true autobiography, and, though the greatest letter-writer of his age in America, was a master at concealing his real feelings. Only his most intimate correspondents learned to read Jefferson's inner thoughts between the lines of his letters.

Thus John Adams—as the present selection of his autobiographical writings by James Bishop Peabody will, I am convinced, readily prove to most readers—emerges not only as one of the indispensable guides to what happened during the birth and early years of the United States of America, but also as one of the most valuable guides to understanding humanity with all its strengths and frailties. The reader of John Adams, like the reader of Pepys or Montaigne, is bound to learn much about himself as well.

EDITORIAL NOTE

Most of the Adams writings reprinted in this biography have been excerpted from the longer original documents in the Massachusetts Historical Society which are being published in their entirety by The Belknap Press of Harvard University Press. Omissions at the beginning or ending of a document are indicated by ellipses only if the extract begins or ends in the middle of a sentence; omissions within a quoted passage are also indicated by ellipses. The quotations from John Adams's *Diary* are highly selective; the omission of entries between quoted passages is not indicated. Some passages of Adams's *Autobiography* have been rearranged for clarity. Original spellings of all documents have been retained; editorial insertions are set within square brackets.

Chronology of Adams and His Times

John Adams born at Braintree (now Quincy), Mass., October 30 (October 19, Old Style)	1735	
	1740	King George's War, 1740–48
Enters Harvard College	1751	
	1754	French and Indian War, 1754–63
Graduates A.B.; becomes Worcester schoolmaster	1755	
Begins legal studies	1756	
Admitted to bar, practices in Braintree	1758	
	1760	Reign of George III, 1760–1820
Records court arguments on writs of assistance	1761	
Begins fourteen years of traveling the court circuit from Maine to Cape Cod	1762	
Begins newspaper writing under the name "Humphrey Ploughjogger"	1763	
Marries Abigail Smith; to the marriage are born (1765–72) two daughters and three sons	1764	Sugar Act; committees of correspondence formed to protest taxation without representation; nonimportation
Assumes active political role, opposing Stamp Act, urging reopening of courts, and asserting American rights	1765	Stamp Act; Sons of Liberty organized
	1766	Stamp Act repealed
	1767	Townshend Acts passed
Wins acquittal for British defendants in Boston Massacre trials; elected to Massachusetts House of Representatives	1770	Boston Massacre; Townshend Acts modified; Lord North's ministry, 1770–82
	1772	Committees of correspondence revived
Election to legislative council rejected by successive governors	1773	Tea Act passed; Boston Tea Party
Elected a Massachusetts delegate to Continental Congress	1774	Coercive Acts; First Continental Congress; reign of Louis XVI of France, 1774–92
In Congress becomes a leader of pro-independence forces and in creation of an American navy; appointed Massachusetts Chief Justice, but does not serve; publishes "Novanglus" papers	1775	Battles of Lexington and Concord, Ticonderoga, and Bunker Hill; Second Continental Congress; Washington becomes Commander in Chief of American forces
Publishes *Thoughts on Government;* becomes a leading advocate of separate state governments and plays a major role in the drafting and adoption of the Declaration of Independence	1776	Tom Paine's *Common Sense* published; British evacuate Boston; Americans retreat from Long Island and New York City
Elected a joint commissioner to France (with Franklin and Arthur Lee), replacing Silas Deane	1777	Battle of Saratoga; Congress adopts Articles of Confederation
	1778	Franco-American alliance
Joint commission dissolved; returns to America, drafts Massachusetts Constitution (adopted 1780); elected minister to negotiate treaties with Britain; sails for France with sons John Quincy and Charles	1779	Spain declares war on Britain
Commissioned by Congress to negotiate treaties and a loan with Dutch	1780	League of Armed Neutrality established; treason of Benedict Arnold

Elected member of joint commission to negotiate peace with Britain	1781	The Netherlands enters war; Articles of Confederation ratified; Battle of Yorktown
Succeeds in gaining Dutch recognition of American sovereignty; signs treaty of amity and commerce with the Netherlands and contract for loan; assists in negotiating preliminary treaty of peace with Britain	1782	Fall of North's ministry; Rockingham and Shelburne ministries, 1782–83
With fellow commissioners, signs definitive peace treaty with Britain at Paris	1783	British evacuate New York; Fox-North coalition ministry; Pitt ministry, 1783–1801
Executes second Dutch loan; elected to commission to negotiate treaties with European and African nations; reunited with wife and daughter; they settle at Auteuil	1784	Diplomatic corps reorganized; John Jay becomes Secretary of Foreign Affairs
On designation as first American minister to Court of St. James's, removes to London	1785	
	1786	Annapolis Convention; Shays's Rebellion
Publishes first two volumes of *A Defence of the Constitutions*; third volume in 1788	1787	Constitutional Convention at Philadelphia
Returns to Braintree after negotiating several European treaties and contracting for two additional Dutch loans	1788	Constitution ratified
Elected Vice President; presides over Senate in 1st to 4th Congresses	1789	Federal government organized in New York; beginning of French Revolution
Begins publishing "Discourses on Davila," leading to breach with Jefferson	1790	Philadelphia temporary U.S. capital, 1790–1800
President of American Academy of Arts and Sciences, 1791–1813	1791	First Bank of the United States; Legislative Assembly rules France, 1791–92
Starts second term as Vice President	1793	Louis XVI beheaded; France at war with Britain; America proclaims neutrality
Elected President; administration marked by continuing crisis in relations with France and by related domestic conflicts	1796	Struggle over ratification of Jay's Treaty; Washington's Farewell Address
Appoints first peace mission to France	1797	XYZ Affair
Signs Alien and Sedition Acts	1798	Second Coalition against France, 1798–99
Appoints second mission to France	1799	Fries's Rebellion; French Consulate, 1799–1804
Following Cabinet defections, attack by Hamilton, and brief residence in the unfinished President's House in Washington, is defeated for re-election	1800	Convention of Mortefontaine ends quasi war between France and the United States; "Federal City" (Washington) becomes the new capital
Names John Marshall Chief Justice of the Supreme Court; retires to Quincy	1801	Presidency of Thomas Jefferson, 1801–9; Tripolitan War, 1801–5
Begins writing *Autobiography*	1802	
	1804	Hamilton killed in duel with Aaron Burr; Napoleon I, Emperor of France, 1804–14
Begins additional memoirs in *Boston Patriot*	1809	Presidency of James Madison, 1809–17
Renews friendship with Jefferson	1812	War with Britain, 1812–15
	1817	Presidency of James Monroe, 1817–25; John Quincy Adams, Secretary of State
Abigail Smith Adams dies, October 28	1818	
Serves as delegate to Massachusetts Convention to revise the state constitution	1820	
Deeds his library to the town of Quincy, provides funds for a new church and academy	1822	
	1825	Presidency of John Quincy Adams, 1825–29
John Adams dies at Quincy, July 4	1826	Thomas Jefferson dies at Monticello, July 4

13

A 1744 engraving of the city of Boston from The American Magazine

Chapter 1

Getting Started

Great Britain was well on the way to building the world's most extensive colonial empire when John Adams was born on October 19, 1735, in the obscure town of Braintree, located in a remote part of that empire called the Massachusetts Bay Colony. The period from 1713 to 1763 was a time of growing prosperity for the American Colonies during which their population increased from 360,000 to 1,600,000. Despite controls imposed by the British Acts of Trade and Navigation at the end of the seventeenth century, the Colonies experienced their greatest growth in commerce and industry. The amenities of eighteenth-century Colonial society—circulating libraries; schools and colleges that provided sound instruction in science, religion, and classical studies; theaters; concert halls; dancing assemblies for the gentle-folk; and finally, taverns where clubs of gentlemen and merchants met to read and discuss the news and opinions printed in the latest London gazettes —were all frequently available in provincial centers of little more than a few thousand persons. Such towns provided more of the means of cultivation than are found today in many American cities of far greater size.

The many imperial wars involving the American Colonies before they won independence resulted not only in Great Britain's mightiest territorial conquests, but also in an accumulation of enthusiastic loyalty to Great Britain in the hearts of the colonials. John Adams was ten years old when he heard stories of the exploits of Sir William Pepperrell, a native-born son of Maine, then part of Massachusetts, who led the expedition, planned and organized by Governor William Shirley of Massachusetts, that in 1745 took the fortress of Louisbourg from the French. Later the young Adams also followed the movements of Lord Loudoun, British Commander in Chief in America, and of Jeffery Amherst and General George Howe. The latter, killed near Ticonderoga in 1758, was the elder brother of General William Howe and Admiral Richard Howe, who were both to play such conspicuous roles in the American Revolution. It was at this time, Adams told a friend many years later, that he had tried unsuccessfully to obtain a captain's commission in His Majesty's service. When Pitt the Elder brought the British Empire to its zenith during the Seven Years' War by taking Canada and India from the French and defeating the Spanish in Cuba and the Philippines, English patriotism and loyalty in the American Colonies reached its peak. James Otis, Jr., at a peace celebration in Boston in 1763, extolled before his countrymen the common interests of the Colonies and the mother country and exhorted them never to pull asunder what God in his providence had united. Meanwhile, a revivalist religious movement called the Great Awakening was stirring up renewed interest in religion throughout the Colonies. In such moving times as these, therefore, it was not surprising that young John Adams, a boy with an ardent temperament, should have been early stimulated to serious study and reflection in order to make sense of his life and his world.

The first influences upon such a boy were the normal ones of locality, family, education, and religion. The eighteenth-century town of Braintree, the home of the Adams family even before its incorporation in May, 1639, consisted of several hundred houses and farms spread out along the coast road between Boston, twelve miles to the north, and Plymouth, twenty-five miles to the south. The locality could boast a colorful history in the early days of the Massachusetts Bay Colony. Those redoubtable Puritans John Endecott and John Winthrop had purged the region in 1630 of one Thomas Morton, self-styled Sachem of Passonagessit, and his gang of vagabond scoundrels for selling rum and firearms to the Indians from their fur-trading post at Mount Wollaston. (The place was referred to in contemporary Puritan records as Dagon's Hill or Merry Mount because of the immoral practices and heathen revelries that took place there around the Maypole.) Governor Winthrop had also seen fit in 1631 to ship back to England the swashbuckling cavalier Sir Christopher Gardiner, who was living in sin with the "known harlot" Mary Grove on the banks of the Neponset River. From John Adams's own zealous efforts as a young lawyer to close taverns and repress pettifoggers in Braintree, it is evident that he did not believe the Puritans had succeeded in ridding the land of undesirable characters.

The house in which John Adams was born still stands today. In the eighteenth century it was situated in old Braintree in a green valley between an abrupt ridge of granite hills to the north and the rugged eminence of Penn's Hill to the south, whose stony soil challenged such resourceful and persistent farmers as John Adams and his father, Deacon John. Lacking those rough granite ledges covered with barberry bushes overlooking the ocean, still so typical of the coast north of Boston, Braintree sloped from its barren and rocky hills to the edge of Boston Bay, whose brackish inlets provided salt marshes on which the farmers harvested eelgrass, mowed the salt hay, and gathered loads of seaweed and mud to add to their manure and compost heaps. John Adams's descriptions of Braintree, from the *Diary* he kept regularly starting at the age of twenty, are those of a practical man with a strong interest in husbandry and an eye for the commercial and industrial potentialities of the place. At Mount Wollaston Farm he saw crops and the signs of trade.

> Aug. 13. Sunday [1769].
> Here is Solitude and Retirement. Still, calm, and serene, cool, tranquil, and peaceful. The cell of the Hermit. Out at one Window, you see Mount Wollaston, the first seat of our Ancestors, and beyond that Stony field Hill, covered over with Corn and fruits.
>
> At the other Window, an Orchard and beyond that the large Marsh called the broad Meadows. From the East Window of the opposite Chamber you see a fine Plain, covered with Corn and beyond that the whole Harbour and all the Islands. From the End Window of the East Chamber, you may see with a prospective Glass, every Ship, Sloop, Schooner, and Brigantine, that comes in, or goes out.

The joys of returning to Braintree after a protracted journey stirred Adams deeply.

> May 1st. 1771. Wednesday.
> Saturday I rode... to Braintree in a Chaise, and when I arrived at my little Retreat, I was quite overcome with Fatigue. Next Morning felt better, and arose early and walked, up Pens Hill and then round, by the Meadow, home.
>
> ...I felt a Joy, I enjoyed a Pleasure, in revisiting my old Haunts, and recollecting my old Meditations among the Rocks and Trees, which was very intense indeed. The rushing Torrent, the purling Stream, the gurgling Rivulet, the dark Thickett, the rugged Ledges and Precipices, are all old Acquaintances of mine. The young Trees, Walnutts and Oaks, which were pruned, and trimmed by me, are grown remarkably. Nay the Pines have grown the better for lopping.

In 1802 John Adams set out to write for his children an account of his life, which he never completed. The care that he took to recount the early history of his family shows the importance he attached to it. Despite his emphasis on the male line, it was through his grandmother, Hannah Bass, that he was descended from John Alden, the last survivor of the Mayflower Compact, and through his mother, Susanna Boylston, that he was exposed to a useful measure of sophistication and urbane refinement in his early youth. We may, nevertheless, discount his preliminary disclaimer of interest on the part of posterity in his writings—a wholly unwarranted expression of humility from a man accustomed to expressing himself openly and decisively on many subjects.

Detail from a water color made by Eliza Susan Quincy showing the house in Braintree (right) in which John Adams was born and (left) the one he lived in after his marriage

Autobiography
Begun Oct. 5. 1802.

As the Lives of Phylosophers, Statesmen or Historians written by them selves have generally been suspected of Vanity, and therefore few People have been able to read them without disgust; there is no reason to expect that any Sketches I may leave of my own Times would be received by the Public with any favour, or read by individuals with much interest. The many great Examples of this practice will not be alledged as a justification, because they were Men of extraordinary Fame, to which I have no pretensions. My Excuse is, that having been the Object of much Misrepresentation, some of my Posterity may probably wish to see in my own hand Writing a proof of the falsehood of that Mass of odious Abuse of my Character, with which News Papers, private Letters and public Pamphlets and Histories have been disgraced for thirty Years. It is not for the Public but for my Children that I commit these Memoirs to writing: and to them and their Posterity I recommend, not the public Course, which the times and the Country in which I was born and the Circumstances which surrounded me compelled me to pursue: but those Moral Sentiments and Sacred Principles, which at all hazards and by every Sacrifice I have endeavoured to preserve through Life.

In a letter to his great friend, Dr. Benjamin Rush of Philadelphia, John Adams summarized the origins of his family.

Quincy [, Mass.] July 19. 1812.

Henry Adams a congregational Dissenter from the Church of England persecuted by the intollerant Spirit of Archbishop Laud, came over to this Country with Eight Sons in the Reign of King Charles the first. One of the Eight returned to England; Seven remained in America and left Families, who by Intermarriages and natural Generation have multiplied like the Sands on the Sea shore or the Starrs in the Milky Way; to such a degree that I know

Book kept by John's father includes entry, Oct. 19, 1735: "Sabath day. John Adams the son of John Adams and Suzanna his wife was born."

not who there is in America to whom I am not related. My Family I believe have cut down more Trees in America than any other Name. What a Family distinction! have I not a right to glory in it? There are however no Parchments to prove it: and the Fact may be disputed. I do not therefore insist upon it.

This Henry and his Son Joseph became original Proprietors of the Town of Braintree incorporated in the Year one thousand six hundred and thirty nine, having previously settled near the foot of Mount Wollaston which was then incorporated with twenty seven thousand Acres of Land in the new Township. This Henry and his son Joseph my Great Grandfather, and his Grandson Joseph my Grandfather, whom I knew, tho he died in 1739, and John my Father who died in 1761 all lie buried in the congregational Church yard in Quincy, half a mile from my house. These were all possessed of landed Estates and all Tradesmen. They wrought on their Farms in Summer and at their Trades in Winter. All reared Families of eight, ten or a dozen Children, except my Father who had but three. All these Children were married and had numerous Families. . . .

You may suppose that We have as steady habits as the pious Folk of Connecticutt when I tell you that of all the Land that was ever owned by any one of the Breed is now owned by some one of the Name and Blood, excepting about ten Acres of miserable barren stony Land, which my Father was compelled to take for a Debt, and which he sold to defray part of the Expense of my Education at Colledge.

The second House that was built by my Ancestor on the original Spot was taken down two or three Years ago at the Age of one hundred and forty Years. The Land remains in two Men direct descendants, of the same Name. I would give twice the Value of it, but I should as soon think of asking them to sell me two Pounds of their Flesh like Shylock. On their first Settlement they erected a Malthouse *pro more Anglicano* [in accordance with the English custom], which converted Barley into Beer for the whole Town and Neighbourhood. Many a time when I was a little Boy have I carried Barley for my Father to be malted by my Great Uncle, Captain and Deacon Peter Adams, who used to pat my Cheeks and pinch my Ears and laugh and play and sport with me as if I were one of his younger schoolmates.

In the month of March last I was called to the House in another part of the Town which was built by my Father, in which he lived and died and from which I buried him; and in the Chamber in which I was born I could not forbear to weep over the remains of a beautiful Child of my son Thomas, that died of the Whooping Cough. Why was I preserved 3/4 of a Century, and that Rose cropped in the Bud? I, almost dead at Top and in all my Limbs, and wholly useless to myself and the world? Great Teacher tell me.

What has preserved this race of Adams's in all their ramifications in such Numbers, health, peace, Comfort and Mediocrity? I believe it is Religion, without which they would have been Rakes, Fops, Sots, Gamblers, starved with hunger, frozen with Cold, scalped by Indians &c. &c. &c., been melted away and disappeared.

John Adams was particularly close to the immediate members of his family, as the following excerpt from his *Autobiography* attests. The uncompleted *Autobiography* is an often-rambling and repetitive document, one that Adams composed intermittently between 1802 and 1807 and never edited for publication. Therefore, it has been necessary to transpose the order of some of the passages included in the present volume.

Autobiography, 1802–7

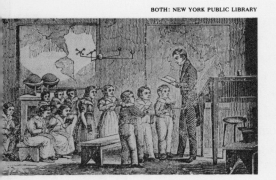

Illustrations from early books show children at work and at play (right).

My Father by his Industry and Enterprize soon became a Person of more Property and Consideration in the Town than his Patron had been. He became a Select Man, a Militia Officer and a Deacon in the Church. He was the honestest Man I ever knew. In Wisdom, Piety, Benevolence and Charity In proportion to his Education and Sphere of Life, I have never seen his Superior....

My Mother was Suzanna Boylston a Daughter of Peter Boylston of Brooklyne, the oldest son of Thomas Boylston a Surgeon and Apothecary who came from London in 1656, and married a Woman by the Name of Gardner of that Town, by whom he had Issue Peter my Grandfather, Zabdiel the Physician, who first introduced into the British Empire the Practice of Inocculation for the Small Pox, Richard, Thomas and Dudley and several Daughters.

My Father had three Sons, John, Peter Boylston, and Elihu. Peter Boylston is still living my Neighbor, my

Friend and beloved Brother. Elihu died at an early Age in 1775. His life was a Sacrifice to the Cause of his Country, having taken in our Army at Cambridge in which he commanded a Company of Volunteers from the Militia, a contagious distemper, which brought him to his Grave leaving three young Children John, Susanna and Elisha.

Deacon Adams could not afford to send more than one son to college. John, the eldest, was selected by his father for this favored opportunity, which, it was hoped, would lead on to a career in the church, as it had for his uncle, the Reverend Joseph Adams of Newington, New Hampshire. John was much happier in Mrs. Belcher's primary school than under the tutelage of the unsympathetic Mr. Joseph Cleverly in the town's secondary school.

Autobiography, 1802–7

As my Parents were both fond of reading, and my father had destined his first born, long before his birth to a public Education I was very early taught to read at home and at a School of Mrs. Belcher the Mother of Deacon Moses Belcher, who lived in the next house on the opposite side of the Road. I shall not consume much paper in relating the Anecdotes of my Youth. I was sent to the public School close by the Stone Church, then kept by Mr. Joseph Cleverly, who died this Year 1802 at the Age of Ninety. Mr. Cleverly was through his whole Life the most indolent Man I ever knew [excepting Mr. Wibirt?] though a tolerable Schollar and a Gentleman. His inattention to his Schollars was such as gave me a disgust to Schools, to books and to study and I spent my time as idle Children do in making and sailing boats and Ships upon the Ponds and Brooks, in making and flying Kites, in driving hoops, playing marbles, playing Quoits, Wrestling, Swimming, Skaiting and above all in shooting, to which Diversion I was addicted to a degree of Ardor which I know not that I ever felt for any other Business, Study or Amusement.

Adams spoke further of his school days in a conversation recorded in 1823 by a Boston relative, Harriet Welsh.

Recollections, 1823

I was about nine or ten years old at that time and soon learn'd the use of the gun and became strong enough to lift it. I used to take it to school and leave it in the entry and the moment it was over went into the field to kill crows and squirrels and I tried to see how many I could kill: at last Mr. Cleverly found this out and gave me a most dreadful scolding and after that I left the gun at an old woman's in the neighborhood. I soon became large enough to go on the marshes to kill wild fowl and to swim and used to beg so hard of my father and mother to let me go that they at last consented and many a cold bois-terous day have I pass'd on the beach without food wait-ing for wild fowl to go over—often *lying* in wait for them on the cold ground—to hide myself from them. I cared not what I did if I could but get away from school, and confess to my shame that I sometimes play'd truant. At last I got to be thirteen years of age and my life had been wasted.

When John Adams was in his mid-twenties, he re-flected in his *Diary* on the deficiencies of his teachers and education and lamented the misspent years of his early youth.

Tuesday, 26 of December [1758]. Mr. Cleverly was chearful, alert, sociable and complai-sant. So much good sense, and knowledge, so much good Humour and Contentment, and so much Poverty, are not to be found, in any other House I believe in this Province. I am amazed that a man of his Inginuity, and sprightliness, can be so shiftless. But what avails a noisy fame, a plenti-ful fortune, and great figure and Consideration in the World?

1760 May 31th. Saturday. Ran over the past Passages of my Life. Little Boats, water mills, wind mills, whirly Giggs, Birds Eggs, Bows and Arrows, Guns, singing, pricking Tunes, Girls &c. Igno-rance of Parents, Masters Cleverly, Marsh, Tutors May-hew &c. By a constant Dissipation among Amuzements, in my Childhood, and by the Ignorance of my Instructors, in the more advanced years of my Youth, my Mind has laid uncultivated so that at 25, I am obliged to study Horace and Homer.—*Proh Dolor!* [Oh grief!]

Deacon John had his own way of dealing with truancy and inattention to study.

Autobiography, 1802–7

My Enthusiasm for Sports and Inattention to Books, alarmed my Father, and he frequently entered into conversation with me upon the Subject. I told him [I did not?] love Books and wished he would lay aside the thoughts of sending me to Colledge. What would you do Child? Be a Farmer. A Farmer? Well I will shew you what it is to be a Farmer. You shall go with me to Penny ferry tomorrow Morning and help me get Thatch. I shall be very glad to go Sir.—Accordingly next morning he took me with him, and with great good humour kept me all day with him at Work. At night at home he said Well John are you satisfied with being a Farmer. Though the Labour had been very hard and very muddy I answered I like it very well Sir. Ay but I dont like it so well: so you shall go to School to day. I went but was not so happy as among the Creek Thatch. My School master neglected to put me into Arithmetick longer than I thought was right, and I resented it. I procured me Cockers [*Cocker's Decimal Arithmetick*] I believe and applyd myself to it at home alone and went through the whole Course, overtook and passed by all the Schollars at School, without any master. I dared not ask my fathers Assistance because he would have disliked my Inattention to my Latin. In this idle Way I passed on till fourteen and upwards, when I said to my Father very seriously I wished he would take me from School and let me go to work upon the Farm. You know said my father I have set my heart upon your Education at Colledge and why will you not comply with my desire. Sir I dont like my Schoolmaster. He is so negligent and so cross that I never can learn any thing under him. If you will be so good as to perswade Mr. Marsh to take me, I will apply myself to my Studies as closely as my nature will admit, and go to Colledge as soon as I can be prepared. Next Morning the first I heard was John I have perswaded Mr. Marsh to take you, and you must go to school there to day. This Mr. Marsh was a Son of our former Minister of that name, who kept a private Boarding School but two doors from my Fathers. To this School I went, where I was kindly treated, and I began to study in Earnest. My Father soon observed the relaxation of my Zeal for my Fowling Piece, and my daily encreasing Attention to my Books. In a little more than a Year Mr. Marsh pronounced me fitted for Colledge.

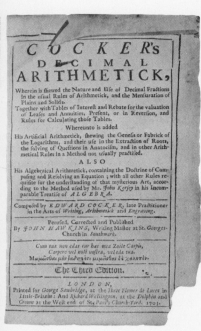

Copy of John's arithmetic book from the notable collection of his books in the Boston Public Library

There was no open entry to college in the eighteenth century, and John Adams had to pass a rigorous entrance examination to be enrolled in Harvard College in 1751, preparation for which was not made easier by conditions unsuited to good study habits. John Adams at a later date noted in his *Diary* the unscholarly customs that prevailed among his friends in Braintree.

Feb. 11. 1759.

I spent one Evening this Week at Billy Belchers. I sat, book in Hand, on one side of the fire, while Dr. Wendell, Billy Belcher and Stephen Cleverly and another young Gentleman sat, in silence, round the Card Table, all the Evening. Two Evenings I spent att Samll. Quincys, in the same manner, Dr. Gardiner, Henry Q., Ned Q., and S. Q. all playing Cards the whole Evening. This is the wise and salutary amuzement, that young Gentlemen take every Evening in this Town, playing Cards, drinking Punch and Wine, Smoaking Tobacco, swearing &c. while 100 of the best Books lie on the shelves, Desks, and Chairs, in the same room. This is not Misspence of Time. This is a wise, a profitable, Improvement of Time. Cards, and Back Gammon, are fashionable Diversions. I'le be curst if any young fellow can study, in this town. What Pleasure can a young Gentleman, who is capable of thinking, take, in playing Cards? It gratifies none of the Senses, nor Sight, Hearing, taste, smell, feeling. It can entertain the Mind only by hushing its Clamours. Cards, Back Gammon are the great antidotes to Reflection, to thinking, that cruel Tyrant within Us. What Learning, or Sense, are we to expect from young Gentlemen, in whom a fondness for Cards, &c. outgrows and choaks the Desire of Knowledge?

House at far right, drawn by Eliza Susan Quincy, was home of Braintree schoolmaster Joseph Marsh, where John Adams prepared for college.

Years later Adams recalled his anxious journey to Cambridge to face his examiners for entrance to Harvard.

Autobiography, 1802–7

In a little more than a Year Mr. Marsh pronounced me fitted for Colledge. On the day appointed at Cambridge for the Examination of Candidates for Admission I mounted my horse and called upon Mr. Marsh, who was to go with me. The Weather was dull and threatened rain. Mr. Marsh said he was unwell and afraid to go out. I must therefore go alone. Thunder struck at this unforeseen disappointment, And terrified at the Thought

One of Adams's earliest bookplates

of introducing myself to such great Men as the President and fellows of a Colledge, I at first resolved to return home: but foreseeing the Grief of my father and apprehending he would not only be offended with me, but my Master too whom I sincerely loved, I arroused my self, and collected Resolution enough to proceed. Although Mr. Marsh had assured me that he had seen one of the Tutors the last Week and had said to him, all that was proper for him to say if he should go to Cambridge; that he was not afraid to trust me to an Examination and was confident I should acquit my self well and be honourably admitted; yet I had not the same confidence in my self, and suffered a very melancholly Journey. Arrived at Cambridge I presented myself according to my directions and underwent the usual Examination by the President Mr. Holyoke and the Tutors Flint, Hancock, Mayhew and Marsh. Mr. Mayhew into whose Class We were to be admitted, presented me a Passage of English to translate into Latin. It was long and casting my Eye over it I found several Words the latin for which did not occur to my memory. Thinking that I must translate it without a dictionary, I was in a great fright and expected to be turned by, an Event that I dreaded above all things. Mr. Mayhew went into his Study and bid me follow him. There Child, said he is a dictionary, there a Grammar, and there Paper, Pen and Ink, and you may take your own time. This was joyfull news to me and I then thought my Admission safe. The Latin was soon made, I was declared Admitted and a Theme given me, to write on in the Vacation. I was as light when I came home as I had been heavy when I went: my Master was well pleased and my parents very happy. I spent the Vacation not very profitably chiefly in reading Magazines and a British Apollo. I went to Colledge at the End of it and took the Chamber assigned me and my place in the Class under Mr. Mayhew.

John Adams's *Autobiography*, as well as his *Diary* entries at college, confirm a particular interest in natural philosophy, which was taught by John Winthrop, Hollis Professor of Mathematics and Natural Philosophy and Fellow of the Royal Society of London.

Autobiography, 1802–7

I soon perceived a growing Curiosity, a Love of Books and

First page of Adams's Diary *begun at "Harvard Colledge June 8th 1753"*

a fondness for Study, which dissipated all my inclination for Sports, and even for the Society of the Ladies. I read forever, but without much method, and with very little Choice. I got my Lessons regularly and performed my recitations without Censure. Mathematicks and natural Phylosophy attracted the most of my Attention, which I have since regretted, because I was destined to a Course of Life, in which these Sciences have been of little Use, and the Classicks would have been of great Importance. I owe to this however perhaps some degree of Patience of Investigation, which I might not otherwise have obtained. Another Advantage ought not to be omitted. It is too near my heart. My Smattering of Mathematicks enabled me afterwards at Auteuil in France to go, with my eldest Son, through a Course of Geometry, Algebra and several Branches of the Sciences, with a degree of pleasure that amply rewarded me for all my time and pains.

20 Wednesday [June, 1753]. At Colledge, a most Charming and Beautifull Scene is this morning displayed. All nature wears a Chearfull garb, after so plentifull a Shower as we were favoured with the Last night, receiving an additionall lustre from the sweet influences of the Sun. — This Day, I (in the religious Phylosopher) read the following experiment, (viz) that the filings of iron, mix'd with sulphur and kneaded to a Dough By the additition of Cold water will in a few hours Become warm, and at last Be set on fire. Which is undoubtedly true, and if so I think that it affords a very probable method of solving the phænomina of subterraneous fires. For it is highly probable that there are abundance of the particles of iron, Sulphur, and water which, (By the flux of water perhaps in the subterraneous Caverns,) may Be Brought together, and then it appears By the precedent experiment, that this effect (viz a fire) will Be produced. At 2 o'Clock heard Mr. Winthrop's lecture in the Hall, in which he was employed in evincing the sphæroidall form of the earth, which he Did, from the vibrations of pendula, the precession of the æquinox, and from the actual mensuration of Degrees at the æquinox and the poles. — After which I extracted the following Hydrostatical Laws from the religious Phylosopher (viz) 1st: if a Body is to be Carried upwards in any liquor, an equall Bulk of said liquor must gravitate or weigh more than such a Body. 2ndly. that in order to

Cause a Body to sink in a liquor, an equal Bulk of said liquor must weigh less than the Body. 3rdly. if you would have the Body, neither to rise or fall But preserve it's place in any part of the liquor, an equal quantity of the said liquor must weigh equally with the Body.

March 8th. [1754]

A Clowdy morning. I am now reading my lord Orrerys letters to his son Concerning Dr. Swift and his writings, which for softness and delicacy of style, accuracy and serenity of sentiment, are absolutely inimitable. Reading also the last volume of Monsieur Rollin's Belles Lettres which are worth their weight in gold. — for his excellent reflections on every remarkable event that occurs in history he informs his readers of the true source of every action and instructs them in the method of forming themselves upon the models of virtue to be met with in History.

19 [March, 1754].

This morning is beyond description, Beautyfull, the Skie bespangled with Clouds which shed a lustre on us by the refraction of the rays of light, together with the healthy and enlivening air, which was purifyed By the thunder, afford most spirited materials for Contemplation. The gaiety of the weather is equally delightfull to the phylosopher, Poet and the man of Pleasure. The Phylosopher finds his passions all Calm, serene, and Pliable so that he finds no Difficulty in subjecting them to the subserviency of his reason, he can now contemplate all the gaudy appearances of nature and like Pythagoras bring Phylosophy down from heaven and make her conversible to men. The Poet thinks this the Best time to Converse with his muse and Consequently gives himself up wholly to her directions. His whole soul is at her disposall and he no more retains the government of himself. While the man of pleasure find such delicacys arising from the objects of sence as are adapted to produce the highest sensations of delight in him.

April 1st. 1754.

Mr. Winthrop began a series of Experimental Phylosophy, and in the 1st place he explained to us the meaning, nature, and excellence of natural phylosophy, which is, (he says) the knowledge of those laws by which all the Bodys, in the universe are restrained, it being evident that not only those great masses of matter the heavenly

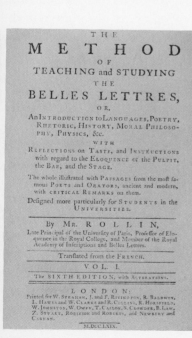

John Adams's own copy of "Monsieur Rollin's Belles Lettres which are worth their weight in gold"

Bodys, but all the minutest combinations of matter in each of them are regulated by the same general laws. For instance it is plain that all the planets observe exactly the same uniform rules in their revolutions round the sun, that every particle of matter observes on the surface of the earth. — As to the usefulness of natural phylosophy, to be convinced of that, it is necessary only to reflect on the state of all the Civilized nations of Europe, compared to many nations, in affrica, of as quick natural parts as Europeans, who live in a manner very little superiour to the Brutes.

But Adams did not spend all his time at Harvard buried in his studies. College had its lighter side, in the form of stories traded about the more colorful professors, such as Henry Flynt. There were also amusing incidents and excursions during the vacations, such as the time — recollected many years later in a letter to his classmate David Sewall — when Adams visited his uncle, the Reverend Joseph Adams of Newington, New Hampshire, in June, 1754. (Montezillo, or Little Hill, from which the letter was dated, was the Italianate name that Adams sometimes gave to his home at Quincy in later years, in whimsical contrast to Jefferson's Monticello, or Lofty Mountain.)

Feb. 11. 1759.

Father Flynt has been very gay and sprightly, this sickness. Coll. Quincy was to see him, a fast day, and was or appeared to be, as he was about taking leave of the old Gentleman, very much affected. The Tears flowed very fast. — I hope Sir says he in [a] Voice of Grief, you will excuse my Passions. — Ay, prithy, says the old Man, I dont care much for you, nor your Passions neither.

F. Morris said to him, "you are going Sir to Abrahams Bosom, but I dont know but I shall reach there first." — "Ay if you are a going there, I dont want to go."

Montezillo [, Mass., December 24, 1821]

I went with a young preacher Ebenezer Adams the son of that uncle up through Chelmsford, to London Derry and a place beyond it called Litchfield if I remember right and from thence down through Kensington to Newington and Portsmouth. Either going or returning we visited Parson Whipple whose lady persecuted me as much as she did afterwards father F[lynt]. The lady had a fine figure and a fair face. At dinner I was very bashful and silent. After dinner Parson W. invited us into another

[room] where he took a pipe himself and offered us pipes. I was an old smoaker and readily took one. The lady very soon came into the room, lifted up her hands and cried out in a masculine voice, I am astonished to see that pretty little boy with a pipe in his mouth smoking that nasty poisoned tobacco. I cant bear the sight. I was as bashful and timorous as a girl, but I resented so much being called a little boy at 15 or 16 years of age and as stout as her husband, that I determined not to be frightened out of my pipe so I continued to puff away. You may well suppose that I bore no very good will to that lady till I afterward became acquainted with the character of Miss Hannah Whipple who afterwards married Dr. Bracket and gave two thousand dollars to the botanical garden [in] Cambridge. The excellences of that daughter very early atoned for all the severity of the mother and I have long since esteemed her an amiable and intelligent woman though sometimes a little too free with her guests.

A view of Harvard College, *from the* Columbian Magazine, *1788*

In another letter written to Sewall in later years, Adams recalled that serious scientific pursuits at Harvard yielded on at least one occasion to more boisterous antics.

Montezillo [, Mass.] 26 November 1821

I spent six weeks at least in Daltons chamber in calculating eclipses in conic sections and algebraic equations and sometimes at midnight we went up on the roof of Old Harvard to view with a tellescope the eclipses of the satellites of Jupiter and gaze at the ring of Saturn. We chose Daltons chamber to avoid the noises in the lower entry chamber which were of great annoyance to my chamber if not to yours. Charles Cushing and my chum and some others made an intolerable racket for though Charles was a very clever fellow and turned out much better than I ever expected he was at college very idle and very obstreperous and I was sometimes not much less so in another way. When Mr. Whitfield preached in Boston I went to Boston to hear him and when I came back, Dalton treated me with some of his exquisite hyson with which his rich father always supplied his only son of which I drank half as many cups as ever drank Dr. Johnson and by the inspiration of that tea I repeated Whitfields sermons, imitating his voice and gestures as well as I could—and I made as much noise two storys high as Charles and his rabble made below.

A solid grounding in Latin and in the elements of Greek at college facilitated John Adams's entry into educated society as well as giving him the greatest pleasure in subsequent years.

Thurdsday [December 21, 1758].

Yesterday and to day I have read loud, Tullius 4 Orations against Cataline. The Sweetness and Grandeur of his sounds, and the Harmony of his Numbers give Pleasure enough to reward the Reading if one understood none of his meaning. Besides I find it, a noble Exercise. It exercises my Lungs, raises my Spirits, opens my Porr[s], quickens the Circulations, and so contributes much to Health.

1760 Aug. 19th.

I began Popes Homer, last Saturday Night was a Week, and last Night, which was Monday night I finished it. Thus I found that in seven days I could have easily read the 6 Volumes, Notes, Preface, Essays, that on Homer, and that on Homers Battles and that on the funeral Games of Homer and Virgil &c. Therefore I will be bound that in 6 months I would conquer him in Greek, and make myself able to translate every Line in him elegantly.

1770. August 19. Sunday.

Gutta cavat lapidem non vi, sed sepe cadendo.... Sic, Homo fit doctus, non vi, sed sepe legendo.

[Not to force does yield the stone,
But falling drops which carve and hone;
And so is man with knowledge filled;
Books, not force, the mind do build.]

Theological controversy stirred up during John Adams's college years by the Great Awakening made him question whether or not he should choose to become a member of the clergy. These doubts were not dispelled while working as a schoolmaster to earn sufficient money to prepare himself for one or another of the learned professions.

Autobiography, 1802–7

Between the Years 1751 when I entered, and 1754 [i.e., 1755] when I left Colledge a Controversy was carried on between Mr. Bryant the Minister of our Parish and some of his People, partly on Account of

Title page of a volume of Plato in Adams's library and signed by him

his Principles which were called Arminian and partly on Account of his Conduct, which was too gay and light if not immoral. Ecclesiastical Councils were called and sat at my Fathers House. Parties and their Accrimonies arose in the Church and Congregation, and Controversies from the Press between Mr. Bryant, Mr. Niles, Mr. Porter, Mr. Bass, concerning the five Points. I read all these Pamphlets and many other Writings on the same Subject and found myself involved in difficulties beyond my Powers of decision. At the same time, I saw such a Spirit of Dogmatism and Bigotry in Clergy and Laity, that if I should be a Priest I must take my side, and pronounce as positively as any of them, or never get a Parish, or getting it must soon leave it. Very strong doubts arose in my mind, whether I was made for a Pulpit in such times, and I began to think of other Professions. I perceived very clearly, as I thought, that the Study of Theology and the pursuit of it as a Profession would involve me in endless Altercations and make my Life miserable, without any prospect of doing any good to my fellow Men.

The last two years of my Residence at Colledge, produced a Clubb of Students, I never knew the History of the first rise of it, who invited me to become one of them. Their plan was to spend their Evenings together, in reading any new publications, or any Poetry or Dramatic Compositions, that might fall in their Way. I was as often requested to read as any other, especially Tragedies, and it was whispered to me and circulated among others that I had some faculty for public Speaking and that I should make a better Lawyer than Divine. This last Idea was easily understood and embraced by me. My Inclination was soon fixed upon the Law: But my Judgment was not so easily determined. There were many difficulties in the Way. Although my Fathers general Expectation was that I should be a Divine, I knew him to be a man of so thoughtful and considerate a turn of mind, to be possessed of so much Candor and moderation, that it would not be difficult to remove any objections he might make to my pursuit of Physick or Law or any other reasonable Course. My Mother although a pious Woman I knew had no partiality for the Life of a Clergyman. But I had Uncles and other relations, full of the most illiberal Prejudices against the

31

Law. I had indeed a proper Affection and veneration for them, but as I was under no Obligation of Gratitude to them, which could give them any colour of Authority to prescribe a course of Life to me, I thought little of their Opinions. Other Obstacles more serious than these presented themselves. A Lawyer must have a Fee, for taking me into his Office. I must be boarded and cloathed for several Years: I had no Money; and my Father having three Sons, had done as much for me, in the Expences of my Education as his Estate and Circumstances could justify and as my Reason or my honor would allow me to ask. I therefore gave out that I would rather take a School, and took my Degree at Colledge undetermined whether I should study Divinity, Law or Physick. In the publick Exercises at Commencement, I was somewhat remarked as a Respondent, and Mr. Maccarty of Worcester who was empowered by the Select Men of that Town to procure them a Latin Master for their Grammar School engaged me to undertake it. About three Weeks after commencement in 1755, when I was not yet twenty Years of Age, a horse was sent me from Worcester and a Man to attend me. We made the Journey about Sixty miles in one day and I entered on my Office.

Although John Adams became a lawyer and not a theologian, the journal entries of 1756, his twenty-first year, show that his religious convictions influenced this decision, as they were to influence other important decisions in his life. These convictions, derived from an earlier and stricter form of Christianity, were brought into reasonable conformity in his own mind with the scientific doctrines of the age. They can be summarized as follows: 1) God is the supreme being who created the universe; 2) God has revealed values in human history by which men should regulate their lives and for which they should be grateful; 3) there is a difference between right and wrong that men are obliged to respect; and 4) each individual should scrutinize his own behavior in order to recognize faults and failures within himself and to try to do better. His thoughts on these important subjects were revealed in three *Diary* entries.

28 [i.e., 29] Saturday [May, 1756].
What is the proper Business of Mankind in this Life? We come into the World naked and destitute of all the Conveniences and necessaries of Life. And if we were not provided for, and nourished by our Parents or others

should inevitably perish as soon as born. We increase in strength of Body and mind by slow and insensible Degrees. 1/3 of our Time is consumed in sleep, and 3/4 of the remainder, is spent in procuring a mere animal sustenance. And if we live to the Age of three score and Ten and then set down to make an estimate in our minds of the Happiness we have enjoyed and the Misery we have suffered, We shall find I am apt to think, that the overballance of Happiness is quite inconsiderable. We shall find that we have been through the greatest Part of our Lives pursuing Shadows, and empty but glittering Phantoms rather than substances. We shall find that we have applied our whole Vigour, all our Faculties, in the Pursuit of Honour, or Wealth, or Learning or some other such delusive Trifle, instead of the real and everlasting Excellences of Piety and Virtue. Habits of Contemplating the Deity and his transcendent Excellences, and correspondent Habits of complacency in and Dependence upon him, Habits of Reverence and Gratitude, to God, and Habits of Love and Compassion to our fellow men and Habits of Temperance, Recollection and self Government will afford us a real and substantial Pleasure. We may then exult in a Consciousness of the Favour of God, and the Prospect of everlasting Felicity.

14 Saturday [August, 1756].

Why am I so unreasonable, as to expect Happiness, and a solid undisturbed Contentment amidst all the Disorders, and the continual Rotations of worldly Affairs? Stability is no where to be found in that Part of the Universe that lies within our observation. The natural and the moral World, are continually changing. The Planets, with all their Appendages, strike out their amazing Circles round the Sun. Upon the Earth, one Day is serene, and clear, no cloud intercepts the kind influence of the Sun, and all Nature seems to flourish and look gay. But these delightfull scenes soon vanish, and are succeeded by the gloom and Darkness of the Night. And before the morning Appears, the Clouds gather, the Winds rise, Lightnings glare, and Thunders bellow through the vast of Heaven. Man is sometimes flushed with Joy and transported with the full Fury of sensual Pleasure, and the next Hour, lies groaning under the bitter Pangs of Disappointments and adverse Fortune. Thus God has told us, by the general Constitution of the World, by the

An eighteenth-century Harvard bookplate, engraved by N. Hurd

Nature of all terrestrial Enjoyments, and by the Constitution of our own Bodies, that This World was not designed for a lasting and a happy State, but rather for a State of moral Discipline, that we might have a fair Opportunity and continual Excitements to labour after a cheerful Resignation to all the Events of Providence, after Habits of Virtue, Self Government, and Piety. And this Temper of mind is in our Power to acquire, and this alone can secure us against all the Adversities of Fortune, against all the Malice of men, against all the Opperations of Nature. A World in Flames, and a whole System tumbling in Ruins to the Center, has nothing terrifying in it to a man whose Security is builded on the adamantine Basis of good Conscience and confirmed Piety. If I could but conform my Life and Conversation to my Speculations, I should be happy. — Have I hardiness enough to contend with omnipotence? Or have I cunning enough to elude infinite Wisdom, or Ingratitude enough to Spurn at infinite Goodness? The Scituation that I am in, and the Advantages that I enjoy, are thought to be the best for me by him who alone is a competent Judge of Fitness and Propriety. Shall I then complain? Oh Madness, Pride, Impiety.

22 Sunday [August, 1756]. The Obligation that is upon us to love God, he says, arises from the Instances of his Love and Goodness to us. He has given us an Existence and a Nature which renders us capable of enjoying Happiness and of suffering Misery. He has given us several senses and has furnished the World around us with a Variety of Objects proper to delight and entertain them. He has hung up in the Heavens over our Heads, and has spread in the Fields of Nature around about us, those glorious Shows and Appearances, by which our Eyes and our Imaginations are so extremely delighted. We are pleased with the Beautyful Appearance of the Flower, we are agreably entertaind with the Prospect of Forrests and Meadows, of verdant Field and mountains coverd with Flocks, we are thrown into a kind of transport and amazement when we behold the amazing concave of Heaven sprinkled and glittering with Starrs. He has also bestowed upon the Vegetable Species a fragrance, that can almost as [agreeably?] entertain our sense of smell. He has so wonderfully constituted the Air that by giving it a par-

First page of a diary started by
Adams after he began teaching in
Worcester and was visiting Braintree

ticular Kind of Vibration, it produces in us as intense sensation of Pleasure as the organs of our Bodies can bear, in all the Varieties of Harmony and Concord. But all the Provision[s] that he has [made?] for the Gratification of our senses, tho very engaging and unmerited Instances of goodness, are much inferior to the Provision, the wonderful Provision that he has made for the gratification of our nobler Powers of Intelligence and Reason. He has given us Reason, to find out the Truth, and the real Design and true End of our Existence, and has made all Endeavours to promote them agreable to our minds, and attended with a conscious pleasure and Complacency. On the Contrary he has made a different Course of Life, a Course of Impiety and Injustice, of Malevolence and Intemperance, appear Shocking and deformed to our first Reflections. And since it was necessary to make us liable to some Infirmities and Distempers of Body, he has plentifully stored the Bowells and the surface of the Earth with Minerals and Vegetables that are proper to defend us from some Deseases and to restore us to health from others. Besides the Powers of our Reason and Invention have enabled us to devize Engines and Instruments to take advantage of the Powers that we find in Nature to avert many Calamities that would other wise befall us, and to procure many Enjoyments and Pleasures that we could not other wise attain. He has connected the greatest Pleasure with the Discovery of Truth and made it our Interest to pursue with Eagerness these intense Pleasures. Have we not the greatest Reason then, yea is it not our indispensible Duty to return our sincere Love and Gratitude to this greatest, kindest and most profuse Benefactor[?] Would it not shew the deepest Baseness and most infamous Ingratitude to despize or to disregard a Being to whose inexhausted Beneficence we are so deeply indebted[?]

Chapter **2**

A Gentleman Lawyer

The young schoolmaster thoroughly enjoyed the congenial atmosphere of Worcester, where he continued to sort out his thoughts, test his beliefs, and form his ambitions. John Adams's earliest surviving correspondence dates from this period, and although his letters reveal a keen interest in public affairs, he was concerned primarily with his choice of profession, his studies and early legal practice in Braintree, and his growing interest in girls. In Worcester the Chandlers and the Putnams provided a well-informed, agreeable company in which Adams could listen to diverse topics of conversation developed by educated persons, and in which he could find an opportunity to test his own opinions. The sensitive young man also had plenty of time to reflect upon his shortcomings in his *Diary* and try to improve himself.

> 4 Wednesday [February, 1756]. A charming warm Day. Dined at Coll. Chandler's with Mr. Pain, Abel Willard and Ebenr. Thayer. Drank Tea at Mr. Paines and supp'd and spent the Eve at Major Chandlers with the same Company, very gaily.
>
> 18 Wednesday [February, 1756]. A charming morning. My Classmate Gardner drank Tea with me. Spent an Hour in the beginning of the evening at Major Gardiners [i.e., Gardiner Chandler's], where it was thought that the design of Christianity was not to make men good Riddle Solvers or good mystery mongers, but good men, good majestrates and good Subjects, good Husbands and good Wives, good Parents and good Children, good masters and good servants. The following Question may be answered some time or other — viz. Where do we find a præcept in the Gospell, requiring Ecclesiastical Synods, Convocations, Councils, Decrees, Creeds, Confessions, Oaths, Subscriptions and whole

Cartloads of other trumpery, that we find Religion incumbered with in these Days?

7 Sunday [March, 1756].

Honesty, Sincerity and openness, I esteem essential marks of a good mind. I am therefore of opinion, that men ought, (after they have examined with unbiassed Judgments, every System of Religion, and chosen one System on their own Authority, for themselves) to avow their Opinions and defend them with boldness.

14 Sunday [March, 1756].

Heard Mr. Maccarty all Day upon Abrahams Faith, in offering up Isaac. Spent the Evening, very Sociably at Mr. Putnams. Several observations concerning Mr. Franklin of Phyladelphia, a prodigious Genius cultivated with prodigious industry.

3 Monday [May, 1756].

A pleasant Day. Spent the Evening and supped at Mr. Maccartys. The Love of Fame naturally betrays a man into several weaknesses and Fopperies that tend very much to diminish his Reputation, and so defeats itself. Vanity I am sensible, is my cardinal Vice and cardinal Folly, and I am in continual Danger, when in Company, of being led an *ignis fatuus* [deceptive] Chase by it, without the strictest Caution and watchfulness over my self.

8 Saturday [May, 1756].

Went a Shooting with Mr. Putnam. Drank Tea with him and his Lady.

12 Wednesday [May, 1756].

Rambled about all Day, gaping and gazing.

13 [i.e., 14]. Friday [May, 1756].

Drank Tea at the Colonels. — Not one new Idea this Week.

14 [i.e., 15]. Saturday [May, 1756].

A lovely Day. Soft vernal Showers. Exercise invigorates, and enlivens all the Faculties of Body and of mind. It arouses our Animal Spirits, it disperses Melancholy. It spreads a gladness and Satisfaction over our minds and qualifies us for every Sort of Buisiness, and every Sort of Pleasure.

Rev. Thaddeus Maccarty

In an early letter written to a college classmate, Adams anticipated the independence of the Colonies and explained his lively interest in politics.

Worcester Oct 12, 1755

The only way to keep us from setting up for ourselves is to disunite us. *Divide et impera* [Divide and rule]. Keep us in distant colonies, and then some great Men in each Colony, desiring the Monarchy of the whole, they will destroy each others influence and keep the Country *in equilibrio* [in balance].

Be not surprised that I am turned Politician. This whole Town is immersed in Politicks. The Interests of Nations and all the *Dira* [terrors] of War, make the subject of every conversation. I sit and hear. And after having been led through a maze, of sage observations I sometimes retire, and by laying things together, form some reflections pleasing to myself. The Produce of one of these Reveries, you have read above. Different employment and different objects, may have drawn your Thought other Ways. I shall think myself happy, if in your turn you communicate your Lucubrations to me.

In his *Diary*, meanwhile, young Adams was recording his reactions to the great events of the day.

22 Thursday [July, 1756].

Fast day. Rose not till 7 o clock. This is the usual Fate of my Resolutions! Wrote the 3 first Chapters of St. James. Wrote in Bolinbroke pretty industriously. Spent the Evening at Mr. Paines. — The Years of my Youth are marked by divine Providence with various and with great Events. The last Year is rendered conspicuous in the memorials of past Ages, by a Series of very remarkable Events, of various Kinds. The Year opened with the Projection of 3 Expeditions, to prevent the further, and remove the present Depredations, and Encroachments of our turbulent french Neighbours. I shall not minute the graduall Steps, advanced by each Army, but only the Issue of each. Braddock the Commander of the Forces, destind against [Fort] Duquesne, and 6 or 700 of his men, were butchered in a manner unexampled in History. All, routed and destroyed without doing the least Injury that we know of, to the Enemy. Johnson, with his Army, was attacked by the Baron Dieskeau, but happily maintaind his Ground and routed the Enemy, taking Dieskeau prisoner. Moncton and Winslow at Nova Scotia, gaind their Point, took the Fortresses and sent of[f] the Inhabitants into these

This view of the main street of Worcester, drawn some years after Adams's stay, shows the "situation" he had found so "pleasant" remained.

Provinces. Boskawen bravely defended our Coast with his Fleet, and made great Havock among the french merchant Ships. All these Actions were performed in a Time of Peace. *Sed paulo majora canamus* [But let us sing a bit of greater things]. God almighty has exerted the Strength of his tremendous Arm and shook one of the finest, richest, and most populous Cities in Europe [Lisbon], into Ruin and Desolation, by an Earthquake. The greatest Part of Europe and the greatest Part of America, has been in violent Convulsions, and admonished the Inhabitants of both, that neither Riches nor Honours, nor the solid Globe itself is a proper Basis, on which to build our hopes of Security. The british Nation has been making very expensive and very formidable Preparations, to Secure its Territories against an Invasion by the French, and to humble the insolent Tempers, and aspiring Prospects of that ambitious and faithless Nation. The gathering of the Clouds, seems to forebode very tempestuous Weather, and none can tell but the Storm will break heavy upon himself in particular. Is it not then the highest Frensy and Distraction to neglect these Expostulations of Providence and continue a Rebellion against that Potentate who alone has Wisdom enough to perceive and Power enough to procure for us the only certain means of Happiness and goodness enough to prompt him to both[?]

Teaching school proved to be a necessary, though only moderately congenial, way of earning money while deciding upon a suitable profession. Nevertheless, it moved Adams to enter in his *Diary* this charming little essay describing the classroom as a miniature commonwealth, with its own distinctive conflicts and personalities.

15 Monday [March, 1756].
I sometimes, in my sprightly moments, consider my self, in my great Chair at School, as some Dictator at the head of a commonwealth. In this little State I can discover all the great Genius's, all the surprizing actions and revolutions of the great World in miniature. I have severall renowned Generalls but 3 feet high, and several deep-projecting Politicians in peticoats. I have others catching and dissecting Flies, accumulating remarkable pebbles, cockle shells &c., with as ardent Curiosity as any Virtuoso in the royal society. Some rattle and Thunder out

A, B, C, with as much Fire and impetuosity, as Alexander fought, and very often sit down and cry as heartily, upon being out spelt, as Cesar did, when at Alexanders sepulchre he recollected that the Macedonian Hero had conquered the World before his Age. At one Table sits Mr. Insipid foppling and fluttering, spinning his whirligig, or playing with his fingers as gaily and wittily as any frenchified coxcomb brandishes his Cane or rattles his snuff box. At another sitts the polemical Divine, plodding and wrangling in his mind about Adam's fall in which we sinned all as his primmer has it. In short my little school like the great World, is made up of Kings, Politicians, Divines, L.D. [LL.D.'s?], Fops, Buffoons, Fidlers, Sychophants, Fools, Coxcombs, chimney sweepers, and every other Character drawn in History or seen in the World. Is it not then the highest Pleasure my Friend to preside in this little World, to bestow the proper applause upon virtuous and generous Actions, to blame and punish every vicious and contracted Trick, to wear out of the tender mind every thing that is mean and little, and fire the new born soul with a noble ardor and Emulation. The World affords no greater Pleasure. Let others waste the bloom of Life, at the Card or biliard Table, among rakes and fools, and when their minds are sufficiently fretted with losses, and inflamed by Wine, ramble through the Streets, assaulting innocent People, breaking Windows or debauching young Girls. I envy not their exalted happiness. I had rather sit in school and consider which of my pupils will turn out in his future Life, a Hero, and which a rake, which a phylosopher, and which a parasite, than change breasts with them, tho possest of 20 lac'd wast coats and £1000 a year. Methinks I hear you say, this is odd talk for J. Adams. I'll tell you, then the Ocasion of it. About 4 months since a poor Girl in this neighbourhood walking by the meeting H[ouse] upon some Ocasion, in the evening, met a fine Gentleman with laced hat and wast coat, and a sword who sollicited her to turn aside with him into the horse Stable. The Girl relucted a little, upon which he gave her 3 Guineas, and wished he might be damned if he did not have her in 3 months. Into the horse Stable they went. The 3 Guineas proved 3 farthings—and the Girl proves with Child, without a Friend upon Earth that will own her, or knowing the father of her 3 farthing Bastard.

This drawing of a small schoolhouse was used to illustrate John Adams's description of his school in Wall's Reminiscences of Worcester, 1877.

21 Saturday [February, 1756].
A Snowy day. Snow about ancle deep. I find by repeated experiment and observation, in my School, that human nature is more easily wrought upon and governed, by promises and incouragement and praise than by punishment, and threatning and Blame. But we must be cautious and sparing of our praise, lest it become too familiar, and cheap and so contemptible. Corporal as well as disgraceful punishments, depress the spirits, but commendation enlivens and stimulates them to a noble ardor and emulation.

21 Wednesday [July, 1756].
Kept School. — I am now entering on another Year, and I am resolved not to neglect my Time as I did last Year. I am resolved to rise with the Sun and to study the Scriptures, on Thurdsday, Fryday, Saturday, and Sunday mornings, and to study some Latin author the other 3 mornings. Noons and Nights I intend to read English Authors. This is my fixt Determination, and I will set down every neglect and every compliance with this Resolution. May I blush whenever I suffer one hour to pass unimproved. I will rouse up my mind, and fix my Attention. I will stand collected within my self and think upon what I read and what I see. I will strive with all my soul to be something more than Persons who have had less Advantages than myself.

In ADAM'S Fall
We sinned all.

Heaven to find,
The Bible Mind.

Christ cruisfy'd
For sinners dy'd.

The Deluge drown'd
The Earth around.

ELIJAH hid
By Ravens fed.

The judgment made
FELIX afraid.

Eighteenth-century primer: "In Adam's Fall, We sinned all."

The previous year the resolute young Adams had written a note to a former college classmate complaining of his waning enthusiasm for schoolteaching as a profession.

Worcester, 2 September, 1755
The situation of the town is quite pleasant, and the inhabitants, as far as I have had opportunity to know their character, are a sociable, generous, and hospitable people; but the school is indeed a school of affliction. A large number of little runtlings, just capable of lisping A B C, and troubling the master. But Dr. Savil tells me, for my comfort "by cultivating and pruning these tender plants in the garden of Worcester, I shall make some of them plants of renown and cedars of Lebanon." However this be, I am certain that keeping this school any length of time, would make a base weed and ignoble shrub of me.

It may have been as an antidote to the classroom that Adams developed at this time a taste for solitude and reflection, which he both cherished and distrusted as tending to idleness. His mood coincided with the appearance of a new sensibility in English literature. Writing after the period of classical rationalism, represented by such figures as Alexander Pope and Samuel Johnson, Adams, in his feeling for the connection between nature and human emotions, displayed the tenderness of a Gray and the moralistic romantic effusiveness of a Wordsworth.

[Spring, 1759]

The Road is walled on each side with a Grove of Trees. The stillness, silence, and the uniformity of the Prospect puts the Mind into a stirring, thoughtful Mood.

But the Reflections that are made in a Grove, are forgotten in the Town, and the Man who resembles a saint in his Thoughts in the first, shall resemble [a] Devil in his Actions in the last.

In such silent scenes, as riding or walking thro the Woods or sitting alone in my Chamber, or lying awake in my Bed, my Thoughts commonly run upon Knowledge, Virtue, Books, &c. tho I am apt to forget these, in the distracting Bustle of the Town, and ceremonious Converse with Mankind.

5 Saturday [June, 1756].

Dreamed away the afternoon.

29 Thursday [July, 1756].

Rose half after 6. Read a little Greek.

30 Fryday [July, 1756].

A very rainy Day. Dreamed away the Time.

Tuesday [January, 1759].

What am I doing? Shall I sleep away my whole 70 Years. No by every Thing I swear I will renounce the Contemplative, and betake myself to an active roving Life by Sea or Land, or else I will attempt some uncommon unexpected Enterprize in Law. Let me lay the Plan and arouse Spirit enough to push boldly. I swear I will push myself into Business. I will watch my Opportunity, to speak in Court, and will strike with surprize—surprize Bench, Bar, Jury, Auditors and all. Activity, Boldness, Forwardness, will draw attention. Ile not lean, with my Elbows on the Table, forever. . . . But I'le not forego the Pleasure of ranging the Woods, Climbing Cliffs, walking in fields, Meadows, by Rivers, Lakes, &c., and confine my self to a Chamber for nothing. Ile have some Boon, in Return, Exchange, fame, fortune, or something.

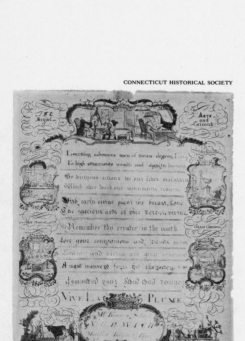

Eighteenth-century writing sheet

By the summer of 1756, John Adams had earned sufficient money to pay for his legal education. Since there were no law schools in America at this time, students learned by way of apprenticeship in the offices of practitioners. In Worcester Adams found his old friend and mentor James Putnam willing to take him on while allowing him to continue to teach school; the event was recorded in his *Diary*.

Detail of a 1766 print showing the skyline of spires in town of Boston

22 Sunday [August, 1756]. Yesterday I compleated a Contract with Mr. Putnam, to study Law under his Inspection for two years. I ought to begin with a Resolution to oblige and please him and his Lady in a particular Manner. I ought to endeavour to oblige and please every Body, but them in particular. Necessity drove me to this Determination, but my Inclination I think was to preach. However that would not do. But I set out with firm Resolutions I think never to commit any meanness or injustice in the Practice of Law. The Study and Practice of Law, I am sure does not dissolve the obligations of morality or of Religion. And altho the Reason of my quitting Divinity was my Opinion concerning some disputed Points, I hope I shall not give Reason of offence to any in that Profession by imprudent Warmth.

When his two years of reading law in Mr. Putnam's office were up, John Adams left Worcester and returned to Braintree. His zeal to excel, reinforced by his interest in knowledge, led him to read more civil law than most of his contemporaries. His scholarly interests and attainments won him the admiration and support of one of Boston's leading lawyers, Jeremiah Gridley, who undertook to present Adams and his neighbor, Samuel Quincy, in court on the same day to take their oaths as attorneys.

Braintree Octr. 5th. 1758. Yesterday arrived here from Worcester. I am this Day about beginning Justinians Institutions with Arnold Vinnius's Notes. I took it out of the Library at Colledge. It is intituled, *D. Justiniani Sacratissimi Principis Institutionum* [Concerning the basis of the Institutes of the most venerable Justinian].... Now I shall have an opportunity of judging of a dutch Commentator whom the Dedicat[ion] calls *celeberrimus suâ Etate in hac Academiâ Doctor* [the most famous teacher of his age in this school]. —Let me read with Attention, Deliberation, Distinction. Let me admire with Knowledge. It is low to admire a Dutch Commentator m[erely] because he uses latin, and greek Phraseology. Let me be able to draw the

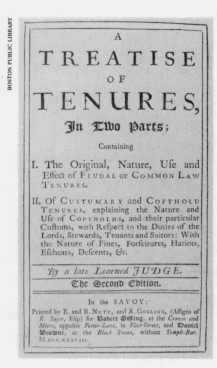

Adams's copy of Gilbert's Tenures

True Character both of the Text of Justinian, and of the Notes of his Commentator, when I have finished the Book. Few of my Contemporary Beginners, in the Study of the Law, have the Resolution, to aim at much Knowledge in the Civil Law. Let me therefore distinguish my self from them, by the Study of the Civil Law, in its native languages, those of Greece and Rome. I shall gain the Consideration and perhaps favour of Mr. Gridley and Mr. Pratt by this means....

I have read about 10 Pages in Justinian and Translated about 4 Pages into English. This is the whole of my Days Work. I have smoaked, chatted, trifled, loitered away this whole day almost. By much the greatest Part of this day has been spent, in unloading a Cart, in cutting oven Wood, in making and recruiting my own fire, in eating nuts and apples, in drinking Tea, cutting and smoking Tobacco and in chatting with the Doctor's Wife at their House and at this. Chores, Chatt, Tobacco, Tea, Steal away Time. But I am resolved to translate Justinian and his Commentators Notes by day light and read Gilberts Tenures by Night till I am master of both, and I will meddle with no other Book in this Chamber on a Week day. On a Sunday I will read the Inquiry into the Nature of the human Soul, and for Amusement I will sometimes read Ovids Art of Love to Mrs. Savel.—This shall be my Method.—I have read Gilberts 1st Section, of feuds, this evening but am not a Master of it.

Wednesday [October 25, 1758]. Went in the morning to Mr. Gridleys, and asked the favour of his Advice what Steps to take for an Introduction to the Practice of Law in this County. He answered "get sworn."

Ego. But in order to that, sir, as I have no Patron, in this County.

G. I will recommend you to the Court. Mark the Day the Court adjourns to in order to make up Judgments. Come to Town that Day, and in the mean Time I will speak to the Bar for the Bar must be consulted, because the Court always inquires, if it be with Consent of the Bar.

Then Mr. Gridley inquired what Method of Study I had pursued, what Latin Books I read, what Greek, what French. What I had read upon Rhetorick. Then he took his Common Place Book and gave me Ld. Hales Advice to a Student of the Common Law, and when I had read

44

that, he gave me Ld. C[hief] J[ustice] Reeves Advice [to] his Nephew, in the Study of the common Law. Then He gave me a Letter from Dr. Dickins, Regius Professor of Law at the University of Cambridge, to him, pointing out a Method of Studying the civil Law. Then he turned to a Letter He wrote himself to Judge Lightfoot, Judge of the Admiralty in Rhode Island, directing to a Method of Studying the Admiralty Law. Then Mr. Gridley run a Comparison between the Business and studies of a Lawyer or Gentleman of the Bar, in England, and that of one here. A Lawyer in this Country must study common Law and civil Law, and natural Law, and Admiralty Law, and must do the duty of a Counsellor, a Lawyer, an Attorney, a sollicitor, and even of a scrivener, so that the Difficulties of the Profession are much greater here than in England.

The Difficulties that attend the study may discourage some, but they never discouraged me. (Here is conscious superiority.)

I have a few Pieces of Advice to give you Mr. Adams. One is to pursue the Study of the Law rather than the Gain of it. Pursue the Gain of it enough to keep out of the Briars, but give your main Attention to the study of it.

The next is, not to marry early. For an early Marriage will obstruct your Improvement, and in the next Place, twill involve you in Expence.

Another Thing is not to keep much Company. For the application of a Man who aims to be a lawyer must be incessant. His Attention to his Books must be constant, which is inconsistent with keeping much Company.

In the study of Law the common Law be sure deserves your first and last Attention. . . .

I asked his Advice about studying Greek. He answered it is a matter of meer Curiosity. — After this long and familiar Conversation we went to Court. Attended all Day and in the Evening I went to ask Mr. Thatchers Concurrence with the Bar. Drank Tea and spent the whole Evening, upon original sin, Origin of Evil, the Plan of the Universe, and at last, upon Law. He says He is sorry that he neglected to keep a common Place Book when he began to study Law, and he is half a mind to begin now. Thatcher thinks, this County is full.

Monday [November 6?, 1758].

Went to Town. Went to Mr. Gridleys office, but he had

Jeremiah Gridley by John Smibert

*Courthouse in Pownalborough,
Maine, where Adams went on his
legal rounds in New England*

not returned to Town from Brookline. Went again. Not returned. Attended Court till after 12 and began to grow uneasy expecting that Quincy would be sworn and I have no Patron, when Mr. Gridly made his Appearance, and on sight of me, whispered to Mr. Prat, Dana, Kent, Thatcher &c. about me. Mr. Prat said no Body knew me. Yes, says Gridley, I have tried him, he is a very sensible Fellow.—At last He rose up and bowed to his right Hand and said "Mr. Quincy," when Quincy rose up, then bowed to me, "Mr. Adams," when I walked out. "May it please your Honours, I have 2 young Gentlemen Mr. Q. and Mr. Adams to present for the Oath of an Attorney. Of Mr. Q. it is sufficient for me to say he has lived 3 Years with Mr. Prat. Of Mr. Adams, as he is unknown to your Honours, It is necessary to say that he has lived between 2 and 3 Years with Mr. Put[nam] of Worcester, has a good Character from him, and all others who know him, and that he was with me the other day several Hours, and I take it he is qualified to study the Law by his scholarship and that he has made a very considerable, a very great Proficiency in the Principles of the Law, and therefore that the Clients Interest may be safely intrusted in his Hands. I therefore recommend him with the Consent of the Bar to your Honors for the Oath." Then Mr. Prat said 2 or 3 Words and the Clerk was ordered to swear us. After the Oath Mr. Gridley took me by the Hand, wished me much Joy and recommended me to the Bar. I shook Hands with the Bar, and received their Congratulations, and invited them over to Stones to drink some Punch. Where the most of us resorted, and had a very chearful [Chat?].

John Adams's first case, *Field* v. *Lambert*, caused him great vexation and much wounded vanity. Adams was an observer at the trial of Field's first action, which was dismissed for want of jurisdiction, and became Field's attorney in his second attempt to obtain damages from Lambert. Lambert's attorney was Samuel Quincy, the young lawyer who was admitted to the bar the same day as Adams, while the Justice of the Peace who presided at the trial was young Quincy's father, the elder Josiah Quincy—a fact that did little to help Adams's case.

Fryday [October 13, 1758].
Read Gilbert. Went in the Evening to Coll. Quincys. Heard a Tryal before him, as a Justice between Jos. Field

and Luke Lambert. The Case was this. Lamberts Horse broke into Fields Inclosure, and lay there some time, damage feasant. When Lambert found that his Horse was there he enters the Inclosure and altho Feild called to him and forbid it, waved his Hat, and Screamed at the Horse, and drove him away, with[out] tendering Feild his Damages. This was a Rescous of the Horse, out of Feilds Hands, for altho Lambert had a Right to enter and take out his [horse] tendering the Damages, yet, as [the] Words [of] the Law are "that whoever shall rescous any Creature out of the Hands of any Person about to drive them to pound, whereby the Party injured shall be liable to lose his Damages, and the Law be eluded, shall forfeit &c.," and as Feild was actually about to drive them to Pound, and Lambert offered him no Damages, this was compleatly a Rescous. Feild, after the Rescous, went to Coll. Quincy, made Complaint against Lambert and requested and obtained a Warrant. The Warrant was directed to the Constable, who brought the Offender before the Justice, attended with the Complainant, and the Witnesses ordered to be summoned. [Samuel] Quincy, for Defendant, took Exception on the Warrant, to the Jurisdiction of the Justice, because the sum originally sued for, consisting of the forfeiture of 40s. to the Poor, and the Parties Damages estimated at 9d. which was 40s. 9d., was a greater sum than the Justice can take Cognisance of, and because the Words of this Act of the Province are, that this 40s. to the Poor, and these Damages to the Party injured shall be recovered, by Action &c., in any of his Majesties Courts of Record. Now as the Court of a single Justice is not one of his Majesties Courts of record the forfeiture and Damages prayed for in this Complaint, cannot be recovered in this Court. The Justice adjourned his Court till 8 o'clock monday morning, in order to inform himself, 1st. Whether the Court of a single Justice of the Peace was one of his Majesties Courts of Record? 2. Whether a single Justice can take Cognisance of any Matter, in which the sum originally prosecuted for is more than 40s.? If upon Examination the Coll. shall find, that, a single Justice has no Authority to hear and determine such a Rescous, at the Adjournment the Proceedings will be quashed, and the Complainant must begin *de Novo,* but if he finds, that a single Justice has Authority, to

Courthouse in Salem, Massachusetts, another stopping place for Adams

determine the matter, he will proceed to Judgment.

Sunday [November 5?, 1758]. Drank Tea at Coll. Quincy's. He read to me a Letter Coll. Gouch wrote him in answer to his Questions, whether a Justices Court was a Court of Record? and then concluded, "So that Sammy was right, for he was all along of that Opinion. I have forgot what your Opinion was?" (This must be a Lye, or else Partiality and parental affection have blotted out the Remembrance that I first started to his son Sam and him too, the Doubt whether he had Jurisdiction as a Justice—and made him really imagine, what he wished had been true viz. that Samll. had started it. If he did remember he knew it was insult to me. But I bore it. Was forgetfulness, was Partiality, or was a cunning Design to try if I was not vain of being the Starter of the Doubt, the true Cause of his saying, He forgot what my Opinion was[?])

Sam has the utmost Reason to be grateful to Mr. Pratt. He will have an opportunity 100 times better than Mr. Prat had of rising into the Practice and Reputation of the Law. I want to see and hear Sam at the Bar. I want to know how he will succeed. I am concerned for him. The Govr. [Colonel Quincy] likes Sam much better than Ned. He has seen or heard some of Neds freaks. This is a Partiality in favor of one Child and against another quite indecent in a father. Tis great Weakness to expose himself so before Strangers.

Tuesday. December 3 or 4 [i.e., 5?, 1758]. Lambert setts up for a Witt and a Humourist. He is like a little nurley [i.e., gnarled] ill natured Horse that kicks at every Horse of his own size, but lears and shears off from every one that is larger. I should mind what I say before him for he [is] always watching for wry Words to make into a droll story to laugh at. He laughs at John Thayer, for saying, "Lambert, I am sorry [I] am your good Friend I am sorry. This will cost you between 2 and 3 hundred Pounds." And it was a silly, ... ignorant Speech. He laughs at Field for being nettled at his laughter. Field complained that he laughed at him. Lambert said, I will laugh when I please. If you carry me to the Rat hole I will laugh all the Way, and after I get there. — Such fellows are hated by all mankind, yet they rise and make a figure, and People dred them.

Altho men of bitter witt, are hated and feared, yet

they are respected, by the World.

Quaere, was there ever a Witt, who had much Humanity and Compassion, much Tenderness of Nature? Mr. Congreve was tender, extreamly tender of giving offence to any man. Dr. Arbuthnot was a[s] great a Wit and Humourist, yet he was tender, and prudent. Mr. Cranch has Witt, and is tender and [gentle?].

Unfortunately, Adams in drafting his writ gave so much thought and attention to selecting the appropriate form of action for his client that he omitted some purely technical words. Justice Quincy appears to have abated the writ, without examining any substantive question, on the ground that Adams had omitted the essential words "the County in the direction to the Constables of Braintree."

Samuel Quincy, who was admitted to the bar at the same time as John Adams, in a portrait by J.S. Copley

Monday. December 18th. 1758
I this Evening delivered to Mr. Field, a Declaration in Trespass for a Rescue. I was obliged to finish it, without sufficient examination. If it should escape an Abatement, it is quite indigested, and unclerklike. I am ashamed of it, and concerned for it. If my first Writt should be abated, if I should throw a large Bill of Costs on my first Client, my Character and Business will suffer greatly. It will be said, I dont understand my Business. No one will trust his Interest in my hands. I never Saw a Writt, on that Law of the Province. I was perplexed, and am very anxious about it. Now I feel the Dissadvantages of Putnams Insociability, and neglect of me. Had he given me now and then a few Hints concerning Practice, I should be able to judge better at this Hour than I can now. I have Reason to complain of him. But, it is my Destiny to dig Treasures with my own fingers. No Body will lend me or sell me a Pick axe. How this first Undertaking will terminate, I know not. I hope the Dispute will be settled between them, or submitted, and so my Writt never come to an Examination. But if it should I must take the Consequences. I must assume a Resolution, to bear without freting.

Friday [December 29, 1758].
Fields Wrath waxed hot this morning. When he found himself defeated a second time. He wished the affair in Hell, called Lambert a Devil and said, "That's always the Way in this Town, when any strange Devil comes into Town, he has all the Priviledges of the Town."

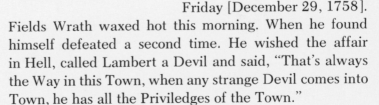

49

Let me Note the fatal Consequences of Precipitation. My first Determination, what to do in this affair was right. I determined not to meddle. But By the cruel Reproaches of my Mother, by the Importunity of Field, and by the fear of having it thought I was incapable of drawing the Writt, I was seduced from that determination, and what is the Consequence? The Writt is defective. It will be said, I undertook the Case but was unable to manage it. This Nonsuit will be in the mouth of every Body. Lambert will proclaim it.

Let me never undertake to draw a Writt, without sufficient Time to examine, and digest in my mind all the Doubts, Queries, Objections that may arise. — But no Body will know of any Abatement except this omission of the County.

An opinion will spread among the People, that I have not Cunning enough to cope with Lambert. I should endeavour at my first setting out to possess the People with an Opinion of my subtilty and Cunning. But this affair certainly looks like a strong Proof of the Contrary.

During his years as a young lawyer, John Adams maintained his sense of humor and his sociability.

"Fiddling and dancing . . . drinking flip and Toddy, and drams. This is the Riot and Revelling of Taverns."

[November] 1760.
Pater was in a very sociable Mood this Evening. He told 3 or 4 merry stories of old Horn. Old Horn, a little crooked old Lawyer in my fathers Youth, who made a Business of Jest and Banter, attacked an old Squaw one Day upon the Neck. The old Squaw made answer, "You poor smitten Boy, you with your Knife in your Tail and your Loaf on your Back, did your Mother born you so?"

A Man, whom he assaulted at another Time, with his Jests, asked him "Did you come straight from Boston?" And upon being answered yes, replied you have been miserably warped by the Way then.

A Market Girl whom he overtook upon the Neck, and asked to let him jigg her? answered by asking what is that? What good will that do? He replied it will make you fat! Pray be so good then says the Girl as to Gigg my Mare. She's miserably lean.

Novr. 25th. 1760.
Rode to the Iron Works Landing to see a Vessell launched. And after Launching went to smoke a Pipe, at Ben.

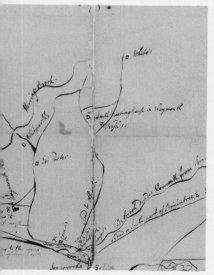

John Adams's opinions on the evils of taverns were supported by a map he drew showing seven taverns in Weymouth and five in Braintree.

Thayers, where the Rabble filled the House. Every Room, kitchen, Chamber was crowded with People. Negroes with a fiddle. Young fellows and Girls dancing in the Chamber as if they would kick the floor thro. Zab Hayward, not finding admittance to the Chamber, gathered a Circle round him in the lower Room. There He began to shew his Tricks and Postures, and Activity. He has had the Reputation, for at least fifteen Years, of the best Dancer in the World in these Towns. Several attempted, but none could equal him, in nimbleness of heels. But he has no Conception of the Grace, the Air nor the Regularity of dancing. His Air is absurd and wild, desultory, and irregular, as his Countenance is low and ignoble. In short the Air of his Countenance, the Motions of his Body, Hands, and Head, are extreamly silly, and affected and mean.

When he first began, his Behaviour and Speeches were softly silly, but as his Blood grew warm by motion and Liquor, he grew droll. He caught a Girl and danced a Gigg with her, and then led her to one side of the Ring and said, "Stand there, I call for you by and by." This was spoke comically enough, and raised a loud laugh. He caught another Girl, with light Hair, and a Patch on her Chin, and held her by the Hand while he sung a song, describing her as he said. This tickled the Girls Vanity, for the song which he applied to her described a very fine Girl indeed.

One of his witty droll sayings he thought, was this. I am a clever fellow, or else the Devil is in me. That is a Clever Girl or else the Devil is in her. Wm. Swan is such another Funmaking animal of diverting Tricks.

Hayward took one Girl by the Hand, and made a Speech to her. "I must confess I am an old Man, and as father Smith says hardly capable of doing my Duty." This raised a broad Laugh too.

Thus, in dancing, singing songs, drinking flip, running after one Girl, and married Woman and another, and making these affected, humorous Speeches, he spent the whole Afternoon.—And Zab and I were foolish enough to spend the whole afternoon in gazing and listening.

Gurney danced, but was modest and said nothing. E. Turner danced not, but bawled aloud.—God dam it, and dam it, and the Devil, &c.—And swore he'd go to Captn.

Thayers and be merry and get as drunk as the Devil. He insisted upon it, drunk he would get. And indeed, not a 2 pence better than drunk he was.

Fiddling and dancing, in a Chamber full of young fellows and Girls, a wild Rable of both sexes, and all Ages, in the lower Room, singing dancing, fiddling, drinking flip and Toddy, and drams.—This is the Riot and Revelling of Taverns And of Thayers frolicks.

In 1761 Adams attended the trial in Boston that tested the infamous writs of assistance, the general search warrants that permitted customs officers to search all premises where they expected to find smuggled goods. In this celebrated case, James Otis argued that the writs violated the natural rights of Englishmen and were therefore null and void. It was this portentous controversy that first focused Adams's attention on those fundamental constitutional questions that were then facing the American Colonies and that he was to wrestle with for the rest of his life.

Autobiography, 1802–7

The next Year after I was sworn, was the memorable Year 1759 when the Conquest of Canada was compleated by the surrender of Montreal to General Amherst. This Event, which was so joyfull to Us and so important to England if she had seen her true Interest, inspired her with a Jealousy, which ultimately lost her thirteen Colonies and made many of Us at the time regret that Canada had ever been conquered. The King sent Instructions to his Custom house officers to carry the Acts of Trade and Navigation into strict Execution. An inferiour Officer of the Customs in Salem whose Name was Cockle petitioned the Justices of the Superiour Court, at their Session in November for the County of Essex, to grant him Writs of Assistants, according to some provisions in one of the Acts of Trade, which had not been executed, to authorize him to break open Ships, Shops, Cellars, Houses &c. to search for prohibited Goods, and merchandizes on which Duties had not been paid. Some Objection was made to this Motion, and Mr. Stephen Sewall, who was then Chief Justice of that Court, and a zealous Friend of Liberty, expressed some doubts of the Legality and Constitutionality of the Writ, and of the Power of the Court to grant it. The Court ordered the question to be argued at Boston, in February term 1761. In the mean time Mr. Sewall died and Mr. Hutch-

Colonel James Otis of Barnstable, father of the famous James Otis, in a portrait by J.S. Copley

Two pages from Adams's Autobiography *describing Otis's great argument in 1761*

inson then Lt. Governor, a Councillor, and Judge of Probate for the County of Suffolk &c. was appointed in his Stead, Chief Justice. The first Vacancy on that Bench, had been promised in two former Administrations, to Colonel James Otis of Barnstable. This Event produced a Dissention between Hutchinson and Otis which had Consequences of great moment. In February Mr. James Otis Junr. a Lawyer of Boston, and a Son of Colonel Otis of Barnstable, appeared at the request of the Merchants in Boston, in Opposition to the Writ. This Gentlemans reputation as a Schollar, a Lawyer, a Reasoner, and a Man of Spirit was then very high. Mr. Putnam while I was with him had often said to me, that Otis was by far the most able, manly and commanding Character of his Age at the Bar, and this appeared to me in Boston to be the universal opinion of Judges, Lawyers and the public. Mr. Oxenbridge Thatcher whose amiable manners and pure principles, united to a very easy and musical Eloquence, made him very popular, was united with Otis, and Mr. Gridley alone appeared for Cockle the Petitioner, in Support of his Writ. The Argument continued several days in the Council Chamber, and the question was analized with great Acuteness and all the learning, which could be connected with the Subject. I took a few minutes, in a very careless manner, which by some means fell into the hands of Mr. Minot, who has inserted them in his history. I was much more attentive to the Information and the Eloquence of the Speakers, than to my minutes, and too much allarmed at the prospect that was opened before me, to care much about writing a report of the Controversy. The Views of the English Government towards the Collonies and the Views of the Collonies towards the English Government, from the first of our History to that time, appeared to me to have been directly in Opposition to each other, and were now by the imprudence of Administration, brought to a Collision. England proud of its power and holding Us in Contempt would never give up its pretentions. The Americans devoutly attached to their Liberties, would never submit, at least without an entire devastation of the Country and a general destruction of their Lives. A Contest appeared to me to be opened, to which I could foresee no End, and which would render my Life a Burden and Property, Industry and every

Thing insecure. There was no Alternative left, but to take the Side, which appeared to be just, to march intrepidly forward in the right path, to trust in providence for the Protection of Truth and right, and to die with a good Conscience and a decent grace, if that Tryal should become indispensible.

Writing to his friend William Tudor many years later, Adams suggested Otis's great argument as the subject of a historical painting, such as Benjamin West or John Trumbull might have conceived. He proceeded to describe what the painter ought to put into the picture, including a portrait of himself.

Quincy 29 March 1817

The scene is the Council Chamber in the old Town House in Boston. The date is in the month of February 1761....

That Council Chamber was as respectable an apartment as the House of Commons or the House of Lords in Great Britain, in proportion, or that in the State House in Philadelphia in which the Declaration of Independence was signed in 1776. In this chamber, round a great fire, were seated five Judges, with Lieutenant-Governor Hutchinson at their Head as Chief Justice, all arrayed in their new, fresh, rich Robes of scarlet English broadcloth; in their cambric bands, and immense judicial wigs. In this Chamber were seated at a long Table all the barristers at law of Boston, and of the neighboring county of Middlesex, in Gowns, Bands and Tie wigs. They were not seated in ivory Chairs, but their Dress was more solemn and more pompous than that of the Roman Senate, when the Gauls broke in upon them.

In a corner of the Room must be placed as a Spectator and Auditor, Wit, Sense, Imagination, Genius, Pathos, Reason, Prudence, Eloquence, Learning and immense Reading, hanging by the shoulders on two Crutches, covered with a great cloth Coat, in the person of Mr. Pratt, who had been solicited on both sides, but would engage on neither, being, as Chief Justice of New York, about to leave Boston forever. Two portraits at more than full length, of King Charles the Second and of King James the Second, in splendid golden Frames, were hung up on the most conspicuous sides of the Apartment....

One circumstance more. Samuel Quincy and John Adams had been admitted barristers at that term. John

The Old State House in Boston

Early engraving of a court of justice

was the youngest; he should be pointed like a short, thick Archbishop of Canterbury, seated at the Table with a pen in his Hand, lost in Admiration, now and then minuting those poor notes which your Pupil, Judge Minot, has printed in his History....

Now for the actors and performers. Mr. Gridley argued with his characteristic learning, ingenuity, and dignity.... But Otis was a Flame of Fire!—with a promptitude of classical Allusions, a depth of Research, a rapid summary of historical Events and Dates, a profusion of legal Authorities, a prophetic glance of his Eye into Futurity, and a Torrent of impetuous Eloquence. He hurried away everything before him. American Independence was then and there born; the Seeds of Patriots and Heroes were then and there sown, to defend vigorous Youth, the *non sine Diis animosus infans* [no speechless youth devoid of divine inspiration]. Every Man of a crowded Audience appeared to me to go away, as I did, ready to take Arms against Writs of Assistance. Then and there was the first scene of the first Act of Opposition to the arbitrary Claims of Great Britain. In fifteen years, namely in 1776, he grew up to Manhood and declared himself Free.

Adams's notes, which he considered no better a reflection of Otis's argument "than the Gleam of a Glow-worm to the meridian blaze of the sun," are the only contemporary written account of this famous speech, which was so important in shaping public opinion.

[February, 1761]

May it please your Honours,
I was desired by one of the court to look into the books and consider the question now before the court, concerning Writs of Assistance. I have accordingly considered it, and now appear not only in obedience to your order, but also in behalf of the inhabitants of this town, who have presented another petition, and out of regard to the liberties of the subject. And I take this opportunity to declare, that whether under a fee or not (for in such a cause as this I despise a fee) I will to my dying day oppose, with all the powers and faculties God has given me, all such instruments of slavery on the one hand, and villainy on the other, as this writ of assistance is. It appears to me (may it please your honours) the worst instrument of arbitrary power, the most destructive of English liberty,

and the fundamental principles of the constitution, that ever was found in an English law-book....

I was sollicited to argue this cause as Advocate-General, and because I would not, I have been charged with a desertion of my office; to this charge I can give a very sufficient answer, I renounced that office, and I argue this cause from the same principle; and I argue it with the greater pleasure as it is in favour of British liberty, at a time, when we hear the greatest monarch upon earth declaring from his throne, that he glories in the name of Briton, and that the privileges of his people are dearer to him than the most valuable prerogatives of his crown....

Let the consequences be what they will, I am determined to proceed. The only principles of public conduct that are worthy a gentleman, or a man are, to sacrifice estate, ease, health and applause, and even life itself to the sacred calls of his country. These manly sentiments in private life make the good citizen, in public life, the patriot and the hero.—I do not say, when brought to the test, I shall be invincible; I pray God I may never be brought to the melancholy trial; but if ever I should, it would be then known, how far I can reduce to practice principles I know founded in truth.—In the mean time I will proceed to the subject of the writ....

What is this but to have the curse of Canaan with a witness on us, to be the servant of servants, the most despicable of God's creation. Now one of the most essential branches of English liberty, is the freedom of one's house. A man's house is his castle; and while he is quiet, he is as well guarded as a prince in his castle. This writ, if it should be declared legal, would totally annihilate this privilege. Custom house officers may enter our houses when they please—we are commanded to permit their entry—their menial servants may enter—may break locks, bars and every thing in their way—and whether they break through malice or revenge, no man, no court can inquire—bare suspicion without oath is sufficient....

But had this writ been in any book whatever it would have been illegal. All precedents are under the controul of the principles of the law. Lord Talbot says, it is better to observe these than any precedents though in the House of Lords, the last resort of the subject. No Acts of Parliament can establish such a writ; Though it should be made

Page of Adams's cramped notes on writs of assistance which, he later wrote, "I took in a few minutes, in a very careless manner"; they are only contemporary written account.

in the very words of the petition it would be void, AN ACT AGAINST THE CONSTITUTION IS VOID. . . .

It is the business of this court to demolish this monster of oppression, and to tear into rags this remnant of Starchamber tyranny—&c.

Jealous mistress though she might be, the Law was not able to occupy all the waking hours and interests of the young attorney, for by his own account John Adams was of an amorous disposition. He greatly enjoyed kissing, "hustling," and "gallanting" the girls, though he frequently later deplored the amount of time spent on these pursuits. His *Diary* entries betray the palpitations of heart and distress of mind that are known to afflict young lovers. The objects of his attentions were Hannah and Esther Quincy, two cousins who lived in Braintree. Hannah was the daughter of Colonel Josiah Quincy and was referred to by Adams in his *Diary* and letters variously as H., O., or Orlinda. She was a lively girl who was flirting simultaneously with Adams, Richard Cranch, Parson Anthony Wibird, and Dr. Bela Lincoln, whom she later married. Adams's interest in her was becoming decidedly serious in the winter of 1758–59.

Friday, Saturday, Sunday, Monday
[October 27–30, 1758].

All Spent in absolute Idleness, or what is worse, gallanting the Girls.

Wednesday [January, 1759].

Drank Tea at Coll. Quincies. Spent the Evening there, and the next morning. In the afternoon, rode out to German Town.

H[annah] Q[uincy] or O. Suppose you was in your Study, engaged in the Investigation of some Point of Law, or Philosophy, and your Wife should interrupt you accidentally and break the Thread of your Thoughts, so that you never could recover it?

Ego. No man, but a crooked Richard, would blame his Wife, for such an accidental Interruption. And No Woman, but a Xantippe, would insist upon her Husbands Company, after he had given her his Reasons for desiring to be alone.

O. Should you like to spend your Evenings, at Home in reading and conversing with your Wife, rather than to spend them abroad in Taverns or with other Company?

Ego. Should prefer the Company of an agreable Wife, to any other Company for the most Part, not always. I should not like to be imprisoned at home.

O. Suppose you had been abroad, and came home fatigued and perplexed, with Business, or came out of your Study, wearied and perplexed with Study, and your Wife should meet you with an unpleasant, or an inattentive face, how should you feel?

[*Ego.*] I would flee my Country, or she should.

O. How shall a Pair avoid falling into Passion or out of humour, upon some Occasions, and treating each other unkindly.

Ego. By resolving against it. Forbid angry words &c.? Every Person knows that all are liable to mistakes, and Errors, and if the Husband finds his Wife in one he should [speak?] reasonably and convince her of it, instead of being angry, and so on the Contrary. But if it happens, that both get out of humour and an angry dispute ensues, yet both will be sorry when their anger subsides, and mutually forgive and ask forgiveness, and love each other the better for it, for the future.

O. thinks more than most of her Sex. She is always thinking or Reading. She sits and looks steadily, one way, very often, several minutes together in thought. E. looks pert, sprightly, gay, but thinks and reads much less than O. . . .

O. Tho O. knows and can practice the Art of pleasing, yet she fails, sometimes. She lets us see a face of Ridicule, and Spying, sometimes, inadvertently, tho she looks familiarly, and pleasantly for the most part. She is apparently frank, but really reserved, seemingly pleased, and almost charmed, when she is really laughing with Contempt. Her face and Hart have no Correspondence.

Hannah checks Parson Wibirt with Irony.—It was very sawcy to disturb you, very sawcy Im sure &c.

I am very thankful for these Checks. Good Treatment makes me think I am admired, beloved, and [my] own Vanity will be indulged in me. So I dismiss my Gard and grow weak, silly, vain, conceited, ostentatious. But a Check, a frown, a sneer, a Sarcasm rouses my Spirits, makes me more careful and considerate. It may in short be made a Question, whether good Treatment or bad is the best for me, i.e. wether Smiles, kind Words, respectful Actions, dont betray me into Weaknesses and Littlenesses, that frowns, Satirical Speeches and contemptuous Behaviour, make me avoid.

Mr. Wibirt has not an unsuspicious openness of face.

Colonel Josiah Quincy, father of one of John's early lady loves

You may see in his face, a silly Pain when he hears the Girls, a whispering, and snickering.

John Borland's house, which the young lovers passed on this particular sentimental stroll in Braintree through Cupid's Grove, was to become the home of John Adams on his return from Europe in 1788. Owned by the United States since 1946, it is now the Adams National Historic Site in Quincy, Massachusetts.

Tuesday [January, 1759].
Took a ride after Dinner to Gullivers Brook in Milton, returned home. Went over to Deacon Belchers and drank Tea, and in the Evening walked home with O. Strolled by the House down to Mr. Borlands, then back down the farm Lane as far as the Gate, then back, up the Hill, and home. Met Mr. Wibirt at the Coll's door, went with him to his Lodgings, slept with him and spent all the next day with him, reading the Reflections on Courtship and Marriage, and afternoon the 4 Satires of John Oldham on the Jesuits.

It was probably about this time that Richard Cranch, friend, rival, and future brother-in-law of John Adams, wrote him a letter enclosing a message from Hannah Quincy. Adams's undated reply reveals all the symptoms of a lover in deep distress.

Say, was there most of Cruelty or of Cunning in sealing up that cruel scroll in a Letter from you. As the Doctor, in order to cheat his Patients' Eyes, conceals his bitterest potions in the sweetest Consalves and Confections, as the Bee conceals herself and her fatal sting in the Center of an Honey Comb, as the Manchineal hides her poisonous juices under the appearance of a fair delicious Fruit, in the same manner Orlinda incloses that paper full of Disappointment, Spleen and Heart Ach, in a Letter from my dearest Friend.

You are sensible that the night working Fancy of a Lover which steals him often over seas and mountains to the company of his Mistress, and which figures in his slumbers a thousand various scenes of Pleasure, only serves to increase his Misery when awake by exciting Desires which he can not gratify: for the remembrance of Pleasure which seemed to be enjoyed in a Dream gives solid Pain when we awake by raising Desires only to be mortified. Just so this Billet has raised in my imagination a sense of Pleasure which my pen can not describe and which seems to be grappled to my Soul with Hooks of Steal, as immovably as I wish to grapple in my arms the Nimph who gives it all its ornaments.

The idea of this has engrossed my whole attention. If I look upon a Law book my Eyes tis true are on the book, but Imagination is at a Tea Table seeing that Hair, those Eyes, that Shape, that familiar friendly look, and hearing Sense divine come mended from her Tongue. When the family are at Devotions, I am paying my Devoirs across a Tea Table to Orlinda. I go to bed and ruminate half the night, then fall asleep and dream of the same enchanting Scenes till morning comes bringing Chagrin, fretfulness and Chaos in exchange for Bliss and Rest.

If, as grave folks say, madness comes by thinking too much on one set of Ideas I shall certainly grow mad, for I have had no Idea in my mind but that of Orlinda or Tea Table and Disappointment since I saw you.

Oh Tea, how shall I curse thy once delightful but now detested stream! May I never taste thy waters more, for they will always recall the remembrance of Orlinda's cruelty, my eager wishes, and fatal Disappointment; or if I must taste, with every cup from thy Stream, may I drink whole Bucketts full from Lethe and forget my Woe.

Richard Cranch—friend, rival, and future brother-in-law of John Adams

An accidental interruption of an intimate conversation saved Hannah Quincy for Dr. Bela Lincoln and John Adams for Abigail Smith.
[Spring, 1759]

Accidents, as we call them, govern a great Part of the World, especially Marriages. Sewal and Esther broke in upon H. and me and interrupted a Conversation that would have terminated in a Courtship, which would in spight of the Dr. have terminated in a Marriage, which Marriage might have depressed me to absolute Poverty and obscurity, to the End of my Life. But the Accident seperated us, and gave room for Lincolns addresses, which have delivered me from very dangerous shackles, and left me at Liberty, if I will but mind my studies, of making a Character and a fortune.

I never began an Explanation of my Designs and Thoughts so that she was obliged to act without certain Knowledge. She had peculiar Reasons to desire an im-

60

mediate Marriage, viz. a young and a very fruitful Mother in Law, on whom her father fondly doats, &c. and she had peculiar Reasons to receive the Drs. Addresses viz. The fondness of her father and his father, for the Match. The Drs. family, Business, and Character. And, in oposition to these Inducements, she had no Certainty of my Passions or Reason or Designs in her favour, but a strong suspicion that I was apprised of the Drs. Designs, and determined to see her no more. — But the Thing is ended. A tender scene! a great sacrifice to Reason!

The epilogue to this affair was told years later by Josiah Quincy, the second mayor of Boston of that name, in a book of reminiscences, *Figures of the Past*. By his account Hannah Quincy, who became Mrs. Ebenezer Storer after the death of her first husband, Dr. Bela Lincoln, was as vivacious in old age as she had been in her youth.

Figures of the Past, 1883
Eventful years rolled by, and I, a young man, just entering life, was deputed to attend my venerable relative on a visit to the equally venerable ex-President. Both parties were verging upon their ninetieth year. They had met very infrequently, if at all, since the days of their early intimacy. When Mrs. Storer entered the room, the old gentleman's face lighted up, as he exclaimed, with ardor, "What! Madam, shall we not go walk in Cupid's Grove together?" To say the truth, the lady seemed somewhat embarrassed by this utterly unlooked-for salutation. It seemed to hurry her back through the past with such rapidity as fairly to take away her breath. But self-possession came at last, and with it a suspicion of girlish archness, as she replied, "Ah, sir, it would not be the first time that we have walked there!"

In later years John Adams recorded his gratitude to his parents for the care they took to inculcate in him at an early age those sound principles and moral scruples that enabled him to master his ardent temperament in his youth.

Autobiography, 1802–7
Here it may be proper to recollect something which makes an Article of great importance in the Life of every Man. I was of an amorous disposition and very early from ten or eleven Years of Age, was very fond of the

Society of females. I had my favorites among the young Women and spent many of my Evenings in their Company and this disposition although controlled for seven Years after my Entrance into College returned and engaged me too much till I was married. I shall draw no Characters nor give any enumeration of my youthfull flames. It would be considered as no compliment to the dead or the living: This I will say—they were all modest and virtuous Girls and always maintained this Character through Life. No Virgin or Matron ever had cause to blush at the sight of me, or to regret her Acquaintance with me. No Father, Brother, Son or Friend ever had cause of Grief or Resentment for any Intercourse between me and any Daughter, Sister, Mother, or any other Relation of the female Sex. My Children may be assured that no illegitimate Brother or Sister exists or ever existed. These Reflections, to me consolatory beyond all expression, I am able to make with truth and sincerity and I presume I am indebted for this blessing to my Education. My Parents held every Species of Libertinage in such Contempt and horror, and held up constantly to view such pictures of disgrace, of baseness and of Ruin, that my natural temperament was always overawed by my Principles and Sense of decorum. This Blessing has been rendered the more prescious to me, as I have seen enough of the Effects of a different practice. Corroding Reflections through Life are the never failing consequence of illicit amours, in old as well as in new Countries. The Happiness of Life depends more upon Innocence in this respect, than upon all the Philosophy of Epicurus, or of Zeno without it. I could write Romances, or Histories as wonderfull as Romances of what I have known or heard in France, Holland and England, and all would serve to confirm what I learned in my Youth in America, that Happiness is lost forever if Innocence is lost, at least untill a Repentance is undergone so severe as to be an overballance to all the gratifications of Licentiousness. Repentance itself cannot restore the Happiness of Innocence, at least in this Life.

Man from Massachusetts

THE BRAINTREE HOMESTEAD

John Adams was born and raised in a small farming community twelve miles down the coast from the bustling city of Boston. Braintree can be seen in its isolated setting at the very bottom of the map at left, just above and to the right of Weymouth, birthplace of Abigail Smith, his future wife. The house in which he was born (at right in the painting above) and the house next door, into which he moved after his marriage, were both plain and simple cottages surrounded by pasture, forest, and swampland. These homesteads were infinitely dear to Adams and the more he was away from them, as he often was for years at a time, the more he yearned to return. He loved the land. After taking a walk one March afternoon, he wrote: "There is very little beauty [in] the face of the Earth now, but the Vegetables will soon spring fresh and green, and young and sprightly Grass, and flowers, and Roses, will appear on the Ground, buds, blossoms, leaves on the Trees, and 100 species of Birds, flying in Air, alighting on the Ground and on Trees, herds of Cattle, Sheep, horses, grazing and lowing in the Pastures. Oh Nature! how [bright?] and beautiful thou art."

A HARVARD EDUCATION

Founded over a hundred years before the fifteen-year-old Adams applied for entrance in 1751, Harvard was the heart of the intellectual life of the Massachusetts Bay Colony. Adams's father had wanted him to enter the ministry after completing his college course. Instead John, while at Harvard, joined "a Clubb of Students" who opined that "I had some faculty for public Speaking and that I should make a better Lawyer than Divine." After much soul-searching, he took this course.

"LOVE SWEETENS LIFE"

In these pastel portraits made of John and Abigail Adams in 1766, two years after their marriage, one can see the intelligence and strength that attracted John to the lively Abigail, virtues that were to sustain her through the long years of separation that lay ahead. John was quick to discover how much "Love sweetens Life," and Abigail happily recognized in her short, stout husband "a Heart Equally warm with my own." For fifty-four years, theirs was to be a close and enduring relationship. The views below, made by a young relative of Abigail's in 1822, depict the church in Quincy in which John Adams was baptized (left) and Mount Wollaston Farm (right), the estate of Abigail's maternal grandfather.

ON TO BOSTON

When John Adams began the practice of law in Boston, the vista above lay before him as he rode toward the city from Braintree. In Boston he found that "My eyes are so diverted with Chimney Sweeps, Carriers of Wood, Merchants, Ladies, Priests, Carts, Horses, Oxen, Coaches, Market men and Women, Soldiers, Sailors, and my Ears with the Rattle Gabble of them all that I cant think long enough in the Street upon any one Thing to start and pursue a Thought." When he was elected in 1770 as a representative from Boston to the provincial legislature, it was to "Phaneul Hall" (right) that he went to say a few words of acceptance. Called "the cradle of American Liberty," Faneuil Hall was the gathering place of the Sons of Liberty during the period of growing unrest prior to the actual outbreak of the Revolution. In contrast, the elegant Province House (right, above) was the home of the royal governor until the British were forced to evacuate Boston after the American victory at Dorchester Heights.

Massachusetts Magazine,

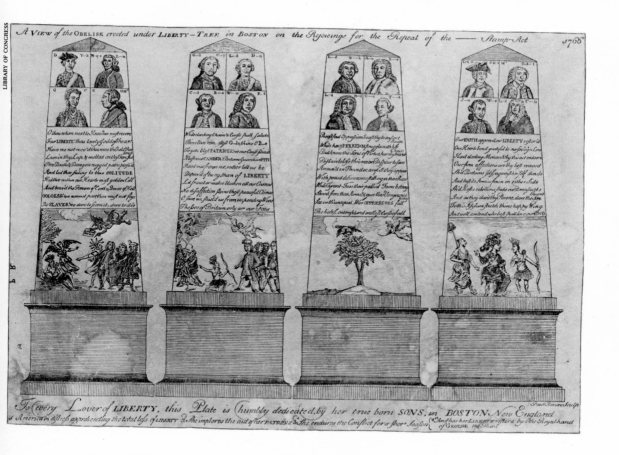

FIRST STIRRINGS OF RESISTANCE

In 1761 the British had authorized warrants that permitted customs officers to search any premises in the Colonies where they expected to find smuggled goods. Adams, a brand new barrister, was present as the able James Otis (left, above) argued that these writs of assistance violated the natural rights of Englishmen, and he left a vivid record of the event: "The scene is the Council Chamber in the old Town House in Boston [center building in the painting at left]. . . . Otis was a Flame of Fire! . . . American Independence was then and there born. . . . Then and there was the first scene of the first Act of Opposition to the arbitrary Claims of Great Britain." Four years later the British imposed another arbitrary claim in the form of the Stamp Act. This time protest swept the Colonies with such force that the act was repealed the following year. In joyful celebration, the Sons of Liberty erected a magnificent obelisk on Boston Common whose four sides are shown in Paul Revere's engraving above, ornamented by portraits of sixteen worthy Englishmen.

HUMILIATING OCCUPATION

The easing of tension after the repeal of the Stamp Act was short-lived. When the British government imposed new duties on paper, tea, and glass, the Bostonians responded with increased smuggling while their assembly conducted itself "in the Stile of a ruling and Sovereign Nation, who acknowledges no Dependence." In the fall of 1768, the British sent a fleet into Boston Harbor (above) and four thousand redcoats disembarked and were quartered throughout the city to maintain order. A local artist, Christian Remick, recorded both events. His original watercolor (right) of the 29th Regiment, forced to make its camp on the Common because no Bostonian would offer lodging, has aged badly; but the stately house of John Hancock on Beacon Hill can be seen dominating the skyline with the tents of the troops pitched directly in front of it. John Adams had been away when all this took place, but as he later recorded: "On my Return I found the Town of Boston full of Troops.... Through the whole succeeding fall and winter a Regiment was exercised, by Major Small, in Brattle Square directly in Front of my house.... Their very Appearance in Boston was a strong proof to me, that the determination in Great Britain to subjugate Us, was too deep and inveterate ever to be altered by Us."

75

THE FRUITS OF ARBITRARY POWER, OR THE BLOODY MASSACRE

PERPETRATED IN KINGSTREET BOSTON ON MARCH 5ᵗʰ 1770. IN WHICH MESSʳˢ SAMˡ GRAY: SAMˡ MAVERICK IAMES CALDWELL

CRISPUS ATTUCKS· PATRICK CARR WERE KILLEᴰ SIX OTHERˢ WOUNDED TWO OF THEM MORTALLY

HOW LONG SHALL THEY UTTER AND SPEAK HARD THINGS AND ALL THE WORKERS OF INIQUITY
BOAST THEMSELVES: THEY BREAK IN PEICES THY PEOPLE O LORD AND AFFLICT
THINE HERITAGE: THEY SLAY THE WIDOW AND THE STRANGER AND MUR-
-DER THE FATHERLESS· YET THEY SAY THE LORD SHALL NOT SEE: NEI-
THER SHALL THE GOD OF JACOB REGARD IT. PSALM XCIV.

"KILL THEM! KILL THEM! KNOCK THEM OVER!"

The continuous sight of redcoats in their streets had an exacerbating effect on the colonists and was bound to result in violence. On the night of March 5, 1770, a group of British soldiers under the command of Captain Thomas Preston fired upon a crowd gathered in front of the Custom House (seen in Paul Revere's plan at right with bodies in front of it). Five persons were killed. John Adams's fiery cousin Sam and his Sons of Liberty immediately labeled this a "Massacre" and saw to it that Revere's print, based on Henry Pelham's original drawing (left), was widely distributed. The real truth emerged from John Adams's defense in the trial of the British soldiers (page from his original notes at right, below). That he undertook the case at all is a tribute to Adams's inherent sense of justice and his willingness to sacrifice his own career if necessary. He recognized that "this would be as important a Cause as was ever tryed in any Court or Country of the World." Skillfully delaying the trial for almost eight months so that the passions of Boston had time to cool, he then placed the blame where it belonged. "We have been entertained with a great variety of phrases to avoid calling this sort of people a mob. Some call them shavers, some call them geniuses. The plain English is, they were, most probably, a motley rabble of saucy boys, Negroes and mulattoes, Irish teagues and outlandish Jack-tars; and why we should scruple to call such a set of people a mob I can't conceive, unless the name is too respectable for them." He went on to describe this "lower order" as crying, "Kill them! Kill them! Knock them over!" In the end Adams succeeded in seeing Captain Preston and all but two of his soldiers acquitted and his own reputation alive and intact.

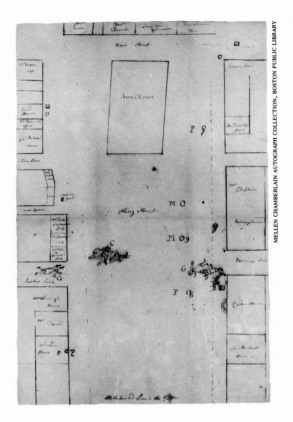

KING GEORGE'S "VILE BOHEA"

The "Brace of Adamses," as John and his cousin Samuel came to be known, kept the fires of resistance well fanned during the years following the Boston Massacre. John said of Sam, seen in John Singleton Copley's fine portrait at right pointing to the Massachusetts Charter, that he was "born and tempered a wedge of steel to split the knot of *lignum vitae* that tied America to England." Thanks to the committees of correspondence, which most of the Colonies had established, word of any British infraction traveled fast and was exploited to the hilt. When the Tea Act of 1773 was imposed and the tea ships arrived in Boston Harbor, seven thousand outraged citizens gathered in the Old South Church for a protest meeting. Sam Adams had made careful preparations, and when the call "To Griffin Wharf!" came, his men knew what to do. The British cartoon below is a satirical comment on the Boston Tea Party that took place on December 16 and shows a teapot exploding in the face of the British soldiers. In Boston, a new song celebrated the "Indians" who dumped the tea in the harbor:

> Rally, Mohawks! bring out your axes,
> And tell King George we'll pay no taxes
>   On his foreign tea.
> His threats are vain; he need not think
> To force our wives and girls to drink
>   His vile Bohea!

John Adams hailed the Tea Party as "the grandest event which has ever yet happened since the controversy with Britain opened."

The Battle of Bunker's Hill BY JOHN TRUMBULL; YALE UNIVERSITY ART GALLERY

"THE REVOLUTION WAS IN THE MINDS
AND HEARTS OF THE PEOPLE"

Sixteen months elapsed between the Tea Party and the actual shooting at Lexington and Concord in April, 1775. But as Adams later wrote, "The Revolution was effected before the war commenced. The Revolution was in the minds and hearts of the people . . . this radical change in the principles, opinions, sentiments, and affections of the people was the real American Revolution." He was in Philadelphia attending the Second Continental Congress when the Battle of Bunker Hill took place on June 17. He had warned Abigail, "In case of real Danger . . . fly to the Woods with our children." Instead, that indomitable woman watched it all from a hill in Braintree with young John Quincy holding her hand. The next day she wrote her husband (right) that she had "heard that our Dear Friend Dr. Warren is no more but fell gloriously fighting for his Country"—an event recorded in John Trumbull's painting above. In Congress it was Adams who proposed Washington for Commander in Chief of the American Army, and in March, 1776, Abigail was to send the joyful news that Washington had forced the British to evacuate Boston.

Dearest Friend   Sunday June 18 1775

in which the fate of America depends - my bursting Heart must find vent
at my pen - I have just heard that our dear Friend Dr Warren is no
more but fell gloriously fighting for his Country - Saying better to die
honourably in the field than ignominiously hang upon the Gallows / great is our
loss he has distinguished himself in every engagement, by his courage
and fortitude, by animating the soldiers & leading them on by his own
example - a particular account of these dreadful, but I hope Glorious
Days will be transmitted you, no doubt in the exacktest manner -

                         the race is not to the swift, nor the
battle to the strong - but the God of Isreal is he that giveth strength & power
unto his people trust in him at all times ye people pour out your hearts
before him, God is a refuge for us - Charlstown is laid in ashes - the Battle
began upon our intrenchments upon Bunkers Hill, a Satturday morning
about 3 oclock & has not ceased yet & tis now 3 o'clock Sabbeth afternoon -

                         Tis expected they will come out over the
Neck to night - & a dreadful Battle must ensue almighty God cover
the heads of our Country men - & be a shield to our dear Friends - how
many have fallen we know not - the constant roar of the cannon
is so [di]stressing that we cannot eat Drink or sleep - may we be supported
and sustaind in the dreadful conflict - I shall tarry here till tis thought
unsafe by my Friends & then I have secured myself a retreat at your
Brothers who has kindly offerd me part of his House - I cannot compose
myself to write any farther at present - I will add more as I hear
farther -

                         Tuesday afternoon -

I have been so much agitated that I have not been able to write
since Sabbeth Day - when I say that ten thousand reports are passing
vague & uncertain as the wind I believe I speak the truth - I am
not able to give you any authentick account of last Saturday - but you
will not be destitute of inteligence - Coll Palmer has just sent
me word that he has an opportunity of conveyance - incorrect as this
Scrawl will be, it shall go - I wrote you last Saturday morning - in the
afternoon I received your kind favour of the 2 June - and that you sent
me by Capt Beals at the same time - I ardently pray that you may be
supported thro the arduous task you have before you - I wish I could contra-
dict the report of the Doctors death - but his a lamentable truth - and the
tears of multitudes pay tribute to his memory - those favorite lines
Collin continually sound in my ears

Chapter 3

Seedtime of the Revolution

John Adams married Abigail Smith on October 25, 1764, in his twenty-ninth year. His law practice enabled him at that time to support a household that would soon be full of growing children. Active in local affairs in Braintree and also intensely devoted to farming, he found that his interests, abilities, and temperament impelled him to take sides in the great political issues of the day. The growing struggle between the royal governor and the independent-minded inhabitants of Boston occasioned the rise of a skillfully directed mob. Never a member of the mob himself nor privy to the maneuverings of the Sons of Liberty, John Adams nevertheless defended ancient British legal rights and constitutional liberties in the press, where he soon won a reputation as a spokesman for the cause of liberty.

That the legality of the writs of assistance was upheld in the Massachusetts courts did not mean that it was politically possible for the royal governor to use them to crack down on smuggling. The government in London eventually felt impelled to raise revenue in the Colonies by more direct means to pay both for the Seven Years' War and for the costs of keeping an army in North America to protect its vast possessions there. Imperial policy soon revealed itself in the Sugar Act of 1764, which increased existing duties, tightened up enforcement procedures, and restricted certain types of colonial trade. The Currency Act of the same year prevented the Colonies from paying their debts in depreciated currency. Disregarding mounting protests in the Colonies, the Grenville ministry in 1765 passed the Stamp Act, which required the purchase of stamped paper for numerous classes of legal documents, pamphlets, newspapers, and playing cards, and the Quartering Act, which obliged the Colonies to quarter troops in public hostelries. The prompt answers to these last measures in the Colonies were mob violence, nonimportation agreements, legislative resolutions, and articles in the press denouncing the tyranny of the home government for passing such oppressive measures in a legislature in which the Colonies were not represented. During this period John Adams attended to his growing family, built up a flourishing legal practice, and still found time to defend the course of liberty in the public press.

The courtship of Abigail Smith seems to have begun in the early 1760s when Adams took on the task of guiding the reading of the intellectually minded girl, whom he referred to as Nabby. In 1761 Abigail was seventeen years old. She was well-bred, clever, and not poor, and she lived with her two lively sisters in the parsonage belonging to their father, the Reverend William Smith of Weymouth. In 1762 Mary (Polly) Smith, an admitted beauty, married Richard Cranch, John Adams's good friend. Betsy Smith, after the death of her first husband, the Reverend John Shaw, became the wife of the Reverend Stephen Peabody. The first references to Abigail and her sisters in John Adams's *Diary*, however, fall short of the lyrical.

[Summer, 1759]

Polly and Nabby are wits....

Q[uery], are fondness and wit compatible? P[arson] S[mith']s Girls have not this fondness, nor this Tenderness....

Are S Gils [the Smith Girls] either Frank or fond, or even candid.—Not fond, not frank, not candid.

A playful message in a letter, sent by John Adams to Mary Smith shortly after the accession to the throne of young King George III, seems today to have been prophetic.

[December 30, 1761]

My—I dont know what—to Mrs. Nabby. Tell her I hear she's about commencing a most loyal subject to young George—and altho my Allegiance has been hitherto inviolate I shall endeavER, all in my Power to foment Rebellion.

A penchant for dreams, names of endearment, and descriptions of nature in its gaudiest and most somber aspects characterize the more emotional letters of the young couple during this period. John complimented Abigail by calling her Diana, while nothing less than the name of Lysander, the great Spartan admiral and victor at Aegospotami, seemed suited to John's courage and abilities. Both writers, however, shifted back and forth in their moods without warning, so that there is pure fun as well as romance in their exchanges. Love of knowledge, which may have prompted John's first attentions to Abigail and which certainly had at one time been strong enough to resist the feminine wiles of Hannah Quincy, now succumbed to a more tender passion.

Saturday morning Aug. 1763

My dear Diana

Germantown is at a great Distance from Weymouth Meeting-House, you know; The No. of Yards indeed is not so prodigious, but the Rowing and Walking that lyes between is a great Discouragement to a weary Traveller. Could my Horse have helped me to Weymouth, Braintree would not have held me last Night.—I lay, in the well known Chamber, and dreamed, I saw a Lady, tripping it over the Hills, on Weymouth shore, and Spreading Light and Beauty and Glory, all around her. At first I thought it was Aurora, with her fair Complexion, her Crimson Blushes and her million Charms and Graces. But I soon found it was Diana, a Lady infinitely dearer to me and more charming.—Should Diana make her Appearance every morning instead of Aurora, I should not sleep as I do, but should be all awake and admiring by four, at latest.—You may be sure I was mortifyed when I found, I had only been dreaming. The Impression however of this dream awaked me thoroughly, and since I had

Adams's letter "For Miss Nabby Smith, Weymouth," his "dear Diana" lost my Diana, I enjoy'd the Opportunity of viewing and admiring Miss Aurora. She's a sweet Girl, upon my Word. Her breath is wholesome as the sweetly blowing Spices of Arabia, and therefore next to her fairer sister Diana, the Properest Physician, for your drooping

                                    J. ADAMS

Abigail showed a very human concern for her Lysander's health when he was being inoculated during the smallpox epidemic of 1764 in Boston, as is revealed in this tender letter.

Fryday Morning April th 20 [1764]
What does it signify, why may not I visit you a Days as well as Nights? I no sooner close my Eyes than some invisible Being, swift as the Alborack of Mahomet, bears me to you. I see you, but cannot make my self visible to you. That tortures me, but it is still worse when I do not come for I am then haunted by half a dozen ugly Sprights. One will catch me and leep into the Sea, an other will carry me up a precipice (like that which Edgar describes to Lear,) then toss me down, and were I not then light as the Gosemore I should shiver into atoms—an other will be pouring down my throat stuff worse than the witches Broth in Macbeth.—Where I shall be carried next I know not, but I had rather have the small pox by inoculation half a dozen times, than be sprighted about as I am. What say you can you give me any encouragement to come? By the time you receive this hope from experience you will be able to say that the distemper is but a triffle. Think you I would not endure a triffle for the pleasure of seeing Lysander, yes were it ten times that triffle I would.—But my own inclinations must not be followed—to Duty I sacrifice them. Yet O my Mamma forgive me if I say, you have forgot, or never knew—but hush.—And do you Lysander excuse me that something I promis'd you, since it was a Speach more undutifull than that which I Just now stop'd my self in—for the present good by.

Eighteenth-century broadside in the form of a poem about inoculation for the dread disease of smallpox

Abigail had the temerity to challenge John to catalog her faults. The courageous hero obliged his fair mistress in a remarkable letter, to which she replied in kind. Together their letters must stand as a tribute to the strength of the bond that already existed between them.

Abigail's uncle, Dr. Cotton Tufts, transmitted John's and Abigail's love letters during their courtship.

Boston May 7th. 1764

I promised you, Sometime agone, a Catalogue of your Faults, Imperfections, Defects, or whatever you please to call them. I feel at present, pretty much at Leisure, and in a very suitable Frame of Mind to perform my Promise. But I must caution you, before I proceed to re-collect yourself, and instead of being vexed or fretted or thrown into a Passion, to resolve upon a Reformation — for this is my sincere Aim, in laying before you, this Picture of yourself.

In the first Place, then, give me leave to say, you have been extreamly negligent, in attending so little to Cards. You have very litle Inclination, to that noble and elegant Diversion, and whenever you have taken an Hand you have held it but aukwardly and played it, with a very un-courtly, and indifferent, Air. Now I have Confidence enough in your good sense, to rely upon it, you will for the future endeavour to make a better Figure in this ele-gant and necessary Accomplishment.

Another Thing which ought to be mentioned, and by all means amended, is, the Effect of a Country Life and Education, I mean, a certain Modesty, sensibility, Bash-fulness, call it by which of these Names you will, that enkindles Blushes forsooth at every Violation of Decency, in Company, and lays a most insupportable Constraint on the freedom of Behaviour. Thanks to the late Refine-ments of modern manners, Hypocrisy, superstition, and Formality have lost all Reputation in the World and the utmost sublimation of Politeness and Gentility lies, in Ease, and Freedom, or in other Words in a natural Air and Behaviour, and in expressing a satisfaction at what-ever is suggested and prompted by Nature, which the aforesaid Violations of Decency, most certainly are.

In the Third Place, you could never yet be prevail'd on to learn to sing. This I take very soberly to be an Imper-fection of the most moment of any. An Ear for Musick would be a source of much Pleasure, and a Voice and skill, would be a private solitary Amusement, of great Value when no other could be had. You must have re-marked an Example of this in Mrs. Cranch, who must in all probability have been deafened to Death with the Cries of her Betcy, if she had not drowned them in Musick of her own.

In the Fourth Place you very often hang your Head like

a Bulrush. You do not sit, erected as you ought, by which Means, it happens that you appear too short for a Beauty, and the Company looses the sweet smiles of that Countenance and the bright sparkles of those Eyes. — This Fault is the Effect and Consequence of another, still more inexcusable in a Lady. I mean an Habit of Reading, Writing and Thinking. But both the Cause and the Effect ought to be repented and amended as soon as possible.

Another Fault, which seems to have been obstinately persisted in, after frequent Remonstrances, Advices and Admonitions of your Friends, is that of sitting with the Leggs across. This ruins the figure and the Air, this injures the Health. And springs I fear from the former source vizt. too much Thinking. — These Things ought not to be!

A sixth Imperfection is that of Walking, with the Toes bending inward. This Imperfection is commonly called Parrot-toed, I think, I know not for what Reason. But it gives an Idea, the reverse of a bold and noble Air, the Reverse of the stately strutt, and the sublime Deportment.

Thus have I given a faithful Portraiture of all the Spotts, I have hitherto discerned in this Luminary. Have not regarded Order, but have painted them as they arose in my Memory. Near Three Weeks have I conned and studied for more, but more are not to be discovered. All the rest is bright and luminous.

Having finished the Picture I finished my Letter, lest while I am recounting Faults, I should commit the greatest in a Letter, that of tedious and excessive Length. There's a prettily turned Conclusion for You! from yr.

LYSANDER

Weymouth May. th 9 1764

Welcome, Welcome thrice welcome is Lysander to Braintree, but ten times more so would he be at Weymouth, whither you are affraid to come. — Once it was not so. May not I come and see you, at least look thro a window at you? Should you not be glad to see your Diana? I flatter myself you would.

Your Brother brought your Letter, tho he did not let me see him, deliverd it the Doctor from whom received it safe. I thank you for your Catalogue, but must confess I was so hardned as to read over most of my Faults with as much pleasure, as an other person would have read their perfections. And Lysander must excuse me if I still

Abigail's father, Rev. William Smith, and the house (below) in Weymouth where she was born in 1744 and where John Adams came to court her

persist in some of them, at least till I am convinced that an alteration would contribute to his happiness. Especially may I avoid that Freedom of Behaviour which according to the plan given, consists in Voilations of Decency, and which would render me unfit to Herd even with the Brutes. And permit me to tell you Sir, nor disdain to be a learner, that there is such a thing as Modesty without either Hypocricy or Formality.

As to a neglect of Singing, that I acknowledg to be a Fault which if posible shall not be complaind of a second time, nor should you have had occasion for it now, if I had not a voice harsh as the screech of a peacock.

The Capotal fault shall be rectified, tho not with any hopes of being lookd upon as a Beauty, to appear agreeable in the Eyes of Lysander, has been for Years past, and still is the height of my ambition.

The 5th fault, will endeavour to amend of it, but you know I think that a gentleman has no business to concern himself about the Leggs of a Lady, for my part I do not apprehend any bad effects from the practise, yet since you desire it, and that you may not for the future trouble Yourself so much about it, will reform.

The sixth and last can be cured only by a Dancing School.

But I must not write more. I borrow a hint from you, therefore will not add to my faults that of a tedious Letter —a fault I never yet had reason to complain of in you, for however long, they never were otherways than agreeable to your own

A SMITH

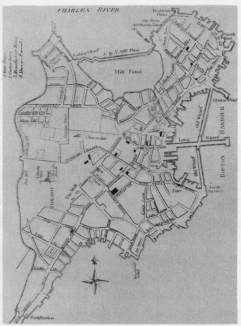

Boston in 1770: John and Abigail lived in houses on Brattle Square, Cole Lane, and Queen Street between the years 1768 and 1774.

Adams's return letter to his "dear Girl," which was written less than a month before their marriage on October 25, 1764, shows a more contrite heart on the part of the young swain.

Septr. 30th. 1764

Oh my dear Girl. I thank Heaven that another Fortnight will restore you to me—after so long a separation. My soul and Body have both been thrown into Disorder, by your Absence, and a Month of two more would make me the most insufferable Cynick, in the World. I see nothing but Faults, Follies, Frailties and Defects in any Body, lately. People have lost all their good Properties or I my Justice, or Discernment.

But you who have always softened and warmed my Heart, shall restore my Benevolence as well as my Health and Tranquility of mind. You shall polish and refine my sentiments of Life and Manners, banish all the unsocial and ill natured Particles in my Composition, and form me to that happy Temper, that can reconcile a quick Discernment with a perfect Candour.

Believe me, now & ever yr. faithful

LYSANDER

On the death of his father in 1761, John Adams inherited a cottage next door to his father's house, together with a barn, ten acres of adjoining land, and some thirty acres of pasture, forest, and swampland elsewhere in Braintree. It was to this house and farm, referred to today as the John Quincy Adams Birthplace, that John and Abigail moved after their marriage. Here they made their home for the next twenty-four years. In 1774, Adams also bought his father's house from his brother, Peter Boylston Adams —the house now referred to as the John Adams Birthplace. Later, when John and Abigail Adams returned from Europe in 1788, they moved to the Borland house in that part of Braintree soon to be called Quincy, where they lived for the rest of their lives. Meanwhile, to be closer to his growing law practice, John Adams rented a house in Brattle Square in Boston in 1768, moving the following year to a house on Cole Lane. In 1772 he decided to buy a house on Queen Street, which was his town residence until 1774. Though never wealthy, the Adams family was able to support a comfortable and well-staffed household, as is evident in a letter that Abigail wrote to her sister Mary Cranch.

Braintree Jan'ry. 31.1767

My Dear Sister

I have just returned from Weymouth, where I have been for a week past. It seems lonesome here, for My Good Man is at Boston; after haveing been in a large family, for a week, to come and set down alone is very solitary; tho we have seven in our family, yet four of them being domestick when my partner is absent and my Babe a sleep, I am still left alone. It gives one a pleasing Sensation my Dear Sister, after haveing been absent a little while to see one's self gladly received upon a return, even by one's Servants. I do not know that I was ever more sensibly affected with it than I was to Day; I could behold joy sparkle in the Eyes of every one of them as I entered the House, whilst they unaffectedly express'd it some to me and some to my Babe.—One runs to the Door, O

89

Mam, I am glad to see you come home again, how do you do? Whilst an other catches the child, and says Dear creature I was affraid she would forget me, and a third hovers round and crys Nab, do you know Polly, and will you come to her?—These little instances shew their regard, and they endear them to us.

John Adams's expanding law practice did not prevent him from farming and improving his land. Husbandry was a source of the greatest satisfaction to him throughout his long life, and he wrote about it in his *Diary* with as much glee as he practiced it.

Octr. 24th. 1762.

Before [sun]rise. My Thoughts have taken a sudden Turn to Husbandry. Have contracted with Jo. T[irrell?] to clear my swamp and to build me a long string of stone Wall, and with Isaac [Tirrell?] to build me 16 Rods more and with Jo Field to build me 6 Rods more. And my Thoughts are running continually from the orchard to the Pasture and from thence to the swamp, and thence to the House and Barn and Land adjoining. Sometimes I am at the orchard Ploughing up Acre after Acre and Planting, pruning Apple Trees, mending Fences, carting Dung. Sometimes in the Pasture, digging stones, clearing Bushes, Pruning Trees, building Wall to redeem Posts and Rails, and sometimes removing Button Trees down to my House. Sometimes I am at the old swamp, burning Bushes, digging stumps and Roots, cutting Ditches, across the Meadow, and against my Uncle, and am sometimes at the other End of the Town, buying Posts and Rails, to Fence against my Uncle and against the Brook, and am sometimes Ploughing the Upland, with 6 Yoke of oxen, and planting Corn, Potatoes, &c. and digging up the Meadow and sowing onions, planting cabbages &c. &c.

Sometimes I am at the Homestead running Cross Fences, and planting Potatoes by the Acre, and Corn by the two Acres, and running a Ditch along the Line between me and Field, and a Fence along the Brook [against] my Brother and another Ditch in the Middle from Fields Line to the Meadow. Sometimes am Carting Gravel from the Neighboring Hills, and sometimes Dust from the streets upon the fresh Meadow. And sometimes plowing, sometimes digging those Meadows, to introduce Clover and other English Grasses.

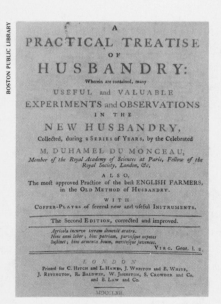

One of the many books on husbandry from John Adams's personal library

In 1763 John Adams's first known newspaper contributions appeared in the *Boston Gazette*. These humorous essays on husbandry were written in rural dialect and were signed with the jocular pen name of "Humphrey Ploughjogger."

Engraving from a contemporary magazine venerating "the plough"

Boston Gazette, 1763

I arnt book larnt enuff, to rite so polytly, as the great gentlefolks, that rite in the News-Papers, about Pollyticks. I think it is pitty, they should know how to rite so well, saving they made better use ont. And that they might do, if they would rite about something else.... What I'me ater is, to get some great larnt gentleman, who has been to Old Ingland, and knows how to raise Hemp there, and can read books about it, and understand um, to print in your News, some direckshon, about it, that we may go to trying, for we cant afford to run venters, by working, may be, a month and then have nothing come of it for want of working right.

A daughter, Abigail, was born in 1765, John Quincy in 1767, Susanna in 1768, Charles in 1770, and Thomas Boylston in 1772. A sixth child, Elizabeth, was stillborn in 1777. With John Adams's growing family responsibilities came the public duties of surveyor of highways, selectman of Braintree, and counsel to the town of Boston in the Stamp Act crisis. Increasing prominence at the bar and in the press as publicist for the cause of liberty led to an association with his second cousin Samuel Adams, the rising leader of Boston's dissident mercantile faction, which was opposed to the exercise of all royal authority over the Colony's commerce. Groups in Boston known as caucuses were soon to produce the Sons of Liberty, a revolutionary party masterminded by Samuel Adams, who skillfully manipulated the Boston mob in order to defeat royal policy. John Adams described a caucus of 1763 in his *Diary*.

Boston Feby. 1763.

This day learned that the Caucas Clubb meets at certain Times in the Garret of Tom Daws, the Adjutant of the Boston Regiment. He has a large House, and he has a moveable Partition in his Garrett, which he takes down and the whole Clubb meets in one Room. There they smoke tobacco till you cannot see from one End of the Garrett to the other. There they drink Phlip I suppose, and there they choose a Moderator, who puts Questions to the Vote regularly, and select Men, Assessors, Collectors, Wardens, Fire Wards, and Representatives are Regularly chosen before they are chosen in the Town.

Uncle Fairfield, Story, Ruddock, Adams, Cooper, and a *rudis indigestaque Moles* [rude, disorderly heap] of others are Members. They send Committees to wait on the Merchants Clubb and to propose, and join, in the Choice of Men and Measures. Captn. Cunningham says they have often solicited him to go to these Caucas, they have assured him Benefit in his Business, &c.

On May 27, 1765, the text of the Stamp Act reached Boston. The people were informed that on and after the first of November taxes up to £10 would have to be paid for prestamped paper, which was required to be used for many sorts of official documents, as well as for newspapers and playing cards. Before the Stamp Act Congress convened in New York on October 7, 1765, to discuss this threat to the business and commerce of the Colonies, the mob was unleashed in Boston. On August 14, 1765, a raging rabble hanged and burned the effigy of Andrew Oliver, Secretary of the Province and designated stamp distributor, and then pillaged Oliver's house. John Adams was seriously disturbed by this violence, and in his *Diary* the next day he questioned "the Grounds and Reasons of the strange Conduct...at Boston.

August 15th. 1765.

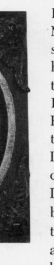

Is it known that he [Andrew Oliver] ever advised the Ministry to lay internal Taxes upon Us? That he ever solicited the office of Distributor of Stamps? or that he has ever done any Thing to injure the People, or to incur their Displeasure, besides barely accepting of that office? If there is no Proof at all of any such Injury done to the People by that Gentleman, has not the blind, undistinguishing Rage of the Rabble done him, irreparable Injustice? To be placed, only in Pageantry, in the most conspicuous Part of the Town, with such ignominous Devices around him, would be thought severity enough by any Man of common sensibility: But to be carried thro the Town, in such insolent Tryumph and burned on an Hill, to have his Garden torn to pieces, his House broken open, his furniture destroyed and his whole family thrown into Confusion and Terror, is a very attrocious Violation of the Peace and of dangerous Tendency and Consequence.

Andrew Oliver by J.S. Copley

On August 25, 1765, the mob sacked the house of Thomas Hutchinson, Chief Justice of the Superior Court and Lieutenant

Governor of the Province. No one was ever punished for these attacks, and it was clear to the authorities that until the troops arrived from England, the people who controlled the mob were the real rulers of Boston. On September 24, 1765, the celebrated Braintree Instructions, drafted by John Adams, were issued. This document contained instructions from the freeholders of Braintree to Mr. Ebenezer Thayer, their representative in the General Court, the legislative body of the Colony. As it was widely read and copied by other towns, it soon enhanced the reputation of its author as a spokesman for the cause of liberty. In the Braintree Instructions Adams pointed out that the Stamp Act did not deprive the Colonies of "Liberty" as such, but of three distinct, fundamental constitutional liberties long since guaranteed to all Englishmen: no taxation without representation; trial by jury; and the independence of the judiciary. Trained in the common law, Adams realized that the people's freedom did not reside in any doctrinaire concept of liberty, but in specific political liberties and legal rights that had been won only after hundreds of years of struggle to limit the extent of the royal prerogative and the powers of the aristocrats in the legislature.

Instructions of the Town of Braintree to their Representative, 1765

We have always understood it to be a grand and fundamental principle of the constitution, that no freeman should be subject to any tax to which he has not given his own consent, in person or by proxy. And the maxims of the law, as we have constantly received them, are to the same effect, that no freeman can be separated from his property but by his own act or fault. We take it clearly, therefore, to be inconsistent with the spirit of the common law, and of the essential fundamental principles of the British constitution, that we should be subject to any tax imposed by the British Parliament; because we are not represented in that assembly in any sense, unless it be by a fiction of the law, as insensible in theory as it would be injurious in practice, if such a taxation should be grounded on it.

Home of Thomas Hutchinson, the only provincial governor who did not inhabit Province House, which was sacked by a mob in August, 1765

But the most grievous innovation of all, is the alarming extension of the power of courts of admiralty. In these courts, one judge presides alone! No juries have any concern there! The law and the fact are both to be decided by the same single judge, whose commission is only during pleasure, and with whom, as we are told, the most mischievous of all customs has become established, that of taking commissions on all condemnations; so that he is under a pecuniary temptation always against the subject.

Among the many articles published by John Adams during the Stamp Act crisis was the so-called third Clarendon letter, which appeared in the *Boston Gazette*. Assuming the name of the late Earl of Clarendon, a conservative British historian and father-in-law of James II, Adams developed for the first time in print some of his most characteristic ideas concerning the concept of mixed government. In this early publication, Adams followed Locke's bipartite division of governmental power between the legislative and executive branches, subsuming the judiciary under the executive. Later, as a result of what he felt were legislative and executive abuses of authority, Adams accepted Montesquieu's tripartite division of powers; and in his *Thoughts on Government*, published in 1776, and his draft of the Massachusetts Constitution, published in 1780, he raised the judiciary to independent status.

Boston Gazette, January, 1766

Were I to define the British constitution, therefore, I should say, it is a limited monarchy, or a mixture of the three forms of government commonly known in the schools, reserving as much of the monarchical splendor, the aristocratical independency, and the democratical freedom, as are necessary that each of these powers may have a control, both in legislation and execution, over the other two, for the preservation of the subject's liberty.

According to this definition, the first grand division of constitutional powers is into those of legislation and those of execution. In the power of legislation, the king, lords, commons, and people are to be considered as essential and fundamental parts of the constitution. . . .

The other grand division of power is that of execution. And here the king is, by the constitution, supreme executor of the laws, and is always present, in person or by his judges, in his courts, distributing justice among the people. But the executive branch of the constitution, as far as respects the administration of justice, has in it a mixture of popular power too. . . .

Thus, it seems to appear, that two branches of popular power, voting for members of the house of commons, and trials by juries, the one in the legislative and the other in the executive part of the constitution, are as essential and fundamental to the great end of it, the preservation of the subject's liberty, to preserve the balance and mixture of the government, and to prevent its running into an oligarchy or aristocracy, as the lords and commons are to prevent its becoming an absolute monarchy. These two popular powers, therefore, are the heart and lungs,

A commission, signed by Governor Hutchinson, appointing one Joseph Moors an adjutant, March 14, 1772

Thomas Hutchinson by E. Truman

the mainspring and the centre wheel, and without them the body must die, the watch must run down, the government must become arbitrary, and this our law books have settled to be the death of the laws and constitution. In these two powers consist wholly the liberty and security of the people. They have no other fortification against wanton, cruel power; no other indemnification against being ridden like horses, fleeced like sheep, worked like cattle, and fed and clothed like swine and hounds; no other defence against fines, imprisonments, whipping-posts, gibbets, bastinadoes, and racks. This is that constitution which has prevailed in Britain from an immense antiquity. It prevailed, and the house of commons and trials by jury made a part of it, in Saxon times, as may be abundantly proved by many monuments still remaining in the Saxon language. That constitution which has been for so long a time the envy and admiration of surrounding nations; which has been no less than five and fifty times since the Norman conquest, attacked in parliament, and attempted to be altered, but without success; which has been so often defended by the people of England, at the expense of oceans of their blood: and which, coöperating with the invincible spirit of liberty inspired by it into the people, has never failed to work the ruin of the authors of all settled attempts to destroy it.

What a fine reflection and consolation is it for a man, that he can be subjected to no laws which he does not make himself, or constitute some of his friends to make for him,—his father, brother, neighbor, friend, a man of his own rank, nearly of his own education, fortune, habits, passions, prejudices, one whose life and fortune and liberty are to be affected, like those of his constituents, by the laws he shall consent to for himself and them! What a satisfaction is it to reflect, that he can lie under the imputation of no guilt, be subjected to no punishment, lose none of his property, or the necessaries, conveniences, or ornaments of life, which indulgent Providence has showered around him, but by the judgment of his peers, his equals, his neighbors, men who know him and to whom he is known, who have no end to serve by punishing him, who wish to find him innocent, if charged with a crime, and are indifferent on which side the truth lies, if he disputes with his neighbor!

John Adams, impressed by the resistance that the Stamp Act had produced throughout all the Colonies, nevertheless worried about the effect it would have on his business as well as on the business of America and Great Britain. Toward the end of the year 1765, he had confided these worries to his *Diary*.

Handbill warning against any use of stamps, distributed the night the British ship bearing stamps arrived

Braintree Decr. 18th. 1765. Wednesday. How great is my Loss, in neglecting to keep a regular Journal, through the last Spring, Summer, and Fall. In the Course of my Business, as a Surveyor of High-Ways, as one of the Committee, for dividing, planning, and selling the North-Commons, in the Course of my two great Journeys to Pounalborough and Marthas Vineyard, and in several smaller Journeys to Plymouth, Taunton and Boston, I had many fine Opportunities and Materials for Speculation. — The Year 1765 has been the most remarkable Year of my Life. That enormous Engine, fabricated by the british Parliament, for battering down all the Rights and Liberties of America, I mean the Stamp Act, has raised and spread, thro the whole Continent, a Spirit that will be recorded to our Honour, with all future Generations. In every Colony, from Georgia to New Hampshire inclusively, the Stamp Distributors and Inspectors have been compelled, by the unconquerable Rage of the People, to renounce their offices. Such and so universal has been the Resentment of the People, that every Man who has dared to speak in favour of the Stamps, or to soften the detestation in which they are held, how great soever his Abilities and Virtues had been esteemed before, or whatever his fortune, Connections and Influence had been, has been seen to sink into universal Contempt and Ignominy. . . .

This Spirit however has not yet been sufficient to banish, from Persons in Authority, that Timidity, which they have discovered from the Beginning. The executive Courts have not yet dared to adjudge the Stamp-Act void nor to proceed with Business as usual, tho it should seem that Necessity alone would be sufficient to justify Business, at present, tho the Act should be allowed to be obligatory. The Stamps are in the Castle. Mr. Oliver has no Commission. The Governor has no Authority to distribute, or even to unpack the Bales, the Act has never been proclaimed nor read in the Province; Yet the Probate office is shut, the Custom House is shut, the Courts of Justice are shut, and all Business seems at a Stand.

Yesterday and the day before, the two last days of Service for January Term, only one Man asked me for a Writ, and he was soon determined to waive his Request. I have not drawn a Writ since 1st. Novr.

How long We are to remain in this languid Condition, this passive Obedience to the Stamp Act, is not certain. But such a Pause cannot be lasting. Debtors grow insolent. Creditors grow angry. And it is to be expected that the Public offices will very soon be forced open, unless such favourable Accounts should be received from England, as to draw away the Fears of the Great, or unless a greater Dread of the Multitude should drive away the Fear of Censure from G. Britain.

It is my Opinion that by this [Timorous] Inactivity we discover Cowardice, and too much Respect [and Regard] to the Act. This Rest appears to be by Implication at least an Acknowledgement of the Authority of Parliament to tax Us. And if this Authority is once acknowledged and established, the Ruin of America will become inevitable.

This long Interval of Indolence and Idleness will make a large Chasm in my affairs if it should not reduce me to Distress and incapacitate me to answer the Demands upon me. But I must endeavour in some degree to compensate the Disadvantage, by posting my Books, reducing my Accounts into better order, and by diminishing my Expences, but above all by improving the Leisure of this Winter, in a diligent Application to my Studies. I find that Idleness lies between Business and Study, i.e. The Transision from the Hurry of a multiplicity of Business, to the Tranquility that is necessary for intense Study, is not easy. There must be a Vacation, an Interval between them, for the Mind to recollect itself.

The Bar seem to me to behave like a Flock of shot Pidgeons. They seem to be stopped, the Net seems to be thrown over them, and they have scarcely Courage left to flounce and to flutter. So sudden an Interruption in my Career, is very unfortunate for me. I was but just getting into my Geers, just getting under Sail, and an Embargo is laid upon the Ship. Thirty Years of my Life are passed in Preparation for Business. I have had Poverty to struggle with—Envy and Jealousy and Malice of Enemies to encounter—no Friends, or but few to assist me, so that I have groped in dark Obscurity, till of late,

A British colonial revenue stamp

and had but just become known, and gained a small degree of Reputation, when this execrable Project was set on foot for my Ruin as well as that of America in General, and of Great Britain.

The call to public service came at last, and John Adams was one of the lawyers selected to represent the town of Boston in the matter of the opening of the courts. He humbly attributed his selection to the operation of some inscrutable law of nature, and his mood changed as abruptly as nature sometimes does.

Decr. 19th. 1765.

A fair Morning after a severe Storm of 3 days and 4 Nights. A vast Quantity of rain fell.

About 12. O Clock came in Messrs. Crafts and Chase and gave me a particular Account of the Proceedings of the Sons of Liberty on Tuesday last, in prevailing on Mr. Oliver to renounce his Office of Distributor of Stamps, by a Declaration under his Hand, and under his Oath, taken before Justice Dana, in Hanover Square, under the very Tree of Liberty, nay under the very Limb where he had been hanged in Effigy, Aug. 14th. 1765. Their absolute Requisition of an Oath, and under that Tree, were Circumstances, extreamly humiliating and mortifying, as Punishment for his receiving a Deputation to be Distributor after his pretended Resignation, and for his faint and indirect Declaration in the News Papers last Monday.

About one O'Clock came in Mr. Clark, one of the Constables of the Town of Boston, with a Letter from Mr. Wm. Cooper their Town Clerk in these Words

Sir

I am directed by the Town to acquaint you, that they have this day voted unanimously, that Jeremiah Gridley, James Otis, and John Adams Esqrs. be applied to, as Council to appear before his Excellency the Governor in Council, in Support of their Memorial, praying that the Courts of Law in this Province may be opened. A Copy of said Memorial will be handed you, on your coming to Town. I am sir, your most obedient hum. sert.,

WM. COOPER TOWN CLERK

Boston Decr. 18th 1765

John Adams Esqr.

The Reasons which induced Boston to choose me, at

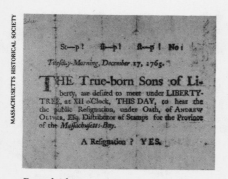

St—p! St—p! St—p! No!

Tuesday-Morning, December 17, 1765.

THE True-born Sons of Liberty, are desired to meet under LIBERTY-TREE, at XII o'Clock, THIS DAY, to hear the the public Resignation, under Oath, of ANDREW OLIVER, Esq; Distributor of Stamps for the Province of the *Massachusetts-Bay.*

A Resignation ? YES.

Broadside issued by Sons of Liberty

a distance, and unknown as I am, The particular Persons concerned and measures concerted to bring this about, I am wholly at a loss to conjecture: as I am, what the future Effects and Consequences will be both with Regard to myself and the Public.

But when I recollect my own Reflections and Speculations Yesterday, a part of which were committed to Writing last Night, and may be seen under Decr. 18th, and compare them with the Proceedings of Boston Yesterday of which the foregoing Letter informed me, I cannot but Wonder, and call to Mind my Ld. Bacons Observation, about secret invisible Laws of Nature, a[nd] Communications and Influences between Places, that are not discoverable by Sense.

But I am now under all obligations of Interest and Ambition as well as Honour, Gratitude and Duty, to exert the Utmost of my Abilities, in this important Cause. How shall it be conducted? Shall we contend that the Stamp-Act is void? That the Parliament have no legal Authority to impose Internal Taxes upon Us?—Because We are not represented in it? And Therefore that the Stamp Act ought to be waived by the Judges, as against natural Equity and the Constitution? Shall we use these, as Arguments for opening the Courts of Law? Or shall We ground ourselves on Necessity only.

Fryday. Decr. 20th. 1765.
Went to Boston. Dined with Mr. Rowe, in Company with Messrs. Gridley, Otis, Kent, and Dudley. After Dinner, went to the Town House, and Attended with the Committee of the Town of Boston and many other Gentlemen in the Representatives Room till about Dark, after Candle Light, when Mr. Adams, the Chairman of the Committee, received a Message from the Governor, by the Deputy Secretary, purporting that his Excellency and the Council were ready to hear the Memorial of the Town of Boston, and their Council in Support of it. But that no other Persons might attend.

We accordingly went in. His Excellency recommended it to Us, who were of Council for the Town, to divide the Points of Law and Topicks of Argument, among ourselves, that Repetition might as much as possible be avoided. Mr. Gridley answered, that, as he was to speak last, he would endeavour to avoid Repetition of what should be said by the two Gentlemen, who were to

Contemporary German engraving of rebellious Bostonians burning papers carrying the stamps they resented

Detail of a 1765 British cartoon showing Britannia (seated, right) handing America (Indian figure) the Stamp Act labeled Pandora's Box

speak before him. Mr. Otis added that as he was to speak second, he would observe the same Rule.

Then it fell upon me, without one Moments Opportunity to consult any Authorities, to open an Argument, upon a Question that was never made before, and I wish I could hope it never would be made again, i.e. Whether the Courts of Law should be open, or not? My old Friend Thatchers *Officina Justitiæ* [workshop of justice]?

I grounded my Argument on the Invalidity of the Stamp Act, it not being in any sense our Act, having never consented to it. But least that foundation should not be sufficient, on the present Necessity to prevent a Failure of Justice, and the present Impossibility of carrying that Act into Execution.

Mr. Otis reasoned with great Learning and Zeal, on the Judges Oaths, &c.

Mr. Gridley on the great Inconveniences that would ensue the Interuption of Justice.

The Governor said many of the Arguments used were very good ones to be used before the Judges of the Executive Courts. But he believed there had been no Instance in America of an Application to the Governor and Council, and said that if the Judges should receive any Directions from the King about a Point of Law, they would scorn to regard them, and would say that while they were in those Seats, they only were to determine Points of Law.

The Council adjourned to the Morning and I repaired to my Lodgings.

John Adams was quick to perceive the political and legal implications of the royal governor's policy of not opening the courts until the colonists were ready to comply with the provisions of the Stamp Act. The story was continued in his *Diary*.

Saturday Decr. 21st. 1765.

Spent the Morning in sauntering about, and chatting with one and another—The Sherriff, Mr. Goldthw[ai]t, Brother Sewal &c.—upon the Times. Dined with Brother Kent; after Dinner received a Hint from the Committee that as I was of Council for the Town I not only had a Right, but it was expected I should attend the Meeting. I went accordingly. The Committee reported the Answer of the Board to their Petition. Which was, in Substance, that the Board had no Authority to direct the Courts of Law, in the manner prayed for. That the Memorial involved a Question of Law, vizt., whether the officers of the Government, in the present Circumstances of the Province, could be justified, in proceeding with Business without Stamps. That the Board were desirous that the Judges should decide that Question freely, without Apprehension of censure from the Board, and that the Board recommended it to the Judges of the Inferior Court for the County of Suffolk and to the other Judges of the other Courts in the Province to determine that Question as soon as may be, at or before their next respective Terms.

The Question was put whether that Paper should be recorded. Passed in the Affirmative.

The next Question was, Whether it was a satisfactory Answer to their Memorial. Unanimously in the Negative. . . .

The Question is "what legal and Constitutional Measures the Town can take to open the Courts of Law?" . . .

My Advice to the Town will be, to take the Board at their Word, and to chuse a Committee immediately, in the first Place to wait on the Governor in Council, as the Supreme Court of Probate, and request of them a determination of the Point, whether the Officers of the Probate Courts in the Province, can be justifyed, in Proceeding with Business without Stamps, in the next Place to wait on the honorable the Judges of the Superiour Court to request their Determination of the same Question, and in the Third Place to wait on the Judges of the Inferior Court for the County of Suffolk with the same Request—in Pursuance of the Recommendation of the honorable Board—and unless a speedy Determination of the Question is obtained in all these Courts in this Way, to request of the Governor a Convention of the two Houses, and if that is refused to endeavour to call one, themselves.

What are the Consequences of the supposition that the Courts are shut up? The King is the Fountain of Justice by the Constitution—And it is a Maxim of the Law, that the King never dies.

Are not Protection and Allegiance reciprocal? And if We are out of the Kings Protection, are we not discharged from our Allegiance. Are not all the Ligaments of Government dissolved? Is it not an Abdication of the Throne? In short where will such an horrid Doctrine terminate? It would run us into Treason!

The Stamp Act divided people into two opposing camps: those who thought that the king's laws and officials should be obeyed, and those who, like John Adams, respected the British constitution but thought it slavery not to resist the imposition of unconstitutional and illegal tyranny.

Decr. 25th. 1765. Christmas. At Home. Thinking, reading, searching, concerning Taxation without Consent, concerning the great Pause and Rest in Business. By the Laws of England Justice flows, with an uninterupted Stream: In that Musick, the Law knows of neither Rests nor Pauses. Nothing but Violence, Invasion or Rebellion can obstruct the River or untune the Instrument.

Decr. 29th. 1765. Sunday. Heard Parson Wibird. Hear O Heavens and give Ear O Earth, "I have nourished and brought up Children and they have rebelled against me."—I began to suspect a Tory Sermon on the Times from this Text. But the Preacher confined himself to Spirituals. But I expect, if the Tories should become the strongest, We shall hear many Sermons against the Ingratitude, Injustice, Disloyalty, Treason, Rebellion, Impiety, and ill Policy of refusing Obedience to the Stamp-Act. The Church Clergy to be sure will be very eloquent. The Church People are, many of them, Favourers of the stamp Act, at present. Major Miller, forsooth, is very fearful, that they will be *stomachful* at Home and angry and resentful. Mr. Vesey insists upon it that, We ought to pay our Proportion of the public Burdens. Mr. Cleverly is fully convinced that they i.e. the Parliament have a Right to tax Us. He thinks it is wrong to go on with Business. We had better stop, and wait till Spring, till we hear from home. He says We put the best face upon it, that Letters have been received in Boston, from the greatest Merchants in the Nation, blaming our Proceedings, and that the Merchants dont second us. Letters from old Mr. Lane, and from Mr. Dubert. He says that Things go on here exactly as they did in the Reign of K[ing] C[harles] 1st. that blessed S[ain]t and Martyr.

Thus, that unaccountable Man goes about sowing

British cartoon of William Pitt on stilts, left one of which is labeled "Sedition" and is based in America; Pitt supported repeal of Stamp Act.

Detail of a cartoon entitled The Ballance, or American's Triumphant *showing William Pitt unseating the several promoters of Stamp Act*

his pernicious Seeds of Mischief, instilling wrong Principles in Church and State into the People, striving to divide and disunite them, and to excite fears to damp their Spirits and lower their Courage.

Etter is another of the poisonous Talkers, but not equally so. Cleverly and Vesey are Slaves in Principle. They are devout religious Slaves—and a religious Bigot is the worst of Men.

Cleverly converses of late at Mr. Lloyds with some of the Seekers of Appointments from the Crown—some of the Dozen in the Town of Boston, who ought as Hancock says to be beheaded, or with some of those, who converse with the Governor, who ought as Tom Boylstone says to be sent Home with all the other Governors on the Continent, with Chains about their Necks.

1765. Decr. 30th. Monday.
We are now concluding the Year 1765, tomorrow is the last day, of a Year in which America has shewn such Magnanimity and Spirit, as never before appeared, in any Country for such a Tract of Country. And Wednesday will open upon Us a new Year 1766, which I hope will procure Us, innumerable Testimonies from Europe in our favour and Applause, and which we all hope will produce the greatest and most extensive Joy ever felt in America, on the Repeal both of the stamp Act and sugar Act, at least of the former.

News of the repeal of the Stamp Act and the passing of the Declaratory Act in March, 1766, was not received in Boston until May 19, 1766. As many of the courts had opened in the meantime without stamps, John Adams was able to resume his law practice, but he followed political events until the crisis was over.

Fryday, March 28th. 1766.
The Jany. Packet, arrived at N. York, has brought the K[ing]'s Speech, the Address of Lords and Commons, 14th. Jany., and many private Letters, which inform that Mr. Pitt was in the House of Commons and declared himself vs. Greenville, and for a Repeal of the Stamp Act, upon Principle. Called it, the most impolitic, arbitrary, oppressive, and unconstitutional Act that ever was passed. Denied that We were represented in the House of Commons. (Q. whether the House of Commons, or the

Parliament). And asserted that the House granted Taxes in their Representative Capacity, not in their Legislative. And therefore, that the Parliament had not Right to tax the Colonies.

Q. What has been said in America which Mr. Pitt has not confirmed? Otis, Adams, Hopkins, &c. have said no more. Hampden, F. A., the Feudal System And Lord Clarendon, have gone no further than Pitt. No Epithets have been used in America worse than impolitic, arbitrary, oppressive, unconstitutional, unless it be cursed, damned, supercursed &c.

What shall we think of Mr. Pitt? What shall we call him? The Genius, and Guardian Angell of Britain and British America? Or what? Is it possible that Greenville, offensive to his K[ing], dissagreable to the People, should prevail vs. the whole new Ministry and Mr. Pitt?

John Adams may have been unduly depressed the day that news of the repeal of the Stamp Act reached Braintree, since that same day he failed in his bid to defeat the incumbent, Ebenezer Thayer, to be the town's representative in the provincial legislature.

Monday May 26th. 1766.

I have been very unfortunate, in running the Gauntlet, thro all the Rejoicings, for the Repeal of the Stamp-Act.

Monday last at 2 O Clock, was our Town Meeting, and the same Evening, were all the Rejoicings in Boston and in Plymouth. After Meeting I mounted for Plymouth, and reached Dr. Halls of Pembroke. The only Rejoicings, I heard or saw were at Hingham, where the Bells rung, Cannons were fired, Drums beaten, and Land Lady Cushing on the Plain, illuminated her House. The County of Plymouth has made a thorough Purgation, Winslow, Clap, Foster, Hayward, Keen, Oliver, Alden, are all omitted, and Warren, Seaver, Thomas, Turner, Vinal, Edson, Sprout are chosen. What a Change!

A duller Day, than last Monday, when the Province was in a Rapture for the Repeal of the Stamp Act, I do not remember to have passed. My Wife who had long depended on going to Boston, and my little Babe were both very ill of an hooping Cough. My self, under Obligation to attend the Superiour Court at Plymouth, the next day, and therefore unable to go to Boston. And the Town of Braintree insensible to the Common Joy!

Chapter 4

Defender of Liberty

The repeal of the Stamp Act in 1766 temporarily relaxed tension in the Massachusetts Bay Colony. When the Townshend Acts of the following year increased duties on paper, tea, and glass, and British troops arrived in Boston in October, 1768, to enforce these measures, the political pot started boiling again. The violence of the Boston mob was unleashed once more against those persons whose activities appeared to condone royal policy. During the night of March 5, 1770, a small contingent of soldiers, provoked by a threatening rabble hurling insults and brickbats, fired in self-defense and killed five persons in Boston. This incident was immediately glorified by the propaganda of Samuel Adams and the Sons of Liberty who called it the Boston Massacre, and its anniversary was for some years celebrated with public ceremonies. When the royal governor announced in 1772 that judges would be paid by the Crown instead of depending upon the vote of the General Court, public opinion was aroused anew.

During this agitated period, John Adams concentrated his energies so successfully upon building up his law practice that, after acting as counsel for the defense in the Boston Massacre trials, he became the acknowledged leader of the Boston bar. In spite of his reluctance to abandon his legal practice for politics, he served a short period in the legislature in 1770 and 1771. Thereafter, he successfully resisted the call of politics until the issue of the judges' salaries brought him once more into the political arena as counselor and journalist. John Adams's development during this period can be clearly traced in his relationships with four of the leading men of Boston: James Otis, Samuel Adams, Thomas Hutchinson, and Jonathan Sewall. His rise to leadership at the bar, for instance, coincided with the eclipse of James Otis's career by madness. As early as the Stamp Act crisis, Adams had noted in his *Diary* the early symptoms of instability in Otis.

> 1765. December. 23D. Monday.
> Otis is fiery and fev'rous. His Imagination flames, his

Passions blaze. He is liable to great Inequalities of Temer—sometimes in Despondency, sometimes in a Rage. The Rashnesses and Imprudences, into which his Excess of Zeal have formerly transported him, have made him Enemies, whose malicious watch over him, occasion more Caution, and more Cunning and more inexplicable Passages in his Conduct than formerly.

By 1770 these symptoms had become alarming.

1770 January 16.
Last Evening at Dr. Peckers with the Clubb.—Otis is in Confusion yet. He looses himself. He rambles and wanders like a Ship without an Helm. Attempted to tell a Story which took up almost all the Evening. The Story may at any Time be told in 3 minutes with all the Graces it is capable of, but he took an Hour. I fear he is not in his perfect Mind. The Nervous, Concise, and pithy were his Character, till lately. Now the verbose, roundabout and rambling, and long winded. He once said He hoped he should never see T[homas] H[utchinson] in Heaven. Dan. Waldo took offence at it, and made a serious Affair of it, said Otis very often bordered upon Prophaneness, if he was not strictly profane. Otis said, if he did see H. there he hoped it would be behind the Door.—In my fathers House are many Mansions, some more and some less honourable.

In one Word, Otis will spoil the Clubb. He talks so much and takes up so much of our Time, and fills it with Trash, Obsceneness, Profaneness, Nonsense and Distraction, that We have no [time] left for rational Amusements or Enquiries.

He mentioned his Wife—said she was a good Wife, too good for him—but she was a tory, an high Tory. She gave him such Curtain Lectures, &c.

In short, I never saw such an Object of Admiration, Reverence, Contempt and Compassion all at once as this. I fear, I tremble, I mourn for the Man, and for his Country. Many others mourne over him with Tears in their Eyes.

During the crisis over the judges' salaries, James Otis became distinctly unreliable.

A 1768 cartoon, engraved by Revere, condemning to "A Warm Place—Hell" seventeen men who voted to rescind a Massachusetts circular letter against the Townshend Acts' duties

BICKERSTAFF'S
BOSTON ALMANACK,
For the Year of our LORD 1770. Being the fecond Year after Leap Year.

The   Hon. JAMES OTIS, jun. Esq;

B O S T O N:
Printed by MEIN and FLEEMING, and to be SOLD by JOHN MEIN, at the
LONDON BOOK-STORE, North-fide of *KING-STREET.*
[Price feven Coppers fingle, and 25 s. Old Tenor, or 3 s. 4. Lawful the Dozen.]

Title page of a 1770 almanac with picture of James Otis, supported on one side by Liberty and on the other by Hercules, or Perseverance

1772. Octr. 27. Tuesday.

At the Printing Office this Morning. Mr. Otis came in, with his Eyes, fishy and fiery, looking and acting as wildly as ever he did.—"You Mr. Edes, You John Gill and you Paul Revere, can you stand there Three Minutes."—Yes. —"Well do. Brother Adams go along with me."—Up Chamber we went. He locks the Door and takes out the Kee. Sit down Tete a Tete.—"You are going to Cambridge to day"—Yes.—"So am I, if I please. I want to know, if I was to come into Court, and ask the Court if they were at Leisure to hear a Motion—and they should say Yes—And I should say 'May it please your Honours—

"'I have heard a Report and read an Account that your Honours are to be paid your Salaries for the future by the Crown, out of a Revenue raised from Us, without our Consent. As an Individual of the Community, as a Citizen of the Town, as an Attorney and Barrister of this Court, I beg your Honours would inform me, whether that Report is true, and if it is, whether your Honours determine to accept of such an Appointment?'

"Or Suppose the substance of this should be reduced to a written Petition, would this be a Contempt? Is mere Impertinence a Contempt?"

In the Course of this curious Conversation it oozed out that Cushing, [Samuel] Adams, and He, had been in Consultation but Yesterday . . . upon that Subject. . . .

After We came down Stairs, something was said about military Matters.—Says Otis to me, Youl never learn military Exercises.—Ay why not?—That You have an Head for it needs no Commentary, but not an Heart.—Ay how do you know—you never searched my Heart.—"Yes I have—tired with one Years Service, dancing from Boston to Braintree and from Braintree to Boston, moaping about the Streets of this Town as hipped as Father Flynt at 90, and seemingly regardless of every Thing, but to get Money enough to carry you smoothly through this World."

This is the Rant of Mr. Otis concerning me, and I suppose of 2 thirds of the Town.—But be it known to Mr. Otis, I have been in the public Cause as long as he, 'tho I was never in the General Court but one Year. I have sacrificed as much to it as he. I have never got [my] Father chosen Speaker and Councillor by it, my Brother in Law chosen into the House and chosen Speaker by it, nor a Brother in Laws Brother in Law into the House and Coun-

cil by it. Nor did I ever turn about in the House, betra
my Friends and rant on the Side of Prerogative, for a
whole Year, to get a father into a Probate Office, and
first Justice of a Court of Common Pleas, and a Brothe
into a Clerks Office.

There is a Complication of Malice, Envy and Jealous
in this Man, in the present disordered State of his Min
that is quite shocking.

I thank God my mind is prepared, for whatever ca
be said of me. The Storm shall blow over me in Silence

John Adams stated later that the example of Otis's a
fliction had deterred him, Adams, from certain kinds of political activity

Autobiography, 1802-

I was solicited to go to the Town Meetings and harrangu
there. This I constantly refused. My Friend Dr. [Joseph
Warren the most frequently urged me to this: My Answe
to him always was "That way madness lies." The Symp
toms of our great Friend Otis, at that time, suggested t
Warren, a sufficient comment on these words, at whicl
he always smiled and said "it was true."

John Adams acted as one of Otis's lawyers in the lawsui
that arose out of a fracas in the British Coffee House about this time. Oti
had tried to thwack a customs officer, one Robinson, on the head with hi
cane, but had unfortunately received a worse drubbing in return. Durin
the trial Otis was observed firing guns from the windows of his house an
was forcibly removed at this time by his friends to the country. Later Adam
went out of his way to defend the memory of Otis before Judge Edmun
Trowbridge, as he reported at the time in a letter to his wife.

Falmouth July 9. 177

At another Time, J. Trowbridge said, it seems by Coll
Barres Speeches that Mr. Otis has acquired Honour, b
releasing his Damages to Robbinson.—Yes, says I, h
has acquired Honour with all Generations.—*Trowbridge*
He did not make much Profit I think.—*Adams.* True
but the less Profit the more Honour. He was a Man o
Honour and Generosity. And those who think he wa
mistaken will pity him.

Thus you see how foolish I am. I cannot avoid exposin
myself, before these high Folk—my Feelings will a
Times overcome my Modesty and Reserve—my Pru

dence, Policy and Discretion.

I have a Zeal at my Heart, for my Country and her Friends, which I cannot smother or conceal: it will burn out at Times and in Companies where it ought to be latent in my Breast. This Zeal will prove fatal to the Fortune and Felicity of my Family, if it is not regulated by a cooler Judgment than mine has hitherto been. Coll. Otis's Phrase is "The Zeal-Pot boils over."

Samuel Adams, one of America's most successful revolutionaries, possessed the same great-grandfather, Joseph Adams of Braintree, as his second cousin John. The two Adamses, who together were to play a conspicuous role in the Continental Congress, came to know each other and to respect each other's very different qualities during the period between the Stamp Act and the outbreak of hostilities in 1775. After one early meeting John Adams recorded his impressions of his older cousin in his *Diary*.

A popular poem, M'Fingal, *contained engravings such as* Town Meeting *with Whigs and Tories doing battle.*

1765. December. 23d. Monday. Went to Boston. After Dinner rambled after Messrs. Gridley and Otis but could find neither. Went into Mr. Dudleys, Mr. Dana's, Mr. Otis's office, and then to Mr. [Samuel] Adams's and went with him to the Monday night Clubb....

Adams is zealous, ardent and keen in the Cause, is always for Softness, and Delicacy, and Prudence where they will do, but is stanch and stiff and strict and rigid and inflexible, in the Cause....

Adams I believe has the most thourough Understanding of Liberty, and her Resources, in the Temper and Character of the People, tho not in the Law and Constitution, as well as the most habitual, radical Love of it, of any of them—as well as the most correct, genteel and artful Pen. He is a Man of refined Policy, stedfast Integrity, exquisite Humanity, genteel Erudition, obliging, engaging Manners, real as well as professed Piety, and a universal good Character, unless it should be admitted that he is too attentive to the Public and not enough so, to himself and his family.

When John Adams was called to represent the town of Boston during the Stamp Act crisis, Samuel Adams encouraged his cousin's patriotic contributions to the cause.

Decr. 25th. 1765. Christmas.
Mr. S. Adams told me he was glad I was nominated for several Reasons. — 1st. Because he hoped that such an Instance of Respect from the Town of Boston, would make an Impression on my Mind, and secure my Friendship to the Town from Gratitude. 2dly. He was in Hopes such a Distinction from Boston, would be of Service to my Business and Interest. 3d. He hoped that Braintree, finding the Eyes of Boston were upon me, would fix their's on me too, next May. His Hopes, in the two first Particulars, may be well grounded, but I am sure not in the Third.

Close as he was to his cousin, John Adams noted certain inconsistencies in his behavior.

1772. Decr. 30. Wednesday.
Spent this Evening with Mr. Samuel Adams at his House. Had much Conversation, about the State of Affairs — Cushing, Hancock, Phillips, Hawley, Gerry, Hutchinson, Sewall, Quincy, &c. &c. Adams was more cool, genteel and agreable than common — concealed, and restrained his Passions — &c. He affects to despize Riches, and not to dread Poverty. But no Man is more ambitious of entertaining his Friends handsomely, or of making a decent, an elegant Appearance than he. He has lately new covered and glased his House and painted it, very neatly, and has new papered, painted and furnished his Rooms. So that you visit at a very genteel House and are very politely received and entertained.

Mr. Adams corresponds with Hawley, Gerry and others. He corresponds in England and in several of the other Provinces. His Time is all employed in the public Service.

Despite the different contributions the two Adamses made to the patriot cause, they were soon coupled in the public mind.

1772. Feby. 9. Sunday.
In the Spring of the Year 1771, several Messages passed between the Governor and the House of Representatives, concerning the Words that are always used in Acts of Parliament, and which were used in all the Laws of this Province, till the Administration of Governor Shirley,

Mr. Samuel Adams, engraved by Paul Revere for Royal American Magazine

"in General Court assembled and by the Authority of the same." Governor Shirley in whose Administration those Words were first omitted in Consequence of an Instruction to him, saw and read these Messages in the Newspapers, and enquired of somebody in Company with him at his Seat in Dorchester, who had raised those Words from Oblivion at this Time?—The Gentleman answered, the Boston Seat.—Who are the Boston Seat? says the Governor.—Mr. Cushing, Mr. Hancock, Mr. Adams and Mr. Adams says the Gentleman.—Mr. Cushing I know, quoth Mr. Shirley, and Mr. Hancock I know, but where the Devil this Brace of Adams's came from, I cant conceive.

Q[uery]. Is it not a Pity, that a Brace of so obscure a Breed, should be the only ones to defend the Household, when the generous Mastiffs, and best blooded Hounds are all hushed to silence by the Bones and Crumbs, that are thrown to them, and even Cerberus himself is bought off, with a Sop?

The Malice of the Court and its Writers seems to be principally directed against these two Gentlemen. They have been stedfast and immoveable in the Cause of their Country, from the Year 1761, and one of them Mr. Samuel Adams for full 20 Years before. They have always since they were acquainted with each other, concurred in Sentiment that the Liberties of this Country had more to fear from one Man the present Governor Hutchinson than from any other Man, nay than from all other Men in the World. This Sentiment was founded in their Knowledge of his Character, his unbounded Ambition and his unbounded Popularity. This Sentiment they have always freely, tho decently, expressed in their Conversation and Writings, Writings which the Governor well knows and which will be remembered as long as his Character and Administration. It is not therefore at all surprizing that his Indignation and that of all his Creatures should fall upon those Gentlemen. Their Maker has given them Nerves that are delicate, and of Consequence their Feelings are exquisite, and their Constitutions tender, and their Health especially of one of them, very infirm: But as a Compensation for this he has been pleased to bestow upon them Spirits that are unconquerable by all the Art and all the Power of Governor Hutchinson, and his Political Creators and

Creatures on both Sides of the Atlantic. That Art and Power which has destroyed a Thatcher, a Mayhew, an Otis, may destroy the Health and the Lives of these Gentlemen, but can never subdue their Principles or their Spirit. They have not the chearing salubrious Prospect of Honours and Emoluments before them, to support them under all the Indignities and Affronts, the Insults and Injuries, the Malice and Slander, that can be thrown upon Men, they have not even the Hope of those Advantages that the suffrages of the People only can bestow, but they have a Sense of Honour and a Love of their Country, the Testimony of a good Conscience, and the Consolation of Phylosophy, if nothing more, which will certainly support them in the Cause of their Country, to their last Gasp of Breath whenever that may happen.

But for all the certainty of his convictions, John Adams occasionally had doubts about his future.

Octr. 19. 1772. Boston.
The Day of the Month reminds me of my Birth day, which will be on the 30th. I was born Octr. 19, 1735. Thirty Seven Years, more than half the Life of Man, are run out. — What an Atom, an Animalcule I am! — The Remainder of my Days I shall rather decline, in Sense, Spirit, and Activity. My Season for acquiring Knowledge is past. And Yet I have my own and my Childrens Fortunes to make. My boyish Habits, and Airs are not yet worn off.

In one of his prominent law cases during this period, John Adams raised fundamental political questions, causing him to become associated in the public mind with the leaders of the radical movement for independence in Massachusetts. In *Sewall* v. *Hancock,* Adams was defending John Hancock, the rich merchant, in a suit brought against him by an old friend of Adams's, Jonathan Sewall, who was then Attorney General. The suit arose out of the seizure of Hancock's sloop *Liberty* for having unloaded goods without paying customs duties imposed by the stringent Townshend Acts of 1767. As a result of Adams's successful defense, the government withdrew the suit, ending the case before a decision was reached. Adams's notes of his argument in court show that his defense consisted of a frontal attack on the validity of the Townshend Acts.

Sewall v. Hancock, 1768–69

Among the Groupe of Hardships which attend this Statute, the first that ought always to be mentioned, and that ought never to be forgotten is that it was made without our Consent. My Clyent Mr. Hancock never consented to it. He never voted for it himself, and he never voted for any Man to make such a Law for him. In this Respect therefore the greatest Consolation of an Englishman, suffering under any Law, is torn from him, I mean the Reflection, that it is a Law of his own Making, a Law that he sees the Necessity of for the Public. Indeed the Consent of the subject to all Laws, is so clearly necessary that no Man has yet been found hardy enough to deny it. And The Patrons of these Acts allow that Consent is necessary, they only contend for a Consent by Construction, by Interpretation, a virtual Consent. But this is only deluding Men with Shadows instead of Substances. Construction has made Treasons where the Law has made none. Constructions, in short and arbitrary Distinctions, made in short only for so many by Words, so many Cries to deceive a Mob have always been the Instruments of arbitrary Power, the means of lulling and ensnaring Men into their own Servitude. For whenever we leave Principles and clear positive Laws, and wander after Constructions, one Construction or Consequence is piled up upon another untill we get at an immense distance from Fact and Truth and Nature, lost in the wild Regions of Imagination and Possibility, where arbitrary Power sitts upon her brazen Throne and governs with an iron Scepter. It is an Hardship therefore, scarcely to be endured that such a pœnal Statute should be made to govern a Man and his Property, without his actual Consent and only upon such a wild Chimæra as a virtual and constructive Consent.

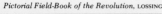

Pictorial Field-Book of the Revolution, LOSSING

John Hancock's handsome residence

Another important issue was raised in the famous impressment case, *Rex* v. *Corbet,* in which John Adams defended Michael Corbet and three other sailors accused of murdering Lieutenant Henry Panton of His Majesty's Royal Navy. Long afterwards, with echoes of this controversy sounding in his mind in the years preceding the War of 1812, John Adams thought Corbet's case to have been more significant in hastening the Revolution than the Boston Massacre trials. Testimony given at the trial revealed that the lieutenant had boarded the salt-laden vessel on which

Corbet and the others were serving and had attempted to persuade them to give themselves up. When the seamen refused and barricaded themselves in a hold below decks, Panton's men knocked down the bulkhead. Finally Corbet, drawing a line in the salt, gave the lieutenant an ultimatum, as was reported in the court record.

Rex v. *Corbet*, 1769

"'If you step over that line, I shall consider it as proof that you are determined to impress me, and by the eternal God of Heaven, you are a dead man.' 'Aye, my lad,' said the lieutenant, 'I have seen many a brave fellow before now.' Taking his snuffbox out of his pocket, and taking a pinch of snuff, he very deliberately stepped over the line, and attempted to seize Corbet. The latter, drawing back his arm, and driving his harpoon with all his force, cut off the carotid artery and jugular vein, and laid the lieutenant dead at his feet."

[The court issued a decree of justifiable homicide and set the prisoner free. John Adams's notes of his argument at the trial show that in this case he upheld the validity of a statute of Queen Anne's reign outlawing the impressment of seamen employed in America.]

This Statute is clear, and decisive, and if it is now in Force, it places the Illegality of all Impresses in America, beyond Controversy. *No Mariner on board any trading Vessell, in any Part of America, shall be liable to be impressed, or shall be impressed, by any officer, impowered by the Ld. Admiral, or any other Person.* If therefore this Statute is now in Force, all that Lt. Panton did on board the Vessell was tortious and illegal, he was a Trespasser from the Beginning, a Trespasser, in coming on board, and in every Act that he did, untill he received the mortal, fatal Wound. He was a Trespasser in going down below, but especially in firing a Pistall among the Men in the Forepeak. It is said that the Lt. with his own Hand discharged this Pistall directly att Michael Corbitt but the Ball missed him and wounded the Man who was next him in the Arm. This therefore was a direct Commencement of Hostilities, it was an open Act of Pyracy, and Corbit and his associates had a Right to defend themselves. It was a direct Attempt upon their Lives. No Custom House officer, no Impress officer has a Right to attempt Life. But it seems that a

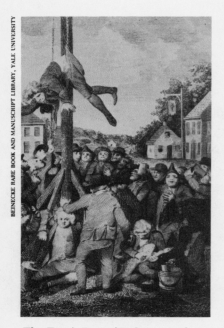

The Tory's Day of Judgment — *hung up on a liberty pole in* M'Fingal

second Pistall was discharged and wounded Corbit in his Cheek, with Powder before the fatal Blow was struck. What could Corbit expect? Should he stand still and be shot? Or should he have surrendered, to a Pyrate? Should he have surrendered to the Impress?

But it has been made a Question whether this Statute of 6. of Ann is now in Force? It has been reported as the Opinion of Sir Dudley Rider, and Sir John Strange, that this Statute expired with the War of Queen Ann. These are venerable Names, but their Opinions are Opinions only of private Men. And there has been no judicial Decision to this Purpose, in any Court of Law, and I trust never will. Their Opinions were expressed so very concisely, that there is great Room to question whether they were given upon the whole Act, or only on some particular Clause in it. Supposing these Opinions to extend to the whole Act, I have taken Pains, to discover what Reasons can be produced in support of them. And I confess I can think of none. There is not the least Colour, for such an Opinion. On the Contrary, there is every Argument, for supposing the Act perpetual.

The growing resentment of the populace to the presence of the British soldiers in Boston in 1768 and 1769, which led directly to the Boston Massacre, was recorded by John Adams in his *Autobiography*. His account clearly shows that this military presence was one of the major causes of patriotic resistance to the exercise of royal authority.

Autobiography, 1802–7

On my Return [from riding the circuit in September, 1768] I found the Town of Boston full of Troops, and as Dr. Byles of punning memory express'd it, our grievances reddressed. Through the whole succeeding fall and Winter a Regiment was exercised, by Major Small, in Brattle Square directly in Front of my house. The Spirit Stirring Drum and the Earpiercing fife arroused me and my family early enough every morning, and the Indignation they excited, though somewhat soothed was not allayed by the sweet Songs, Violins and flutes of the serenading Sons of Liberty, under my Windows in the Evening. In this Way and a thousand others I had sufficient Intimations that the hopes and Confidence of the People, were placed on me, as one of their Friends: and I was determined, that as far as depended on me

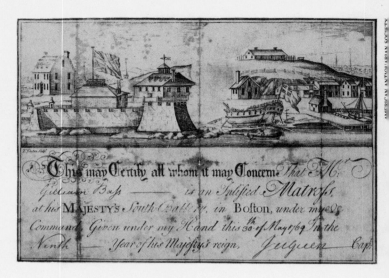

Certificate with an engraving of "his Majesty's South Battery in Boston," dated May 1769, with ship and battery flying British flags

they should not be disappointed: and that if I could render them no positive Assistance, at least I would never take any part against them. My daily Reflections for two Years, at the Sight of those Soldiers before my door were serious enough. Their very Appearance in Boston was a strong proof to me, that the determination in Great Britain to subjugate Us, was too deep and inveterate ever to be altered by Us: For every thing We could do, was misrepresent[ed], and Nothing We could say was credited.

John Adams later described in his *Autobiography* some of the events connected with the Boston Massacre of March 5, 1770, together with a description of his subsequent role in successfully defending Captain Thomas Preston and the soldiers accused of murder.

Autobiography, 1802–7

The Year 1770 was memorable enough, in these little Annals of my Pilgrimage. The Evening of the fifth of March, I spent at Mr. Henderson Inches's House at the South End of Boston, in Company with a Clubb, with whom I had been associated for several Years. About nine O Clock We were allarmed with the ringing of Bells, and supposing it to be the Signal of fire, We snatched our Hats and Cloaks, broke up the Clubb, and went out to assist in quenching the fire or aiding our friends who might be in danger. In the Street We were informed that the British Soldiers had fired on the Inhabitants, killed some and wounded others near the

Town house. A Croud of People was flowing down the Street, to the Scene of Action. When We arrived We saw nothing but some field Pieces placed before the south door of the Town house and some Engineers and Grenadiers drawn up to protect them. Mrs. Adams was in Circumstances, and I was apprehensive of the Effect of the Surprise upon her, who [was] alone, excepting her Maids and a Boy in the House. Having therefore surveyed round the Town house and seeing all quiet, I walked down Boylstons Alley into Brattle Square, where a Company or two of regular Soldiers were drawn up in Front of Dr. Coopers old Church with their Musquets all shouldered and their Bayonetts all fixed. I had no other way to proceed but along the whole front in a very narrow Space which they had left for foot passengers. Pursuing my Way, without taking the least notice of them or they of me, any more than if they had been marble Statues, I went directly home to Cold Lane. My Wife having heard that the Town was still and likely to continue so, had recovered from her first Apprehensions, and We had nothing but our Reflections to interrupt our Repose. These Reflections were to me, disquieting enough. Endeavours had been systematically pursued for many Months, by certain busy Characters, to excite Quarrells, Rencounters and Combats single or compound in the night between the Inhabitants of the lower Class and the Soldiers, and at all risques to inkindle an immortal hatred between them. I suspected that this was the Explosion, which had been intentionally wrought up by designing Men, who knew what they were aiming at better than the Instrument employed. If these poor Tools should be prosecuted for any of their illegal Conduct they must be punished. If the Soldiers in self defence should kill any of them they must be tryed, and if Truth was respected and the Law prevailed must be acquitted. To depend upon the perversion of Law and the Corruption or partiality of Juries, would insensibly disgrace the Jurisprudence of the Country and corrupt the Morals of the People. It would be better for the whole People to rise in their Majesty, and insist on the removal of the Army, and take upon themselves the Consequences, than to excite such Passions between the People and the Soldiers [as] would expose both to continual prosecution civil or criminal and keep the Town boiling

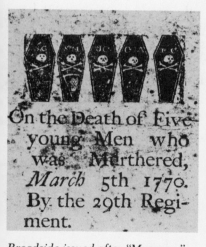

Broadside issued after "Massacre"

in a continual fermentation. The real and full Intentions of the British Government and Nation were not yet developed: and We knew not whether the Town would be supported by the Country: whether the Province would be supported by even our neighbouring States of New England; nor whether New England would be supported by the Continent. These were my Meditations in the night. The next Morning I think it was, sitting in my Office, near the Steps of the Town house Stairs, Mr. Forrest came in, who was then called the Irish Infant. I had some Acquaintance with him. With tears streaming from his Eyes, he said I am come with a very solemn Message from a very unfortunate Man, Captain Preston in Prison. He wishes for Council, and can get none. I have waited on Mr. Quincy, who says he will engage if you will give him your Assistance: without it possitively he will not. Even Mr. Auchmuty declines unless you will engage . . . . I had no hesitation in answering that Council ought to be the very last thing that an accused Person should want in a free Country. That the Bar ought in my opinion to be independent and impartial at all Times And in every Circumstance. And that Persons whose Lives were at Stake ought to have the Council they preferred: But he must be sensible this would be as important a Cause as ever was tryed in any Court or Country of the World: and that every Lawyer must hold himself responsible not only to his Country, but to the highest and most infallible of all Trybunals for the Part he should Act. He must therefore expect from me no Art or Address, No Sophistry or Prevarication in such a Cause; not any thing more than Fact, Evidence and Law would justify. Captain Preston he said requested and desired no more: and that he had such an Opinion, from all he had heard from all Parties of me, that he could chearfully trust his Life with me, upon those Principles. And said Forrest, as God almighty is my Judge I believe him an innocent Man. I replied that must be ascertained by his Tryal, and if he thinks he cannot have a fair Tryal of that Issue without my Assistance, without hesitation he shall have it. Upon this, Forrest offered me a single Guinea as a retaining fee and I readily accepted it. . . . The Tryal of the Soldiers was continued for one Term, and in the Mean time an Election came on, for a Representative of Boston.

A summons issued to witnesses to "give such Evidence as ye know . . . on an indictment against Preston for Murder," October 20, 1770

In June, 1770, Adams was elected a representative from Boston to the provincial legislature. His decision to serve was a courageous one, since it put him in the politically ambiguous position of defending British military personnel while at the same time representing the rebellious town of Boston in its struggle with the royal governor.

Old Landmarks and Historic Personages of Boston
BY SAMUEL ADAMS DRAKE, 1900

Two Boston landmarks familiar to Adams: the Old Corner Bookstore (above), erected in 1710, and the Old Feather Store (below) in 1680

MASSACHUSETTS HISTORICAL SOCIETY

Autobiography, 1802–7

A Town Meeting was called for the Choice of a Successor to Mr. Bowdoin; Mr. Ruddock a very respectable Justice of the Peace, who had risen to Wealth and Consequence, by a long Course of Industry as a Master Shipwright, was sett up in Opposition to me. Notwithstanding the late Clamour against me, and although Mr. Ruddock was very popular among all the Tradesmen and Mechanicks in Town, I was chosen by a large Majority. I had never been at a Boston Town Meeting, and was not at this, till Messengers were sent to me, to inform me that I was chosen. I went down to Phanuel Hall and in a few Words expressive of my sense of the difficulty and danger of the Times; of the importance of the Trust, and of my own Insuffi[ci]ency to fulfill the Expectations of the People, I accepted the Choice. Many Congratulations were offered, which I received civilly, but they gave no Joy to me. I considered the Step as a devotion of my family to ruin and myself to death, for I could scarce perceive a possibility that I should ever go through the Thorns and leap all the Precipices before me, and escape with my Life. At this time I had more Business at the Bar, than any Man in the Province: My health was feeble: I was throwing away as bright prospects [as] any Man ever had before him: and had devoted myself to endless labour and Anxiety if not to infamy and to death, and that for nothing, except, what indeed was and ought to be all in all, a sense of duty. In the Evening I expressed to Mrs. Adams all my Apprehensions: That excellent Lady, who has always encouraged me, burst into a flood of Tears, but said she was very sensible of all the Danger to her and to our Children as well as to me, but she thought I had done as I ought, she was very willing to share in all that was to come and place her trust in Providence. I immediately attended the General Court at Cambridge, to which place the Governor had removed it, to punish the Town of Boston, in Obedience however, as he said I suppose truly to an Instruction he had received from the King.... This was to me a

119

fatiguing Session, for they put me upon all the Drudgery of managing all the disputes, and an executive Court had a long Session which obliged me to attend, allmost constantly there upon a Number of very disagreable Causes. Not long after the Adjournment of the General Court came on the Tryals of Preston and the Soldiers.

John Adams found that he had to refuse some agreeable invitations if he was to prepare an adequate defense of the soldiers. He wrote about it in his *Diary*.

June 28. Thursday [1770].

Mr. Goldthwait. Do you call tomorrow and dine with Us at flax Pond near Salem. Rowe, Davis, Brattle and half a dozen, as clever fellows as ever were born, are to dine there under the shady Trees, by the Pond, upon fish, and Bacon and Pees &c. and as to the Madeira, nothing can come up to it. Do you call. We'll give a genteell Dinner and fix you off on your Journey.

Rumours of Ships and Troops, a Fleet and an Army, 10 Regiments and a No. of line of Battle Ships, were talked of to day.

If an Armament should come, what will be done by the People? Will they oppose them?

"If, by supporting the Rights of Mankind, and of invincible Truth, I shall contribute to save from the Agonies of Death one unfortunate Victim of Tyranny, or of Ignorance, equally fatal; his Blessing and Tears of Transport, will be a sufficient Consolation to me, for the Contempt of all Mankind." Essay on Crimes and Punishments [by the Marchese di Beccaria, an eighteenth-century Italian jurist and criminologist].

Adams succeeded in postponing the trials for almost eight months, during which period emotions had time to subside. After a long trial, Captain Preston was acquitted by a jury of the charge of murder and set free. The succeeding trial of the soldiers resulted on December 5, 1770, in a verdict of acquittal for all but two, who were convicted of manslaughter only and discharged after being branded on the thumb. During the trial of the soldiers, John Adams skillfully depicted the soldiers' plight, as well as eloquently invoking the justice of the law.

Rex v. *William Wemms et al.*, 1770

You must place yourselves in the situation of *Wemms* or

Two pages from Adams's brief in defense of Captain Thomas Preston

Killroy—consider yourselves, as knowing that the prejudices of the world about you, were against you; that the people about you, thought you came to dragoon them into obedience to statutes, instructions, mandates and edicts, which they thoroughly detested; that many of these people were thoughtless and inconsiderate, old and young, sailors and landmen, negroes and molattos; that they, the soldiers had no friends about them, the rest were in opposition to them; with all the bells ringing, to call the town together to assist the people in *King-street*; for they knew by that time, that there was no fire; the people shouting, huzzaing, and making the mob whistle as they call it, which when a boy makes it in the street, is no formidable thing, but when made by a multitude, is a most hideous shriek, almost as terrible as an Indian yell; the people crying Kill them! Kill them! Knock them over! heaving snow-balls, oyster shells, clubs, white birch sticks three inches and a half diameter, consider yourselves, in this situation, and then judge, whether a reasonable man in the soldiers situation, would not have concluded they were going to kill him. I believe, if I was to reverse the scene, I should bring it home to our own bosoms; suppose Colonel *Marshall,* when he came out of his own door, and saw these grenadiers coming down with swords, &c. had thought it proper to have appointed a military watch; suppose he had assembled *Gray* and *Attucks* that were killed, or any other persons in town, and had planted them in that station as a military watch, and there had come from *Murray's* barracks, thirty or forty soldiers, with no other arms than snow-balls, cakes of ice, oyster-shells, cinders and clubs, and attacked this military watch in this manner, what do you suppose would have been the feelings and reasonings of any of our householders; I confess I believe they would not have borne the one half of what the witnesses have sworn the soldiers bore, till they had shot down as many as were necessary to intimidate and disperse the rest; because, the law does not oblige us to bear insults to the danger of our lives, to stand still with such a number of people round us, throwing such things at us, and threatening our lives, until we are disabled to defend ourselves. . . .

I will enlarge no more on the evidence, but submit it to you.—Facts are stubborn things; and whatever may be our wishes, our inclinations, or the dictates of our passions, they cannot alter the state of facts and evidence: nor is the law less stable than the fact; if an assault was made to endanger their lives, the law is clear, they had a right to kill in their own defence; if it was not so severe as to endanger their lives, yet if they were assaulted at all, struck and abused by blows of any sort, by snow-balls, oyster-shells, cinders, clubs, or sticks of any kind; this was a provocation, for which the law reduces the offence of killing, down to manslaughter, in consideration of those passions in our nature, which cannot be eradicated. To your candour and justice I submit the prisoners and their cause.

The law, in all vicissitudes of government, fluctuations of the passions, or flights of enthusiasm, will preserve a steady undeviating course; it will not bend to the uncertain wishes, imaginations, and wanton tempers of men. To use the words of a great and worthy man, a patriot, and an hero, and enlightned friend of mankind, and a martyr to liberty; I mean ALGERNON SIDNEY, who from his earliest infancy sought a tranquil retirement under the shadow of the tree of liberty, with his tongue, his pen, and his sword, "The law, (says he,) no passion can disturb. 'Tis void of desire and fear, lust and anger. 'Tis *mens sine affectu;* written reason; retaining some measure of the divine perfection. It does not enjoin that which pleases a weak, frail man, but without any regard to persons, commands that which is good, and punishes evil in all, whether rich, or poor, high or low, — 'Tis deaf, inexorable, inflexible." On the one hand it is inexorable to the cries and lamentations of the prisoners; on the other it is deaf, deaf as an adder to the clamours of the populace.

Page of Adams's law docket with the name of John Hancock, April 1, 1771

In his *Autobiography* John Adams later recorded he felt that the juries had given correct verdicts in the trials of Captain Prescott and the soldiers.

Autobiography, 1802–7

It appeared to me, that the greatest Service which could be rendered to the People of the Town, was to lay before them, the Law as it stood that the[y] might be fully apprized of the Dangers of various kinds, which must arise from intemperate heats and irregular commotions. Although the Clamour was very loud, among some Sorts of People, it has been a great Consolation to me through

Life, that I acted in this Business with steady impartiality, and conducted it to so happy an Issue.

By the end of May, 1771, general fatigue, a lung condition, and a pain in his chest prompted John Adams to take a trip down the beautiful Connecticut Valley on horseback. Along the way he stopped to take the mineral waters at Stafford Springs. His *Diary* contains the narrative of the pleasant interlude.

1771. Thursday May 30. Mounted my Horse for Connecticutt. Stopped, and chatted an Hour with Tom Crafts who is very low with Rheumatism and an Hectic, but the same honest, good humoured Man as ever. Stopped again at little Cambridge at the House by the Meeting House, and gave my Horse Hay and Oats, at Mr. Jacksons. Rode alone. My Mind has been running chiefly upon my Farm and its Inhabitants and Furniture, my Horses, Oxen, Cows, Swine, Walls, Fences &c. I have in several late Rambles very particularly traced, and pursued every Swamp and Spring upon the North Side of Penns Hill from its Sourse to its Outlet. And I think if I owned the whole of that Side of the Hill I could make great Improvements upon it, by Means of Springs, and Descents and falls of Water.

1771. Monday June 3d. A fine Morning—a soft, sweet S. W. Wind, Oated in Spencer—turned my Horse to grass at Wolcotts in Brookfield. I ride alone, I find no Amusement, no Conversation, and have nothing to think about. But my Office and Farm frequently steal into my Mind, and seem to demand my Return. They must both suffer for Want of my Presence.

The Road to Stafford turns off, by Brookfield Meeting House, into Brimfield in the County of Hampshire.

Dined at Cheneys of Western in the County of Hampshire. An old Man came in, and after some Conversation with the old Landlady, she asked him, if he was not the Man who called here about 17 Years ago and was intrusted with a Jill of W. India Rum? He said Yes. Hant you had your Money?—No.—Well I sent it by a Brimfield Man, within a fortnight after. I'le at him about it. I'm desperate glad you mentioned it. I had the Rum. I was driving down a drove of Hogs. My two Boys were with me, I lost em both in the Year 1759, one at Crownpoint and one about 10 mile from Albany. They drinked the Rum with me. I'm glad you mentioned it—the Money is justly your due. I'le pay you now—how much is it.— 2s:4d.—But says I, interposing for Curiosity, that will hardly do justice for the Interest is as much as the Principall. The whole Debt is 4s:8d.—I'm a poor Man says he. Landlady wont ask me Interest.—I was much amused with the old Womans quick and tenacious Memory, and with the old Mans Honesty. But it seems to be, that the whole Anecdote shews that these are but two Penny People.

This honest Man whose Name is Frost, hearing that I was bound to the Spring, and unacquainted with the Way, very obligingly waited for me, to shew me the Way as far as he went which was several Miles. His father came from Billerica, to Springfield. Mrs. Cheney says her Husband came from Roxbury. I found that Frost was a great Partisan of the mineral Spring. He said, He had been weakly this 30 Year, and the Spring had done him more good in a few days, than all the Drs. had done, in 30 Year—and he went on and told of a great Number of marvellous Instances of Cures wrought there by Washing and drinking while he was there.

1771. Tuesday. June 4th. Rode over to the Spring. One Childs had built a little House, within a few Yards of the Spring, and there some of the lame and infirm People keep. The Spring arises at the Foot of a Steep high Hill, between a Cluster of Rocks very near the Side of a River. The Water is very clear, limpid and transparent, the Rocks And Stones and Earth at the Bottom are tinged with a reddish yellow colour, and so is the little Wooden Gutter that is placed at the Mouth of the Spring to carry the Water off—indeed the Water communicates that Colour, which resembles that of the Rust of Iron, to whatever Object it washes. Mrs. Child furnished me with a Glass Mugg, broken to Pieces and painted together again, and with that I drank pretty plentifully of the Water. It has the Taste of fair Water with an Infusion of some Preparation of steel in it, which I have taken, heretofore—Sal Martis, somewhat like Copperas. They have built a shed over a little Reservoir made of Wood, about 3 feet deep and into that have conveyed the Water from the Spring, and there People bath, Wash and plunge, for which Childs has 8d. a time. I plunged in twice—but the 2d time was superfluous and did me more hurt than good, it is very cold indeed.

1771. Wednesday June 5th.
Rode to the Spring, drank and plunged. Dipped but once. Sky cloudy.

1771. Fryday. June 7th.
Went to the Spring with the Dr. and drank a Glass and an half i.e. a Jill and an half....

I begin to grow weary of this idle, romantic Jaunt. I believe it would have been as well to have staid in my own Country and amused myself with my farm, and rode to Boston every day. I shall not suddenly take such a Ramble again, merely for my Health. I want to see my Wife, my Children, my Farm, my Horse, Oxen, Cows, Walls, Fences, Workmen, Office, Books, and Clerks. I want to hear the News, and Politicks of the Day. But here I am, at Bissels in Windsor, hearing my Landlord read a Chapter in the Kitchen and go to Prayers with his Family, in the genuine Tone of a Puritan.

1771. Saturday June 8th.
At eleven O Clock arrived at Wrights in Weathersfield. I have spent this Morning in Riding thro Paradise. My Eyes never beheld so fine a Country. From Bissills in Windsor to Hartford Ferry, 8 Miles, is one continued Street—Houses all along, and a vast Prospect of level Country on each Hand, the Lands very rich and the Husbandry pretty good. The Town of Hartford is not very compact, there are some very handsome and large Houses, some of brick. The State House is pretty large, and looks well. I stopped only to oat my Horse and get my Head and Face shaved, and then rode to Weathersfield 4 miles, on the West Side of the River.—Here is the finest Ride in America, I believe. Nothing can exceed the Beauty, and Fertility of the Country. The Lands upon the River, the flatt low Lands, are loaded with rich, noble Crops of Grass, and Grain and Corn. Wright says, some of their Lands, will yeild 2 Crops of English Grass, and two Ton and an half at each Crop, and plenty of after feed besides—but these must be nicely managed and largely dunged. They have in Weathersfield a large brick Meeting House, Lockwood the Minister. A Gentleman came in and told me, that there was not such another Street in America as this at Weathersfield excepting one

*View of the hotel and buildings at
Mineral Springs, Stafford, in 1810*

at Hadley, and that Mr. Ingersol the Stamp Master told him, he had never seen in Phyladelphia nor in England, any Place equal to Hartford and Weathersfield.—One Joseph Webb, one Deane and one Verstille, are the principal Traders here, both in English and W. India Goods. . . .

Rode to Middletown, and put up for the Sabbath at Shalers, near the Court House. Middleton I think is the most beautifull Town of all. When I first opened into the Town which was upon the Top of a Hill, there opened before me the most beautifull Prospect of the River, and the Intervals and Improvements, on each Side of it, and the Mountains at about 10 Miles distance both on the East and West Side of the River, and of the main Body of the Town at a Distance. I went down this Hill, and into a great Gate, which led me to the very Banks of the River. The Road lies here along the Bank of the River and on the right Hand is a fine level Tract of Interval Land as rich as the Soil of Egypt. The Lotts are divided by no Fence, but here are Strips runing back at right Angles from the River, on one is Indian Corn, on another Parrallell to it is Rye, on another Barley, on another Flax, on another a rich Burden of Clover and other English Grasses, and after riding in this enchanting Meadow for some Time you come to another Gate, which lets you into the main Body of the Town, which is ornamented as is the Meadow I just mentioned, with fine Rows of Trees and appears to me as populous, as compact and as polite as Hartford.

The Air all along from Somers to Middleton appears to me to be very clear, dry, and elastic. And therefore, if I were to plan another Journey for my Health, I would go from Boston to Lancaster and Lunenbourg, thence to No. 4. and thence down to N. Hampton, Deerfield, Hadley, Springfield, then to Endfield, and along the River down to Seabrook [Saybrook], and from thence over to Rhode Island and from thence to Braintree. And here I might possibly, i.e. at No. 4. look up some Land to purchase for my Benefit, or the Benefit of my Children. But I hope I shall not take another Journey merely for my Health very soon. I feel sometimes sick of this—I feel guilty—I feel as if I ought not to saunter and loyter and trifle away this Time—I feel as if I ought to be employed, for the Benefit of my fellow Men, in some Way or other.

In all this Ramble from Stafford, I have met with no-

The Charter Oak in Hartford, Conn.

Webb House in Wethersfield, Conn.

body that I knew, excepting Jo. Trumble, who with his father the Governor were crossing the ferry for the East Side when I was for the West.

Bespoke Entertainment for the Sabbath, at Shalers, and drank Tea. She brought me in the finest and sweetest of Wheat Bread, and Butter, as yellow as Gold, and fine Radishes, very good Tea and sugar. I regaled without Reserve. But my Wife is 150 Miles from me at least, and I am not yet homeward bound. I wish Connecticutt River flowed through Braintree. But the barren rocky Mountains of Braintree are as great a Contrast as can be conceived to the level smoth, fertile Plains of this Country. Yet Braintree pleases me more.

I long to be foul of Deacon Belchers Orchard. I am impatient to begin my Canal, and banks, to convey the Water all round, by the Road and the House. I must make a Pool in the Road by the Corner of my Land at the Yard in front of the House, for the cool Spring Water to come into the Road there—that the Cattle, and Hogs, and Ducks may regale themselves there.

Looking into the Almanac, I am startled. S[uperior] C[ourt] Ipswich is the 18th. day of June. I thought it a Week later 25. So that I have only next Week to go home 150 Miles. I must improve every Moment. It is 25 miles a day if I ride every day next Week.

ALL.: *Connecticut Historical Collections*
BY JOHN WARNER BARBER, 1836

Public buildings in Middletown

The last *Diary* entry of this picturesque journey records the return of the traveler to his native country and to his thoughts concerning familiar problems.

1771. Thursday June 13th.
I read to day an Address from the Convention of Ministers, and from the Clergy in the northern Part of the County of Hampshire and from the Town of Almesbury, all conceived in very high Terms, of Respect and Confidence and Affection. Posterity will scarcely find it possible, to form a just Idea of this Gentlemans Character. But if this wretched Journal should ever be read, by my own Family, let them know that there was upon the Scene of Action with Mr. Hutchinson, one determined Enemy to those Principles and that Political System to which alone he owes his own and his Family's late Advancement —one who thinks that his Character and Conduct have been the Cause of laying a Foundation for perpetual Dis-

A commission signed by Hutchinson, "Captain General and Governor in Chief, in and over His Majesty's Province of Massachusetts-Bay"

content and Uneasiness between Britain and the Colonies, of perpetual Struggles of one Party for Wealth and Power at the Expence of the Liberties of this Country, and of perpetual Contention and Opposition in the other Party to preserve them, and that this Contention will never be fully terminated but by Warrs, and Confusions and Carnage. Cæsar, by destroying the Roman Republic, made himself perpetual Dictator, Hutchinson, by countenancing and supporting a System of Corruption and all Tyranny, has made himself Governor—and the mad Idolatry of the People, always the surest Instruments of their own Servitude, laid prostrate at the Feet of both. With great Anxiety, and Hazard, with continual Application to Business, with loss of Health, Reputation, Profit, and as fair Prospects and Opportunities of Advancement, as others who have greedily embraced them, I have for 10 Years together invariably opposed this System, and its fautors. It has prevailed in some Measure, and the People are now worshipping the Authors and Abetters of it, and despizing, insulting, and abusing, the Opposers of it....

As I came over Sudbury Causey, I saw a Chaplain of one of the Kings Ships fishing in the River, a thick fat Man, with rosy Cheeks and black Eyes. At Night he came in with his fish. I was in the Yard and he spoke to me, and told me the News.—The Governor gave a very elegant Entertainment to the Gentlemen of the Army and Navy and Revenue, and Mrs. Gambier in the Evening a very elegant Ball—as elegant a cold Collation as perhaps you ever see—all in figures &c. &c. &c.

Read this days Paper. The melodious Harmony, the perfect Concords, the entire Confidence and Affection, that seems to be restored greatly surprizes me. Will it be lasting. I believe there is no Man in so curious a Situation as I am. I am for what I can see, quite left alone, in the World.

Thomas Hutchinson had incurred Adams's censure long before news of his appointment as Governor of Massachusetts interrupted Adams's pastoral idyll. While still Lieutenant Governor, Hutchinson had angered Adams by his overweening ambition, his multiple office-holding, and his practice of appointing friends and relatives to the highest places in government. But Hutchinson continued in the public favor until 1773, when letters written by himself and others to correspondents in England were purloined and turned over to Benjamin Franklin, London agent for the Massachusetts Bay Colony's legislature. The letters revealed Hutchinson's preference for further restrictions on colonial liberties rather than a severance of ties with Great Britain—an alternative he thought would be disastrous for the colony. Sent to Boston, the letters were copied and circulated clandestinely among the Sons of Liberty and their friends, in whom they aroused great indignation. Again, Adams took pen in hand and recorded the progress of events in his *Diary*.

1773. March 22d. Monday.
This Afternoon received a Collection of Seventeen Letters, written from this Prov[ince], Rhode Island, Connecticutt and N. York, by Hut[chinson], Oli[ver], Moff[at], Paxt[on], and Rome, in the Years 1767, 8, 9.

They came from England under such Injunctions of Secrecy, as to the Person to whom they were written, by whom and to whom they are sent here, and as to the contents of them, no Copies of the whole or any Part to be taken, that it is difficult to make any use of them.

These curious Projectors and Speculators in Politicks, will ruin this Country—cool, thinking, deliberate Villain[s], malicious, and vindictive, as well as ambitious and avaricious.

The Secrecy of these epistolary Genii is very remarkable—profoundly secret, dark, and deep.

1773. April 7th: Wednesday.
At Charlestown. What shall I write?—say?—do?

Sterility, Vacuity, Barrenness of Thought, and Reflection.

What News shall we hear?

1773 April 24th. Saturday.
I have communicated to Mr. Norton Quincy, and to Mr. Wibird the important Secret. They are as much affected, by it, as any others. Bone of our Bone, born and educated among us! Mr. Hancock is deeply affected, is determined in Conjunction with Majr. Hawley to watch the vile Serpent, and his deputy Serpent Brattle.

The Subtilty, of this Serpent, is equal to that of the old one.

Framed silhouette of Hutchinson

Thomas Hutchinson sailed for England in 1774. His departure out of John Adams's life was not mourned. On the other hand, Jonathan Sewall, an old and dear friend with whom Adams had been acquainted since 1757 when they were law students in Worcester, had been deeply influenced, Adams felt, by Hutchinson and Toryism. In the preface to the 1819 edition of *Novanglus and Massachusettensis*, a history of Britain's dispute with America, John Adams recalled the course of his friendship with Sewall.

Novanglus and Massachusettensis, 1819

After the surrender of Montreal, in 1759, rumors were everywhere spread, that the English would now new-model the Colonies, demolish the charters, and reduce all to royal governments. These rumors I had heard as often as he had. One morning I met him accidentally on the floor of the old town-house. "John," said he, "I want to speak with you." He always called me John, and I him Jonathan; and I often said to him, I wish my name were David. He took me to a window-seat and said, "These Englishmen are going to play the devil with us. They will overturn every thing. We must resist them, and that by force. I wish you would write in the newspapers, and urge a general attention to the militia, to their exercises and discipline, for we must resist in arms." I answered, "All this, I fear is true; but why do you not write yourself? You are older than I am, have more experience than I have, are more intimate with the grandees than I am, and you can write ten times better than I can." There had been a correspondence between us, by which I knew his refined style, as well as he knew my coarse one. "Why," said Mr. Sewall, "I would write, but Goffe will find me out, and I shall grieve his righteous soul, and you know what influence he has in Middlesex." This Goffe had been attorney-general for twenty years, and commanded the practice in Middlesex and Worcester and several other counties. He had power to crush, by his frown or his nod, any young lawyer in his county. He was afterwards Judge Trowbridge, but at that time as ardent as any of Hutchinson's disciples, though he afterwards became alienated from his pursuits and principles.

John Adams recounted in his *Autobiography* the details surrounding an important decision, taken with respect to his own life, that involved his friend Sewall.

Autobiography, 1802–7

In the Course of this Year 1768 My Friend Mr. Jonathan Sewall who was then Attorney General called on me in

When Hutchinson was about to leave, he was hung in effigy along with Alexander Wedderburn, and these epitaphs were issued as a broadside in Philadelphia, May 3, 1774.

MASSACHUSETTS HISTORICAL SOCIETY

Brattle Street, and told me he was come to dine with me. This was always an acceptable favour from him, for although We were at Antipodes in Politicks We had never abated in mutual Esteem or cooled in the Warmth of our Friendship. After Dinner Mr. Sewall desired to have some Conversation with me alone and proposed adjourning to the office. Mrs. Adams arose and chose to Adjourn to her Chamber. We were accordingly left alone. Mr. Sewall then said he waited on me at that time at the request of the Governor Mr. Bernard, who had sent for him a few days before and charged him with a Message to me. The Office of Advocate General in the Court of Admiralty was then vacant, and the Governor had made Enquiry of Gentlemen the best qualified to give him information, and particularly of one of great Authority (meaning Lt. Governor and Chief Justice Hutchinson), and although he was not particularly acquainted with me himself the Result of his Inquiries was that in point of Talents, Integrity, Reputation and consequence at the Bar, Mr. Adams was the best entitled to the Office and he had determined Accordingly, to give it to me. It was true he had not Power to give me more than a temporary Appointment, till his Majestys Pleasure should be known: but that he would give immediately all the Appointment in his Power, and would write an immediate Recommendation of me to his Majesty and transmitt it to his Ministers and there was no doubt I should receive the Kings Commission, as soon as an Answer could be returned from England: for there had been no Instance of a refusal to confirm the Appointment of a Governor in such Cases.

Although this Offer was unexpected to me, I was in an instant prepared for an Answer. The Office was lucrative in itself, and a sure introduction to the most profitable Business in the Province: and what was of more consequence still, it was a first Step in the Ladder of Royal Favour and promotion. But I had long weighed this Subject in my own Mind. For seven Years I had been solicited by some of my friends and Relations, as well as others, and Offers had been made me by Persons who had Influence, to apply to the Governor or to the Lieutenant Governor, to procure me a Commission for the Peace. Such an Officer was wanted in the Country where I had lived and it would have been of very considerable Advantage to me. But I had always rejected these proposals, on Account of the unsettled State of the Country, and my Scruples about laying myself under any restraints, or Obligations of Gratitude to the Government for any of their favours. The new Statutes had been passed in Parliament laying Duties on Glass, Paint &c. and a Board of Commissioners of the Revenue was expected, which must excite a great fermentation in the Country, of the Consequences of which I could see no End.

My Answer to Mr. Sewall was very prompt, that I was sensible of the honor done me by the Governor: but I must be excused from Accepting his Offer. Mr. Sewall enquired why, what was my Objection. I answered that he knew very well my political Principles, the System I had adopted and the Connections and Friendships I had formed in Consequence of them: He also knew that the British Government, including the King, his Ministers and Parliament, apparently supported by a great Majority of the Nation, were persevering in a System, wholly inconsistent with all my Ideas of Right, Justice and Policy, and therefore I could not place myself in a Situation in which my Duty and my Inclination would be so much at Variance. To this Mr. Sewall returned that he was instructed by the Governor to say that he knew my political Sentiments very well: but they should be no Objection with him. I should be at full Liberty to entertain my own Opinions, which he did not wish to influence by this office. He had offered it to me, merely because he believed I was the best qualified for it and because he relied on my Integrity. I replied This was going as far in the generosity and Liberality of his sentiments as the Governor could go or as I could desire, if I could Accept the Office: but that I knew it would lay me under restraints and Obligations that I could not submit to and therefore I could not in honor or Conscience Accept it.

Mr. Sewall paused, and then resuming the Subject asked, why are you so quick, and sudden in your determination? You had better take it into consideration, and give me an Answer at some future day. I told him my Answer had been ready because my mind was clear and my determination decided and unalterable. That my Advice would be that Mr. Fitch should be appointed, to whose Views the Office would be perfectly agreable. Mr. Sewal said he should certainly give me time to think of it: I said that time would produce no change and he had better make his report immediately. We parted, and about three Weeks afterwards he came to me again and hoped I had thought more favourably on the Subject: that the Governor had sent for him and told him the public Business suffered and the office must be filled. I told him my Judgment and Inclination and determination were unalterably fixed, and that I had hoped that Mr. Fitch would have been appointed before that time. Mr. Fitch however never was appointed. He acted for the Crown, by the Appointment of the Judge from day to day, but never had any Commission from the Crown or Appointment of the Governor.

The break in this friendship, which did not come until 1774, had its epilogue in 1788.

Novanglus and Massachusettensis, 1819
We continued our friendship and confidential intercourse, though professedly in boxes of politics as opposite as east and west, until the year 1774, when we both attended the superior court in Falmouth, Casco Bay, now Portland. I had then been chosen a delegate to Congress. Mr. Sewall invited me to take a walk with him, very early in the morning, on the great hill. In the course of our rambles, he very soon began to remonstrate against my going to Congress. He said, that "Great Britain was determined on her system; her power was irresistible, and would certainly be destructive to me, and to all those who should persevere in opposition to her designs." I answered, "that I knew Great Britain was determined on her system, and that very determination determined me on mine; that he knew I had been constant and uniform in opposition to all her measures; that the die was now cast; I had passed the Rubicon; swim or sink, live or die, survive or perish with my country, was my unalterable determination." The conversation was protracted into length, but this was the substance of the whole. It terminated in my saying to him, "I see we must part, and with a bleeding heart I say, I fear forever; but you may depend upon it, this adieu is the sharpest thorn on which I ever set my foot." I never conversed with him

again till the year 1788. Mr. Sewall retired, in 1775, to England, where he remained and resided in Bristol. . . .

In 1788, Mr. Sewall came to London to embark for Halifax. I inquired for his lodgings, and instantly drove to them, laying aside all etiquette to make him a visit. I ordered my servant to announce John Adams, was instantly admitted, and both of us, forgetting that we had ever been enemies, embraced each other as cordially as ever. I had two hours conversation with him, in a most delightful freedom, upon a multitude of subjects. He told me he had lived for the sake of his two children; he had spared no pains nor expense in their education, and he was going to Halifax in hope of making some provision for them. They are now two of the most respectable gentlemen in Canada. One of them a chief justice, the other an attorney-general. Their father lived but a short time after his return to America; evidently broken down by his anxieties, and probably dying of a broken heart. He always lamented the conduct of Great Britain towards America. No man more constantly congratulated me, while we lived together in America, upon any news, true or false, favorable to a repeal of the obnoxious statutes and a redress of our grievances; but the society in which he lived had convinced him that all resistance was not only useless but ruinous.

Chapter **5**

The Road to Philadelphia

Political events in the Massachusetts Bay Colony during the years 1773 and 1774 were so skillfully manipulated and exploited by Samuel and John Adams as to put the colony in the van of resistance to royal authority. If Samuel was the artificer of resistance, John was the publicist who justified it.

The committees of correspondence, which most of the colonies had established in an effort to coordinate resistance to Britain, were doing their utmost to exploit colonial objections to British importation duties and to the payment of judges' salaries by the Crown. During the night of December 16, 1773, a group of patriots, disguised as Indians, dumped several cargoes of tea from England into Boston Harbor to prevent taxes being paid on it. This act of purposeful destruction of property immediately provoked punitive measures from London. Early in 1774 the so-called Intolerable Acts were passed by Parliament closing the Port of Boston on June 1, 1774, and depriving the inhabitants of Massachusetts of many of the cherished civil rights guaranteed them under their charter.

The colonial response to this punishment was a resolution of the Virginia House of Burgesses, passed on May 28, 1774, calling for a congress of representatives from each colony to consider the king's latest measures. John Adams was a member of the Massachusetts delegation to this First Continental Congress, which met in Philadelphia from September 5 to October 26, 1774. Precipitated by rumors that British troops had committed atrocities in Boston, and by the resolutions of Suffolk County, Massachusetts, against "the attempts of a wicked administration to enslave America," and spurred on by Samuel Adams and the radicals, the Congress rejected a plan for a peaceful adjustment of difficulties. Instead the delegates adopted a declaration of rights and grievances addressed to the people of Great Britain and the colonies. They also sent a petition to the king and created the Continental Association, consisting of committees of inspection from each colony, which were to supervise colonial agreements of nonimportation, nonexportation, and nonconsumption. The creation of this powerful extra-legal machinery, by and in the hands of the radicals, supported the king's growing conviction that the American Colonies were in a state of active rebellion, a belief that was soon to be confirmed with the opening of hostilities in 1775.

It was during this period that John Adams came to the conclusion that he must commit his life entirely to the cause of liberty by quitting his law practice to serve in the First Continental Congress. His letters reveal his anguish and his exultation as he confronted the call to participate in colonial leadership. His political writings display a growing mastery of the science of government, and his *Autobiography* shows that during the crisis of 1773 over judges' salaries his published reflections on the operation of the British constitution were capable of producing practical results.

Autobiography, 1802–7

At this Period [winter of 1773–74], the Universal Cry, among the Friends of their Country was "What shall We do to be saved?" It was by all Agreed, As the Governor was entirely dependent on the Crown, and the Council in danger of becoming so if the Judges were made so too, the Liberties of the Country would be totally lost, and every Man at the Mercy of a few Slaves of the Governor. But no Man presumed to say what ought to be done, or what could be done. Intimations were frequently given, that this Arrangement should not be submitted to.—I understood very well what was meant, and I fully expected that if no Expedient could be suggested, that the Judges would be obliged to go where Secretary Oliver had gone to Liberty Tree, and compelled to take an Oath to renounce the Royal Salaries. Some of these Judges were men of Resolution and the Chief Justice in particular, piqued himself so much upon it and had so often gloried in it on the Bench, that I shuddered at the expectation that the Mob might put on him a Coat of Tar and Feathers, if not put him to death. I had a real respect for the Judges. Three of them Trowbridge, Cushing and Brown I could call my Friends. Oliver and Ropes abstracted from their politicks were amiable Men, and all of them were very respectable and virtuous Characters. I dreaded the Effect upon the Morals and temper of the People, which must be produced, by any violence offered to the Persons of those who wore the Robes and bore the sacred Characters of Judges, and moreover I felt a strong Aversion to such partial and irregular Recurrences to original Power. The poor People

The Liberty Tree in Boston,
rallying place for the patriots

themselves who by secret manoeuvres are excited to insurrection are seldom aware of the purposes for which they are set in motion: or of the Consequences which may happen to themselves: and when once heated and in full Career, they can neither manage themselves, nor be regulated by others. Full of these Reflections, I happened to dine with Mr. Samuel Winthrop at New Bost[on], who was then Clerk of the Superior Court, in company with several Members of the General Court of both Houses and with several other Gentlemen of the Town. Dr. John Winthrop Phylosophical Professor at Colledge and Dr. Cooper of Boston both of them very much my Friends, were of the Company. The Conversation turned wholly on the Topic of the Day—the Case of the Judges. All agreed that it was a fatal Measure and would be the Ruin of the Liberties of the Country: But what was the Remedy? It seemed to be a measure that would execute itself. There was no imaginable Way of resisting or eluding it. There was lamentation and mourning enough: but no light and no hope. The Storm was terrible and no blue Sky to be discovered. I had been entirely silent, and in the midst of all this gloom, Dr. Winthrop, addressing himself to me, said Mr. Adams We have not heard your Sentiments on this Subject, how do you consider it? I answered that my Sentiments accorded perfectly with all which had been expressed. The Measure had created a Crisis, and if it could not be defeated, the Liberties of the Province would be lost. The Stroke was levelled at the Essence of the Constitution, and nothing was too dear to be hazarded in warding it off. It levelled the Axe at the Root, and if not opposed the Tree would be overthrown from the foundation. It appeared so to me at that time and I have seen no reason, to suspect that I was in an Error, to this day. But said Dr. Winthrop, What can be done? I answered, that I knew not whether any one would approve of my Opinion but I believed there was one constitutional Resource, but I knew not whether it would be possible to persuade the proper Authority to have recourse to it. Several Voices at once cryed out, a constitutional Resource! what can it be? I said it was nothing more nor less than an Impeachment of the Judges by the House of Representatives before the Council. An Impeachment! Why such a thing is without Precedent. I believed it was, in

Chief Justice Peter Oliver

137

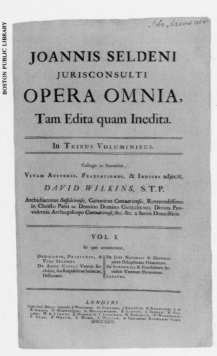

Adams's copy of "Seldens Works in which is a Treatise on Judicature"

this Province: but there had been precedents enough, and by much too many in England: It was a dangerous Experiment at all times: but it was essential to the preservation of the Constitution in some Cases, that could be reached by no other Power, but that of Impeachment. But whence can We pretend to derive such a Power? From our Charter, which gives Us, in Words as express, as clear and as strong as the Language affords, all the Rights and Priviledges of Englishmen: and if the House of Commons in England is the grand Inquest of the Nation, the House of Representatives is the Grand Inquest of this Province, and the Council must have the Powers of Judicature of the House of Lords in Great Britain. This Doctrine was said by the Company to be wholly new. They knew not how far it could be supported, but it deserved to be considered and examined. After all if it should be approved by the House, the Council would not convict the Judges.—That, I said, was an after consideration, if the House was convinced that they had the Power, and that it was their duty to exercise it, they ought to do it, and oblige the Council to enquire into their Rights and Powers and Duties. If the Council would not hearken to Law or Evidence, they must be responsible for the consequences, and the Guilt and blame must lie at their door. The Company seperated, and I knew that the Governor and the Judges would soon have Information of this Conversation, and as several Members of both Houses were present, and several Gentlemen of the Town, I was sensible that it would soon become the Talk of the Legislatures as well as of the Town. The next day, I believe, Major Hawley came to my House and told me, he heard I had broached a strange Doctrine. He hardly knew what an Impeachment was, he had never read any one and never had thought on the Subject. I told him he might read as many of them as he pleased. There stood the State Tryals on the Shelf which were full of them, of all sorts good and bad. I shewed him Seldens Works in which is a Treatise on Judicature in Parliament, and gave it him to read. That judicature in Parliament was as ancient as common Law and as Parliament itself; that without this high Jurisdiction it was thought impossible to defend the Constitution against Princes and Nobles and great Ministers, who might commit high Crimes and Misdemeanors which no other Authority would be powerfull enough to prevent or punish. That our Constitution was a Miniature of the British: that the Charter had given Us every Power, Jurisdiction and right within our Limits which could be claimed by the People or Government of England, with no other exceptions than those in the Charter expressed. We looked into the Charter together, and after a long conversation and a considerable Research he said he knew not how to get rid of it. In a Day or two another Lawyer in the House came to me, full of doubts and difficulties, He said he heard I had shown Major Hawley some Books relative to the Subject and desired to see them. I shewed them to him and made nearly the same comment upon them. It soon became the common Topick and research of the Bar. Major Hawley had a long Friendship for Judge Trowbridge and a high Opinion of his Knowledge of Law which was indeed extensive: he determined to converse with the Judge upon the Subject, went to Cambridge on Saturday and staid till monday. On this Visit he introduced this subject, and appealed to Lord Coke and Selden, as well as to the Charter, and advanced all the Arguments which occurred to him. The Judge although he had renounced the Salary We may suppose was not much delighted with the Subject, on Account of his Brothers. He did however declare to the Major that he could not deny, that the Constitution had given the Power to the House of Representatives, the Charter was so full and express, but that the Exercise of it, in this Case would be vain as the Council would undoubtedly acquit the Judges even if they heard and tryed the Impeachment. Hawley was not so much concerned about that as he was to ascertain the Law. The first time I saw Judge Trowbridge, he said to me, I see Mr. Adams you are determined to explore the Constitution and bring to Life all its dormant and latent Powers, in defence of your Liberties as you understand them. I answered I should be very happy if the Constitution could carry Us safely through all our difficulties without having recourse to higher Powers not written. The Members of the House, becoming soon convinced that there was something for them to do, appointed a Committee to draw up Articles of Impeachment against the Chief Justice Oliver. Major Hawley who was one of this Committee, would do nothing without me, and insisted on bringing them to my house, to examine and discuss the Articles paragraph by Paragraph, which was readily consented to by the Committee. Several Evenings were spent in my Office, upon this Business, till very late at night. One Morning, meeting Ben. Gridley, he said to me Brother Adams you keep late Hours at your House: as I passed it last night long after midnight, I saw your Street door vomit forth a Crowd of Senators. The Articles when prepared were reported to the House of Representatives, adopted by them and sent up to the Council Board. The Council would do nothing and there they rested. The Friends of Administration thought they had obtained a Tryumph but they were mistaken. The Articles were printed in the Journals of the House and in the Newspapers, and the People meditated on them at their Leisure. When the Superior Court came to sit in Boston, the Grand Jurors and Petit Jurors as their names were called over refused to take the Oaths. When examined and demanded their reasons for this extraordinary Conduct, they answered to a Man, that the Chief Justice of that Court stood impeached of high Crimes and Misdemeanors, before his Majestys Council, and they would not sit as Jurors while that Accusation was depending. Att the Charlestown Court the Jurors unanimously refused in the same manner: They did so at Worcester and all the other Counties. The Court never sat again untill a new one was appointed by the Council exercising the Powers of a Governor under the Charter after the Battle of Lexington on the 19th of April 1775.

The Green Dragon Tavern, where a group "met to Plan the Consignment of a few Shiploads of Tea," 1773

The Boston Tea Party in December, 1773, was indeed a decisive act, the implications of which John Adams clearly discerned the following day in a letter to his friend James Warren.

Boston, 17 December, 1773.
The die is cast. The people have passed the river and cut away the bridge. Last night three cargoes of tea were emptied into the harbor. This is the grandest event which has ever yet happened since the controversy with Britain opened. The sublimity of it charms me!

For my part, I cannot express my own sentiments of it better than in the words of Colonel D. to me, last evening.... "The worst that can happen, I think," said

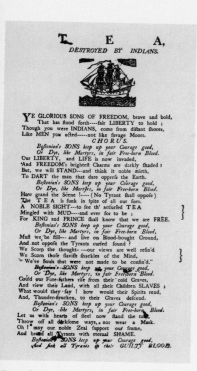

T E A,

DESTROYED BY INDIANS.

YE GLORIOUS SONS OF FREEDOM, brave and bold,
    That has stood forth----fair LIBERTY to hold ;
Though you were INDIANS, come from distant shores,
Like MEN you acted-----not like savage Moors.
        C H O R U S.
    Boftonian's SONS keep up your Courage good,
    Or Dye, like Martyrs, in fair Free-born Blood.
Our LIBERTY, and LIFE is now invaded,
'And FREEDOM's brighteft Charms are darkly fhaded ;
But, we will STAND---and think it noble mirth,
To DART the man that dare opprefs the Earth.
    Boftonian's SONS keep up your Courage good,
    Or Dye, like Martyrs, in fair Free-born Blood.
How grand the Scene !----(No Tyrant fhall oppofe)
The T E A is funk in fpite of all our foes.
A NOBLE SIGHT---to fee th' accurfed T E A
Mingled with MUD----and ever for to be ;
For KING and PRINCE fhall know that we are FREE.
    Boftonian's SONS keep up your Courage good,
    Or Dye, like Martyrs, in fair Free-born Blood,
Muft we be fill'---and live on Blood-bought Ground,
And not oppofe the Tyrants curfed found ?
We Scorn the thought---our views are well refin'd
We Scorn thofe flavifh fhackles of the Mind,
" We've Souls that were not made to be confin'd."
    Boftonian's SONS keep up your Courage good,
    Or Dye, like Martyrs, in fair Free-born Blood.
Could our Fore-fathers rife from their cold Graves,
And view their Land, with all their Children SLAVES ;
What would they fay ! how would their Spirits rend,
And, Thunder-ftrucken, to their Graves defcend.
    Boftonian's SONS keep up your Courage good,
    Or Dye, like Martyrs, in fair Free-born Blood.
Let us with hearts of fteel now ftand the tatt,
Throw off all irkfome ways, nor wear a Mask.
Oh ! may our noble Zeal fupport our frame,
And brand all Tyrants with eternal SHAME.
    Boftonian's SONS keep up your Courage good,
    And fink all Tyrants in their GUILTY BLOOD.

*Broadside verse hails "*A NOBLE SIGHT
to see th' accursed TEA, *Mingled
with* MUD — *and ever for to be."*

*Detail of an English cartoon depicts
British ministers forcing
America to swallow their tea.*

he, "in consequence of it, will be that the province must pay for it. Now, I think the province may pay for it, if it is drowned, as easily as if it is drunk; and I think it is a matter of indifference whether it is drunk or drowned. The province must pay for it in either case. But there is this difference; I believe it will take them ten years to get the province to pay for it; if so, we shall save ten years' interest of the money, whereas, if it is drunk, it must be paid for immediately." Thus he.—However, he agreed with me, that the province would never pay for it; and also in this, that the final ruin of our constitution of government, and of all American liberties, would be the certain consequence of suffering it to be landed.

Governor Hutchinson and his family and friends will never have done with their good services to Great Britain and the colonies. But for him, this tea might have been saved to the East India Company. Whereas this loss, if the rest of the colonies should follow our example, will, in the opinion of many persons, bankrupt the company. However, I dare say, the governor and consignees and custom-house officers in the other colonies will have more wisdom than ours have had, and take effectual care that their tea shall be sent back to England untouched; if not, it will as surely be destroyed there as it has been here.

Threats, phantoms, bugbears, by the million, will be invented and propagated among the people upon this occasion. Individuals will be threatened with suits and prosecutions. Armies and navies will be talked of. Military executions, charters annulled, treason trials in England, and all that. But these terms are all but imaginations. Yet, if they should become realities, they had better be suffered than the great principle of parliamentary taxation be given up.

The town of Boston never was more still and calm of a Saturday night than it was last night. All things were conducted with great order, decency, and *perfect submission to government.* No doubt we all thought the administration in better hands than it had been.

A few days later, John Adams was still gloating over the Boston Tea Party in another letter to James Warren.

Boston, 22 December, 1773

The spirit of liberty is very high in the country, and universal. Worcester is aroused. Last week a monument to liberty was erected there in the heart of the town, within a few yards of Colonel Chandler's door. A gentleman of as good sense and character as any in that county, told me this day, that nothing which has been ever done, is more universally approved, applauded, and admired than these last efforts. He says, that whole towns in that county were on tiptoe to come down.

General Thomas Gage, who had replaced Thomas Hutchinson in his capacity as Royal Governor of the Province, adjourned the legislature to Salem in June, 1774. Before Gage realized what was happening and could dissolve the legislature, the representatives selected a committee to represent Massachusetts in what would later be known as the First Continental Congress, to be held in Philadelphia in September, 1774.

Autobiography, 1802–7

It is well known that in June 1774 The General Court at Cambridge appointed Members to meet with others from the other States in Congress on the fifth of August [September]. Mr. Bowdoin, Mr. Cushing, Mr. Samuel Adams, Mr. John Adams and Mr. Robert Treat Paine were appointed. After this Election I went for the tenth and last time on the Eastern Circuit: At York at Dinner with the Court, happening to sit at Table next to Mr. Justice Seward, a Representative of York, but of the unpopular Side, We entered very sociably and pleasantly into conversation, and among other Things he said to me, Mr. Adams you are going to Congress, and great Things are in Agitation. I recommend to you the Doctrine of my former Minister Mr. Moody. Upon an Occasion of some gloomy prospect for the Country, he preached a Sermon from this text "And they know not what to do." After a customary introduction, he raised this Doctrine from his Text, that "in times of great difficulty and danger, when Men know not what to do, it is the Duty of a Person or a People to be very careful that they do not do, they know not what." This oracular Jingle of Words, which seemed, however to contain some good Sense, made Us all very gay. But I thought the venerable Preacher when he had beat the Drum ecclesiastic to animate the Country to undertake the Expedi-

A British cartoon of 1774 shows General Thomas Gage thrown by Massachusetts' resistance to the harsh measures taken against the colony.

tion to Louisbourg in 1745, and had gone himself with it as a Chaplain, had ventured to do he knew not what, as much as I was likely to do in the Expedition to Congress. I told the Deacon that I must trust Providence as Mr. Moody had done, when he did his duty though he could not foresee the Consequences.

John Adams's private thoughts at this critical time do not reflect the nonchalance he may have affected in public. His letters to his wife are full of deep concern for his family, his finances, and his future.

York [Maine] June 29. 1774

I was first sworn in 1758; My Life has been a continual Scaene of Fatigue, Vexation, Labour and Anxiety. I have four Children. I had a pretty Estate from my Father, I have been assisted by your Father. I have done the greatest Business in the Province. I have had the very richest Clients in the Province: Yet I am Poor in Comparison of others.

This I confess is grievous, and discouraging. I ought however, to be candid enough to acknowledge that I have been imprudent. I have spent an Estate in Books. I have spent a Sum of Money indiscreetly in a Lighter, another in a Pew, and a much greater in an House in Boston. These would have been Indiscretions, if the Impeachment of the Judges, the Boston Port Bill, &c. &c. had never happened; but by the unfortunate Interruption of my Business from these Causes, these Indiscretions become almost fatal to me, to be sure much more detrimental.

John Lowell, at Newbury Port, has built him an House, like the Palace of a Nobleman and lives in great Splendor. His Business is very profitable. In short every Lawyer who [has] the least Appearance of Abilities makes it do in the Co[untry.] In Town, nobody does, or ever can, who Either is not obstinately determined never to have any Connection with Politicks or does not engage on the Side of the Government, the Administration and the Court.

Let us therefore my dear Partner, from that Affection which we feel for our lovely Babes, apply ourselves by every Way, we can, to the Cultivation of our Farm. Let Frugality, And Industry, be our Virtues, if they are not of any others. And above all Cares of this Life let our

Broadside of June, 1774, lists the addresses and occupations of people who had signed a testimonial to Hutchinson on his departure, so that "every Friend to his Country" would know who British sympathizers were.

ardent Anxiety be, to mould the Minds and Manners of our Children. Let us teach them not only to do virtuously but to excell. To excell they must be taught to be steady, active, and industrious.

York July 1st: 1774

I am so idle, that I have not an easy Moment, without my Pen in my Hand. My Time might have been improved to some Purpose, in mowing Grass, raking Hay, or hoeing Corn, weeding Carrotts, picking or shelling Peas. Much better should I have been employed in schooling my Children, in teaching them to write, cypher, Latin, French, English and Greek.

I sometimes think I must come to this—to be the Foreman upon my own Farm, and the School Master to my own Children. I confess myself to be full of Fears that the Ministry and their Friends and Instruments, will prevail, and crush the Cause and Friends of Liberty. The Minds of that Party are so filled with Prejudices, against me, that they will take all Advantages, and do me all the Damage they can. These Thoughts have their Turns in my Mind, but in general my Hopes are predominant. In a Tryal of a Cause here to Day, some Facts were mentioned, which are worth writing to you. It was sworn, by Dr. Lyman, Elder Bradbury and others, that there had been a Number of Instances in this Town of fatal Accidents, happening from sudden Noises striking the Ears of Babes and young Children. A Gun was fired near one Child, as likely as any; the Child fell immediately into fits, which impaired his Reason, and is still living an Ideot. Another Child was sitting on a Chamber floor. A Man rapped suddenly and violently on the Boards which made the floor under the Child [tremble?]. The Child was so startled, and frightened, that it fell into fits, which never were cured.

This may suggest a Caution to keep Children from sudden Frights and surprizes.

Dr. Gardiner arrived here to day, from Boston, brings us News of a Battle at the Town Meeting, between Whigs and Tories, in which the Whiggs after a Day and an Halfs obstinate Engagement were finally victorious by two to one. He says the Tories are preparing a flaming Protest.

I am determined to be cool, if I can; I have suffered

such Torments in my Mind, heretofore, as have almost overpowered my Constitution, without any Advantage: and now I will laugh and be easy if I can, let the Conflict of Parties, terminate as it will—let my own Estate and Interest suffer what it will. Nay whether I stand high or low in the Estimation of the World, so long as I keep a Conscience void of Offence towards God and Man. And thus I am determined by the Will of God, to do, let what will become of me or mine, my Country, or the World.

I shall arouse myself ere long I believe, and exert an Industry, a Frugality, a hard Labour, that will serve my family, if I cant serve my Country. I will not lie down and die in Dispair. If I cannot serve my Children by the Law, I will serve them by Agriculture, by Trade, by some Way, or other. I thank God I have a Head, an Heart and Hands which if once fully exerted alltogether, will succeed in the World as well as those of the mean spirited, low minded, fawning obsequious scoundrells who have long hoped, that my Integrity would be an Obstacle in my Way, and enable them to out strip me in the Race.

But what I want in Comparison of them, of Villany and servility, I will make up in Industry and Capacity. If I dont they shall laugh and triumph.

I will not willingly see Blockheads, whom I have a Right to despise, elevated above me, and insolently triumphing over me. Nor shall Knavery, through any Negligence of mine, get the better of Honesty, nor Ignorance of Knowledge, nor Folly of Wisdom, nor Vice of Virtue.

I must intreat you, my dear Partner in all the Joys and Sorrows, Prosperity and Adversity of my Life, to take a Part with me in the Struggle. I pray God for your Health—intreat you to rouse your whole Attention to the Family, the stock, the Farm, the Dairy. Let every Article of Expence which can possibly be spared be retrench'd. Keep the Hands attentive to their Business, and [let] the most prudent Measures of every kind be adopted and pursued with Alacrity and Spirit.

Falmouth [Portland, Maine] July 6th: 1774
I believe it is Time to think a little about my Family and Farm. The fine Weather, we have had for 8 or 10 days

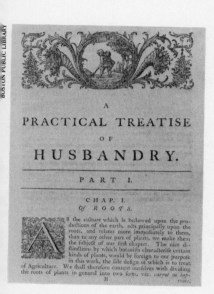

A

PRACTICAL TREATISE

OF

HUSBANDRY.

PART I.

CHAP. I.
OF ROOTS.

First page of an eighteenth-century book on husbandry owned by Adams

A New Method of Reaping, *woodcut from* Columbian Magazine *of 1778*

past I hope has been carefully improved to get in my Hay. It is a great Mortification to me that I could not attend every Step of their Progress in mowing, making and carting. I long to see [t]hat Burden.

But I long more still to see to the procuring more Sea Weed and Marsh Mud and Sand &c.

However my Prospect is interrupted again. I shall have no Time. I must prepare for a Journey to Philadelphia, a long Journey indeed! But if the Length of the Journey was all, it would be no burden. But the Consideration of What is to be done, is of great Weight. Great Things are wanted to be done, and little Things only I fear can be done. I dread the Thought of the Congress's falling short of the Expectations of the Continent, but especially of the People of this Province.

Vapours avaunt! I will do my Duty, and leave the Event. If I have the Approbation of my own Mind, whether applauded or censured, blessed or cursed, by the World, I will not be unhappy.

Certainly I shall enjoy good Company, good Conversation, and shall have a fine Ride, and see a little more of the World than I have seen before.

I think it will be necessary to make me up, a Couple of Pieces of new Linnen. I am told, they wash miserably, at N. York, the Jerseys and Philadelphia too in Comparison of Boston, and am advised to carry a great deal of Linnen.

Whether to make me a Suit of new Cloaths, at Boston or to make them at Phyladelphia, and what to make I know not, nor do I know how I shall go—whether on Horse back, in a Curricle, a Phaeton, or altogether in a Stage Coach I know not.

The Letters I have written or may write...must be kept secret or at least shewn with great Caution....

Kiss my dear Babes for me. Your

JOHN ADAMS

I believe I forgot to tell you one Anecdote: When I first came to this House it was late in the Afternoon, and I had ridden 35 miles at least. "Madam" said I to Mrs. Huston, "is it lawfull for a weary Traveller to refresh himself with a Dish of Tea provided it has been honestly smuggled, or paid no Duties?"

"No sir, said she, we have renounced all Tea in this Place. I cant make Tea, but I'le make you Coffee." Accordingly I have drank Coffee every Afternoon since, and have borne it very well. Tea must be universally renounced. I must be weaned, and the sooner, the better.

Falmouth July 7th: 1774

I am engaged in a famous Cause: The Cause of [Richard] King, of Scarborough vs. a Mob, that broke into his House, and rifled his Papers, and terrifyed him, his Wife, Children and Servants in the Night. The Terror, and Distress, the Distraction and Horror of this Family cannot be described by Words or painted upon Canvass. It is enough to move a Statue, to melt an Heart of Stone, to read the Story. A Mind susceptible of the Feelings of Humanity, an Heart which can be touch'd with Sensibi[li]ty for human Misery and Wretchedness, must reluct, must burn with Resentment and Indignation, at such outragious Injuries. These private Mobs, I do and will detest. If Popular Commotions can be justifyed, in Opposition to Attacks upon the Constitution, it can be only when Fundamentals are invaded, nor then unless for absolute Necessity and with great Caution. But these Tarrings and Featherings, these breaking open Houses by rude and insolent Rabbles, in Resentment for private Wrongs or in pursuance of private Prejudices and Passions, must be discountenanced, cannot be even excused upon any Principle which can be entertained by a good Citizen—a worthy Member of Society....

I shant be able to get away, till next Week. I am concerned only in 2 or 3 Cases and none of them are come on yet. Such an Eastern Circuit I never made. I shall bring home as much as I brought from home I hope, and not much more, I fear.

I go mourning in my Heart, all the Day long, tho I say nothing. I am melancholly for the Public, and anxious for my Family, as for myself a Frock and Trowsers, an Hoe and Spade, would do for my Remaining Days.

For God Sake make your Children, *hardy, active* and *industrious*, for Strength, Activity and Industry will be their only Resource and Dependance.

A British cartoon of 1775 shows a group of American ladies signing a paper promising not to drink tea.

Richard King, whose "Cause" Adams was defending, was a rich farmer, merchant, and timber exporter of Scarborough, Maine, and also the father of the young Rufus King, the future Federalist leader and Minister to the Court of St. James's during John Adams's Presidency. King was hated by his local debtors and vilified by others who suspected him of Loyalist leanings. Adams, deeply involved in the patriot movement for ten years, did not scruple to take the case of a notorious Tory on the eve of setting off for the Continental Congress. The notes of his closing address to the jury in July, 1774, suggest that John Adams's eloquence could soar to great heights in the cause of justice.

King v. *Stewart*, 1773–74

An Englishmans dwelling House is his Castle. The Law has erected a Fortification round it—and as every Man is Party to the Law, i.e. the Law is a Covenant of every Member of society with every other Member, therefore every Member of Society has entered into a Solemn Covenant with every other that he shall enjoy in his own dwelling House as compleat a security, safety and Peace and Tranquility as if it was surrounded with Walls of Brass, with Ramparts and Palisades and defended with a Garrison and Artillery.—This covenant has been broken in a most outragious manner. We are all bound then to make good to the Plaintiff his Damages.

Every English[man] values himself exceedingly, he takes a Pride and he glories justly in that strong Protection, that sweet Security, that delightfull Tranquillity which the Laws have thus secured to him in his own House, especially in the Night. Now to deprive a Man of this Protection, this quiet and Security in the dead of Night, when himself and Family confiding in it are asleep, is treat[ing] him not like an Englishman nor like a Freeman but like a Slave—like a miserable Turk, or Tartar. Is not this a base Affront? No Man who has a Soul, who has the Spirit of a Man in him can ever after during his whole Life, ever forget such an Indignity, tho he may forgive it. He can never think of it without Pain of Mind, without Impatience, Anger, Resentment, Shame and Grief....

Be pleased then to imagine yourselves each one for himself—in bed with his pregnant Wife, in the dead of Midnight, five Children also asleep, and all the servants. 3 Children in the same Chamber, two above. The Doors and Windows all barrd, bolted and locked—all asleep, suspecting nothing, harbouring no Malice, Envy or Revenge in your own Bosoms nor dreaming of any in your Neighbours. In the Darkness, the stillness the silence of Midnight.

Paul Revere's engraving of a snake made up of united colonies pitted against the British griffin was used on masthead of a patriot paper.

British cartoon of 1774 showing the Bostonians forcing a tarred and feathered exciseman to swallow tea while men in background dump it out

All of a sudden, in an Instant, in a twinkling of an Eye, an armed Banditti of Felons, Thieves, Robbers, and Burglars, rush upon the House. Like Savages from the Wilderness, or like Legions from the Blackness of Darkness, they yell and Houl, they dash in all the Windows and enter. Enterd they Roar, they stamp, they Yell, they houl, they cutt break tear and burn all before them.

Do you see a tender and affectionate Husband, an amiable deserving Wife near her Time, 3 young Children, all in one Chamber, awakened all at once, ignorant what was the Cause, terrifyd, inquisitive to know it. The Husband attempting to run down stairs, his Wife, laying hold of his Arm, to stay him and sinking fainting dying away in his Arms. The Children crying and clinging round their Parents—*father will they kill me*—father save me! The other Children and servants in other Parts of the House, joining in the Cries of Distress.

What sum of Money Mr. Foreman would tempt you, to be Mr. King, and to let your Wife undergo what Mrs. King underwent, and your Children what theirs did for one Night?

I freely confess that the whole sum sued for would be no temptation to me, if there was no other Damage than this.

But how can the Impression of it be erased out of his Mind and hers and the Childrens. It will lessen and frequently interrupt his Happiness as long as he lives, it will be a continual Sourse of Grief to him.

On August 10, 1774, the Massachusetts delegation left Boston in considerable style for the First Continental Congress in Philadelphia. It was reported by a contemporary that "they made a very respectable parade, in sight of five of the Regiments encamped on the Common, being in a coach and four, preceded by two white servants well mounted and arm'd, with four blacks behind in livery, two on horseback and two footmen." John Adams's *Diary* betrays the turmoil of his inner thoughts before the departure and illustrates his remarkable capacity for adjusting to great events once they were under way.

1774. June 25th. Saturday. Since the Court adjourned without Day this afternoon I have taken a long Walk, through the Neck as they call it, a fine Tract of Land in a general Field—Corn, Rye, Grass interspersed in great Perfection this fine season.

I wander alone, and ponder.—I muse, I mope, I ruminate.—I am often In Reveries and Brown Studies.—The Objects before me, are too grand, and multifarious for my Comprehension.—We have not Men, fit for the Times. We are deficient in Genius, in Education, in Travel, in Fortune—in every Thing. I feel unutterable Anxiety.—God grant us Wisdom, and Fortitude!

Should the Opposition be suppressed, should this Country submit, what Infamy and Ruin! God forbid. Death in any Form is less terrible.

Boston. August 10. Wednesday [1774]. The committee for the Congress took their departure from Boston, from Mr. Cushing's house, and rode to Coolidge's, where they dined in company with a large number of gentlemen, who went out and prepared an entertainment for them at that place. A most kindly and affectionate meeting we had, and about four in the afternoon we took our leave of them, amidst the kind wishes and fervent prayers of every man in the company for our health and success. This scene was truly affecting, beyond all description affecting.

15. Monday [August, 1774]. Mr. Silas Deane, of Wethersfield, came over to Hartford to see us. He is a gentleman of a liberal education, about forty years of age; first kept a school, then studied law, then married the rich widow of Mr. Webb, since which he has been in trade. Two young gentlemen, his sons-in-law, Messrs. Webbs, came over with him. They are genteel, agreeable men, largely in trade, and are willing to renounce all their trade.

Mr. Deane gave us an account of the delegates of New York. Duane and Jay are lawyers. Livingston, Low, and Alsop are merchants. Livingston is very popular. Jay married a Livingston, Peter's daughter, and is supposed to be of his side.

Mr. Deane says the sense of Connecticut is, that the resolutions of the Congress shall be the laws of the Medes and Persians; that the Congress is the grandest and most important assembly ever held in America, and that *all* of America is intrusted to it and depends upon it.

John Adams could not be expected to find New York equal to Boston, but at least he was impressed with its architecture.

1774 Aug. 20. Saturday.

Lodged at Cocks at Kingsbridge, a pretty Place—Uncas River running before the Door and verdant Hills all round. This Place is about 15 Miles from N. York. Uncas River is the Bound between the County of Westchester and the County of N. York. This Place is 10 Miles from Hell Gate, which is supposed to be occasioned by a large Cavern under the Rocks, into which the Water rushes at certain Times of the Tide. This Whirlpool is 5 Miles from the City.

We breakfasted at Days, and arrived in the City of New York at 10 O Clock—at Hulls, a Tavern, the Sign the Bunch of Grapes. We rode by several very elegant Country Seats, before we came to the City....

From Hulls We went to private Lodgings at Mr. Tobias Stoutenberg's, in Kings Street, very near the City Hall one way and the French Church the other. Mr. McDougal and Mr. Platt came to see us. Mr. Platt asked us to dinner next Monday. Mr. McDougal stayed longer, and talk'd a good deal. He is a very sensible Man, and an open one. He has none of the mean Cunning which disgraces so many of my Country men. He offers to wait on us this afternoon to see the City.

After Dinner, Mr. McDougal and Mr. Platt came and walked with Us, to every Part of the City. First We went to the Fort where We saw the Ruins of that magnificent Building the Governors House. From the Parade before the Fort you have a fine Prospect of Hudsons River and of the East River or the Sound and of the Harbour—of Long Island, beyond the Sound River, and of New Jersey, beyond Hudsons River. The Walk round this Fort is very pleasant, tho the Fortifications are not strong. Between the Fort and the City is a beautifull Elipsis of Land, railed in with solid Iron, in the Center of which is a Statue of his Majesty on Horse back, very large, of solid Lead, gilded with Gold, standing on a Pedastal of Marble very high. We then walked up the broad Way, a fine Street, very wide, and in a right Line from one End to the other of the City. In this rout We saw the old Church, and the new Church. The new is a very magnificent Building—cost 20,000 £ York Currency. The Prison is a large and an handsome stone building. There are two setts of Barracks. We saw the New York Colledge which is also a large Stone Building. A new Hospital is

Detail of an engraving of New York City shortly after Adams visited it

building of Stone. We then walked down to a ship Yard, where a Dutch East India Ship is building of 800 Tons burden. Then We walked round thro another Street which is the Principal Street of Business. Saw the several Marketts. After this We went to the Coffee House, which was full of Gentlemen, read the News Papers, &c. Here were introduced to Us Mr. [John Morin] Scott and a Mr. Litchfield, who invited us to Hulls Tavern, where we went and staid till 11 o Clock. We supped together, and had much Conversation. Mr. Scott is a Lawyer, of about 50 years of Age, a sensible Man, but not very polite. He is said to be one of the readiest Speakers upon the Continent. It was he who harrangued the People, and prevailed upon them to discard the Resolves of their Committee of 51, as void of Vigour, Sense and Integrity.

Mr. Scott was censuring McDougal in a friendly free Way for not insisting upon choosing Delegates by Ballot, &c.

Mr. Platt said but little. But McDougal was talkative, and appears to have a thorough Knowledge of Politicks. The two great Families in this Province, upon whose Motions all their Politicks turn, are the Delanceys and Livingstones. There is Virtue and Abilities as well as fortune, in the Livingstones, but not much of either of the three in the Delanceys, according to him.

The Streets of this Town are vastly more regular and elegant than those in Boston, and the Houses are more grand as well as neat. They are almost all painted— brick buildings and all.

1774. Aug. 22. Monday. This Morning We took Mr. McDougal into our Coach and rode three Miles out of Town, to Mr. Morine Scotts to break fast. A very pleasant Ride! Mr. Scott has an elegant Seat there, with Hudsons River just behind his House, and a rural Prospect all around him. Mr. Scott, his Lady and Daughter, and her Husband Mr. Litchfield were dressed to receive Us. We satt in a fine Airy Entry, till called into a front Room to break fast. A more elegant Breakfast, I never saw—rich Plate—a very large Silver Coffee Pott, a very large Silver Tea Pott—Napkins of the very finest Materials, and toast and bread and butter in great Perfection. After breakfast, a Plate of beautifull Peaches, another of Pairs and another of

Plumbs and a Muskmellen were placed on the Table.

Mr. Scott, Mr. William Smith and Mr. William Livingston, are the Triumvirate, who figured away in younger Life, against the Church of England—who wrote the independent Reflecter, the Watch Tower, and other Papers. They are all of them Children of Yale Colledge. Scott and Livingston are said to be lazy. Smith improves every Moment of his Time. Livingstone is lately removed into N. Jersey, and is one of the Delegates for that Province....

View of City Hall in New York

Mr. Morin Scott called upon Us at our Lodgings, and politely insisted upon our taking a Seat in his Chariot, to Mr. Platts. We accepted the Invitation and when We came there were shewn into as elegant a Chamber as ever I saw—the furniture as rich and splendid as any of Mr. Boylstones. Mr. Low, Mr. Peter Vanbrugh Livingston, Mr. Phillip Livingston, Dr. Treat a Brother of the Minister, and Mr. McDougal, Mr. Scott and Mr. Litchfield dined with us and spent the Afternoon.

P. V. Livingston is a sensible Man, and a Gentleman—he has been in Trade, is rich, and now lives upon his Income. Phill. Livingston is a great, rough, rappid Mortal. There is no holding any Conversation with him. He blusters away. Says if England should turn us adrift we should instantly go to civil Wars among ourselves to determine which Colony should govern all the rest. Seems to dread N. England—the Levelling Spirit &c. Hints were thrown out of the Goths and Vandalls—mention was made of our hanging the Quakers, &c. I told him, the very Existence of the Colony was at that Time at Stake—surrounded with Indians at War, against whom they could not have defended the Colony, if the Quakers had been permitted to go on.

1774 Aug. 23. Tuesday.
With all the Opulence and Splendor of this City, there is very little good Breeding to be found. We have been treated with an assiduous Respect. But I have not seen one real Gentleman, one well bred Man since I came to Town. At their Entertainments there is no Conversation that is agreable. There is no Modesty—No Attention to one another. They talk very loud, very fast, and all-together. If they ask you a Question, before you can utter 3 Words of your Answer, they will break out upon you, again—and talk away.

When the delegates reached Princeton, New Jersey, the reception they received was in keeping with their academic surroundings. John Adams met here two men, the Reverend John Witherspoon and Richard Stockton, who were to become colleagues in Congress and signers of the Declaration of Independence.

1774 Aug. 27. Saturday. About 12 O Clock We arrived at the Tavern in Prince Town, which holds out the Sign of Hudibrass, near Nassau Hall Colledge. The Tavern Keepers Name is Hire.

The Colledge is a stone building about as large as that at New York. It stands upon rising Ground and so Commands a Prospect of the Country.

After Dinner Mr. Pidgeon a student of Nassau Hall, Son of Mr. Pidgeon of Watertown from whom we brought a Letter, took a Walk with us and shewed us the Seat of Mr. Stockton a Lawyer in this Place and one of the Council, and one of the Trustees of the Colledge. As we returned we met Mr. [Houston], the Professor of Mathematicks and natural Philosophy, who kindly invited Us to his Chamber. We went. The Colledge is conveniently constructed. Instead of Entries across the Building, the Entries are from End to End, and the Chambers are on each side of the Entries. There are such Entries one above another in every Story. Each Chamber has 3 Windows, two studies, with one Window in each, and one Window between the studies to enlighten the Chamber.

Mr. [Houston] then shewed us the Library. It is not large, but has some good Books.... By this Time the Bell rang for Prayers. We went into the Chappell, the President [Dr. John Witherspoon] soon came in, and we attended. The Schollars sing as badly as the Presbyterians at New York. After Prayers the President attended Us to the Balcony of the Colledge, where We have a Prospect of an Horizon of about 80 Miles Diameter. We went into the Presidents House, and drank a Glass of Wine. He is as high a Son of Liberty, as any Man in America. He says it is necessary that the Congress should raise Money and employ a Number of Writers in the Newspapers in England, to explain to the Public the American Plea, and remove the Prejudices of Britons. He says also We should recommend it to every Colony to form a Society for the Encouragement of Protestant Emigrants from the 3 Kingdoms. The Dr. waited on us to our

Pictorial Field-Book of the Revolution, LOSSING

Nassau Hall at Princeton College

Lodgings and took a Dish of Coffee. He is one of the Committee of Correspondence, and was upon the Provincial Congress for appointing Delegates from this Province to the general Congress. Mr. William Livingston and He laboured he says to procure an Instruction that the Tea should not be paid for. Livingston he says is very sincere and very able in the public Cause, but a bad Speaker, tho a good Writer.

Just before they reached Philadelphia, the Massachusetts delegation did some politicking with the representatives of the local Sons of Liberty, which John Adams described many years later in a letter to Timothy Pickering.

6 August, 1822.

We were met at Frankfort by Dr. Rush, Mr. Mifflin, Mr. Bayard, and several other of the most active sons of liberty in Philadelphia, who desired a conference with us. We invited them to take tea with us in a private apartment. They asked leave to give us some information and advice, which we thankfully granted. They represented to us that the friends of government in Boston and in the Eastern States, in their correspondence with their friends in Pennsylvania and all the Southern States, had represented us as four desperate adventurers. "Mr. Cushing was a harmless kind of man, but poor, and wholly dependent on the popularity for his subsistence. Mr. Samuel Adams was a very artful, designing man, but desperately poor, and wholly dependent on his popularity with the lowest vulgar for his living. John Adams and Mr. Paine were two young lawyers, of no great talents, reputation, or weight, who had no other means of raising themselves into consequence, than by courting popularity." We were all suspected of having independence in view. Now, said they, you must not utter the word independence, nor give the least hint or insinuation of the idea, either in Congress or any private conversation; if you do, you are undone; for the idea of independence is as unpopular in Pennsylvania, and in all the Middle and Southern States, as the Stamp Act itself. No man dares to speak of it. Moreover, you are the representatives of the suffering State. Boston and Massachusetts are under a rod of iron. British fleets and armies are tyrannizing over you; you yourselves are personally obnoxious to them and all the friends of government; you have been long persecuted by them all; your feelings have been hurt, your passions excited; you are thought to be too warm, too zealous, too sanguine. You must be, therefore, very cautious; you must not come forward with any bold measures, you must not pretend to take the lead. You know Virginia is the most populous State in the Union. They are very proud of their ancient dominion, as they call it; they think they have a right to take the lead, and the Southern States, and Middle States too, are too much disposed to yield it to them."

This was plain dealing, Mr. Pickering; and I must confess that there appeared so much widsom and good sense in it, that it made a deep impression on my mind, and it had an equal effect on all my colleagues.

The brilliant gathering in Philadelphia of America's ablest men provided John Adams with many fine occasions for observation, which he recorded in his *Diary.*

1774 Aug. 31. Wednesday.
Made a Visit to Governor Ward of Rhode Island at his Lodgings. There We were introduced to several Gentlemen.

Mr. Dickenson, the Farmer of Pennsylvania, came to Mr. Wards Lodgings to see us, in his Coach and four beautifull Horses. He was introduced to Us, and very politely said he was exceedingly glad to have the Pleasure of seeing these Gentlemen, made some Enquiry after the Health of his Brother and Sister, who are now in Boston. Gave us some Account of his late ill Health and his present Gout. This was the first Time of his getting out.

Mr. Dickenson has been Subject to Hectic Complaints. He is a Shadow—tall, but slender as a Reed—pale as ashes. One would think at first Sight that he could not live a Month. Yet upon a more attentive Inspection, he looks as if the Springs of Life were strong enough to last many Years.

1774 Septr. 10. Saturday.
Mr. Reed returned with Mr. [Samuel] Adams and me to our Lodgings, and a very social, agreable and communicative Evening We had.

He says We never were guilty of a more Masterly Stroke of Policy, than in moving that Mr. Duchè might read Prayers, it has had a very good Effect, &c. He says the Sentiments of People here, are growing more and more favourable every day.

1774. Thursday. Septr. 22. Dined with Mr. Chew, Chief Justice of the Province, with all the Gentlemen from Virginia, Dr. Shippen, Mr. Tilghman and many others. We were shewn into a grand Entry and Stair Case, and into an elegant and most magnificent Chamber, untill Dinner. About four O Clock We were called down to Dinner. The Furniture was all rich. — Turttle, and every other Thing — Flummery, Jellies, Sweetmeats of 20 sorts, Trifles, Whip'd Syllabubbs, floating Islands, fools — &c., and then a Desert of Fruits, Raisins, Almonds, Pears, Peaches — Wines most excellent and admirable. I drank Madeira at a great Rate and found no Inconvenience in it.

In the Evening General Lee and Coll. Lee, and Coll. Dyer and Mr. Deane, and half a Score friends from Boston came to our Lodgings. Coll. Lee staid till 12 o Clock and was very social and agreable.

The American Congress as engraved for Cowley's History of England

1774. Wednesday. Sept. 28. Dined with Mr. R. Penn. A magnificent House, and a most splendid Feast, and a very large Company. Mr. Dickinson and General Lee were there, and Mr. Moylan, besides a great number of the Delegates. — Spent the Evening at Home, with Coll. Lee, Coll. Washington and Dr. Shippen who came in to consult with us.

1774. Sunday [October 9]. The Multiplicity of Business and Ceremonies, and Company that we are perpetually engaged in, prevents my Writing to my Friends in Mass. as I ought, and prevents my recording many Material Things in my Journal.

Phyladelphia with all its Trade, and Wealth, and Regularity is not Boston. The Morals of our People are much better, their Manners are more polite, and agreable — they are purer English. Our Language is better, our Persons are handsomer, our Spirit is greater, our Laws are wiser, our Religion is superiour, our Education is better. We exceed them in every Thing, but in a Markett, and in charitable public foundations.

Went in the Afternoon to the Romish Chappell and heard a good discourse upon the Duty of Parents to their Children, founded in Justice and Charity. The Scenery and the Musick is so callculated to take in Mankind that

I wonder, the Reformation ever succeeded. The Paint-
ings, the Bells, the Candles, the Gold and Silver. Our
Saviour on the Cross, over the Altar, at full Length, and
all his Wounds a bleeding. The Chanting is exquisitely
soft and sweet.

1774 Monday. Octr. 10th.
The Deliberations of the Congress, are spun out to an
immeasurable Length. There is so much Wit, Sense,
Learning, Acuteness, Subtilty, Eloquence, &c. among
fifty Gentlemen, each of whom has been habituated to
lead and guide in his own Province, that an immensity
of Time, is spent unnecessarily.

1774 Tuesday Octr. 11.
Dined with Mr. McKean in Markett Street, with Mr.
Reed, Rodney, Chace, Johnson, Paca, Dr. Morgan, Mr.
R. Penn, &c.

Spent the Evening with Mr. [Patrick] Henry at his
Lodgings consulting about a Petition to the King.

Henry said he had no public Education. At fifteen he
read Virgill and Livy, and has not looked into a Latin
Book since. His father left him at that Age, and he has
been struggling thro Life ever since. He has high Notions.
Talks about exalted Minds, &c. He has a horrid Opinion
of Galloway, Jay, and the Rutledges. Their System he
says would ruin the Cause of America. He is very impatient to see such Fellows, and not be at Liberty to
describe them in their true Colours.

The First Continental Congress provided the best
occasion possible for the leaders of the colonial resistance to get to know each
other, to test opinions, and to work together in the common cause. In spite
of many deep-seated divergences of opinion about fundamental questions,
the Congress achieved a remarkable unanimity of opinion on many matters.
The spirit of toleration that prevailed is illustrated in John Adams's account
to his wife of the salutary effect the reading of Christian prayers had upon
the Congress.

Phyladelphia Septr. 16. 1774
Having a Leisure Moment, while the Congress is assem-
bling, I gladly embrace it to write you a Line.

When the Congress first met, Mr. Cushing made a
Motion, that it should be opened with Prayer. It was
opposed by Mr. Jay of N. York and Mr. Rutledge of
South Carolina, because we were so divided in religious

Highly romanticized painting of Mr. Duché's first prayer in Congress

Sentiments, some Episcopalians, some Quakers, some Aanabaptists, some Presbyterians and some Congregationalists, so that We could not join in the same Act of Worship.—Mr. S. Adams arose and said he was no Bigot, and could hear a Prayer from a Gentleman of Piety and Virtue, who was at the same Time a Friend to his Country. He was a Stranger in Phyladelphia, but had heard that Mr. Duché (Dushay they pronounce it) deserved that Character, and therefore he moved that Mr. Duché, an episcopal Clergyman, might be desired, to read Prayers to the Congress, tomorrow Morning. The Motion was seconded and passed in the Affirmative. Mr. Randolph our President, waited on Mr. Duché, and received for Answer that if his Health would permit, he certainly would. Accordingly next Morning he appeared with his Clerk and in his Pontificallibus, and read several Prayers, in the established Form; and then read the Collect for the seventh day of September, which was the Thirty fifth Psalm.—You must remember this was the next Morning after we heard the horrible Rumour, of the Cannonade of Boston.—I never saw a greater Effect upon an Audience. It seemed as if Heaven had ordained that Psalm to be read on that Morning.

After this Mr. Duché, unexpected to every Body struck out into an extemporary Prayer, which filled the Bosom of every Man present. I must confess I never heard a better Prayer or one, so well pronounced.

Many years later Adams recollected some of the critical moments and accomplishments of the First Continental Congress, which had moved Pitt the Elder to allow that "for solidity of reason, force of sagacity and wisdom of conclusion under a complication of difficult circumstances, no nation or body of men can stand in preference to the general Congress at Philadelphia." However, John Adams, writing three decades later, without referring to his *Diary* or to the printed journals of the Congress, did not always give an accurate account when he described the work of the various committees and subcommittees.

Autobiography, 1802–7

On the 5th of August [September] Congress assembled in Carpenters Hall. The Day before, I dined with Mr. Lynch a Delegate from South Carolina, who, in conversation on the Unhappy State of Boston and its inhabitants, after some Observations had been made on the Elo-

quence of Mr. Patrick Henry and Mr. Richard Henry
Lee, which had been very loudly celebrated by the
Virginians, said that the most eloquent Speech that had
ever been made in Virginia or any where else, upon
American Affairs had been made by Colonel Washington.
This was the first time I had ever heard the Name of
Washington, as a Patriot in our present Controversy, I
asked who is Colonel Washington and what was his
Speech? Colonel Washington he said was the officer who
had been famous in the late french War and in the Battle
in which Braddock fell. His Speech was that if the
Bostonians should be involved in Hostilities with the
British Army he would march to their relief at the head
of a Thousand Men at his own expence. This Sentence
Mr. Lynch said, had more Oratory in it, in his Judgment,
than all that he had ever heard or read. We all agreed
that it was both sublime, pathetic and beautifull.

The more We conversed with the Gentlemen of the
Country, and with the Members of Congress the more
We were encouraged to hope for a general Union of the
Continent. As the Proceedings of this Congress are in
Print, I shall have Occasion to say little of them. A few
Observations may not be amiss. After some days of
general discussions, two Committees were appointed of
twelve members each, one from each State, Georgia not
having yet come in. The first Committee was instructed
to prepare a Bill of Rights as it was called or a Declaration of the Rights of the Colonies: the second, a List of
Infringements or Violations of those Rights. Congress
was pleased to appoint me, on the first Committee, as
the Member for Massachusetts. It would be endless to
attempt even an Abridgment of the Discussions in this
Committee, which met regularly every Morning, for
many days successively, till it became an Object of
Jealousy to all the other Members of Congress. It was
indeed very much against my Judgment, that the Committee was so soon appointed, as I wished to hear all the
great Topicks handled in Congress at large in the first
Place. They were very deliberately considered and debated in the Committee however. The two Points which
laboured the most, were 1. Whether We should recur to
the Law of Nature, as well as to the British Constitution
and our American Charters and Grants. Mr. Galloway
and Mr. Duane were for excluding the Law of Nature. I

was very strenuous for retaining and insisting on it, as a Resource to which We might be driven, by Parliament much sooner than We were aware. The other great question was what Authority We should conceed to Parliament: whether We should allow any Authority to it, in our internal Affairs: or whether We should allow it to regulate the Trade of the Empire, with or without any restrictions. These discussions spun into great Length, and nothing was decided. After many fruitless Essays, The Committee determined to appoint a Sub committee, to make a draught of a Sett of Articles, that might be laid in Writing before the grand Committee and become the foundation of a more regular debate and final decision. I was appointed on the Subcommittee, in which after going over the ground again, a Sett of Articles were drawn and debated one by one. After several days deliberation, We agreed upon all the Articles excepting one, and that was the Authority of Parliament, which was indeed the Essence of the whole Controversy. Some were for a flatt denial of all Authority: others for denying the Power of Taxation only. Some for denying internal but admitting [ex]ternal Taxation. After a multitude of Motions had [been] made, discussed [and] negatived, it seems as if We should never agree upon any Thing. Mr. John Rutledge of South Carolina, one of the Committee, addressing himself to me, was pleased to say "Adams We must agree upon Something: You appear to be as familiar with the Subject as any of Us, and I like your Expressions *the necessity of the Case* and *excluding all Ideas of Taxation external and internal.* I have a great Opinion of that same Idea of the Necessity of the Case and I am determined against all taxation for revenue. Come take the Pen and see if you cant produce something that will unite Us." Some others of the Committee seconding Mr. Rutledge, I took a sheet of paper and drew up an Article. When it was read I believe not one of the Committee were fully satisfied with it, but they all soon acknowledged that there was no hope of hitting on any thing, in which We could all agree with more Satisfaction. All therefore agreed to this, and upon this depended the Union of the Colonies. The Sub Committee reported their draught to the grand Committee, and another long debate ensued especially on this Article, and various changes and modifications

Carpenters Hall, where the First Continental Congress held meetings

161

America in Flames, a British view of 1775 showing patriots trying to douse fire being fanned by Quebec Bill, withdrawal of the charter of Massachusetts, and Boston Port Bill

of it were Attempted, but none adopted. The Articles were then reported to Congress, and debated Paragraph by Paragraph. The difficult Article was again attacked and defended. Congress rejected all Amendments to it, and the general Sense of the Members was that the Article demanded as little as could be demanded, and conceeded as much as could be conceeded with Safety, and certainly as little as would be accepted by Great Britain: and that the Country must take its fate, in consequence of it. When Congress had gone through the Articles, I was appointed to put them into form and report a fair Draught for their final Acceptance. This was done and they were finally accepted.

The Committee of Violations of Rights reported a sett of Articles which were drawn by Mr. John Sullivan of New Hampshire: and These two Declarations, the one of Rights and the other of Violations, which are printed in the Journal of Congress for 1774, were two Years afterwards recapitulated in the Declaration of Independence on the fourth of July 1776. The Results of the Procedings of Congress for this Year remain in the Journals: and I shall not attempt any Account of the debates, nor of any thing of the share I took in them. I never wrote a Speech beforehand, either at the Bar or in any public Assembly, nor committed one to writing after it was delivered, and it would be idle to attempt a Recollection, of Arguments from day to day, through a whole session, at the distance of Thirty Years. The Delegates from Massachusetts, representing the State in most immediate danger, were much visited, not only by the members of Congress but by all the Gentlemen in Phyladelphia and its neighbourhood, as well as Strangers and Occasional Travellers. We took Lodgings all together at the Stone House opposite the City Tavern then held by Mrs. Yard, which was by some Complimented with the Title of Head Quarters, but by Mr. Richard Henry Lee, more decently called Liberty Hall. We were much caressed and feasted by all the principal People, for the Allens, and Penns and others were then with Us, though afterwards some of them cooled and fell off, on the declaration of Independence. We were invited to Visit all the public Buildings and places of resort, and became pretty well acquainted with Men and things in Philadelphia.

Chapter **6**

The Fight for Independence

During the year 1775, John Adams reached the conclusion that independence was the key to the restoration of liberties in America. His intense and active promotion in the Second Continental Congress of a policy of independence constitutes the busiest, and quite possibly the most triumphant, period of his life.

Adams realized that American independence was not worth anything if it could not be maintained. With the efforts of the world's mightiest empire directed, however clumsily, toward preventing independence, an army and a navy were needed to repulse that empire's attacks. New governments had to be created in the Colonies capable of raising soldiers, levying taxes, and operating essential services; the ports had to be opened to trade to pay for the war and to receive the succor of friendly nations; a national government had to be created capable of conducting its own affairs as well as relations with foreign powers; alliances had to be made to obtain military aid, and foreign loans had to be negotiated to pay for expenses. It was the Second Continental Congress that had to deal with all these matters. Though certainly not a government when it met on May 10, 1775, the Congress began assuming and exercising powers that enabled it to function as a government and to transform thirteen rebellious and disunited colonies into the independent United States of America.

Adams's early espousal in Congress of independence as a policy for the Thirteen Colonies immediately classed him as a radical. It was fortunate for the radicals, however, that they had such a zealous and capable leader, for Congress contained powerful men impelled by strong views in favor of conciliation with the mother country. The instructions of the delegates from New York, Delaware, Maryland, and the Carolinas limited these members to promoting the restoration of harmony between Great Britain and the Colonies and to achieving the redress of grievances. Loyalty to the Crown remained strong in the Continental Army, where as late as January,

1776, a toast to the health of the king was drunk every evening in George Washington's officers' mess at Cambridge.

John Adams's single-minded dedication in Congress, molding public opinion and creating governmental institutions capable of supporting independence, is a dramatic tale. He wrote that he was "engaged in constant business from seven to ten in the morning in committee, from ten to four in Congress, and from six to ten again in Committee." He was forced to draw upon all the resources of his character, education, professional training, and natural good health to accomplish his purposes. The skill with which he debated and deployed his forces in Congress marked him as a man of outstanding effectiveness, clear judgment, and unquestioned integrity in the eyes of his contemporaries, a man capable of filling offices of the highest trust.

The First Continental Congress had resolved in its closing days in October, 1774, that another Congress should convene in Philadelphia on May 10, 1775, if the Colonies' grievances had not been redressed by that time. John Adams's *Diary* entry the day following Congress's adjournment showed that —if he was aware of such a possibility—he did not consider his own return to the city a likely possibility.

> 1774. Fryday. Octr. 28.
> Took our Departure in a very great Rain, from the happy, the peacefull, the elegant, the hospitable, and polite City of Phyladelphia.—It is not very likely that I shall ever see this Part of the World again, but I shall ever retain a most greatefull, pleasing Sense, of the many Civilities I have received, in it.

John Adams had anticipated separation from the mother country as early as 1755, but he did not favor independence as long as the British government was just and individual liberties in America were protected. At the end of December, 1774, he was still working for reconciliation, as he made clear in a letter to James Burgh.

> Braintree, 28 December, 1774.
> For my own part, I have bent my chief attention to prevent a rupture, and to impress my friends with the importance of preventing it.

In a series of political essays that he signed "Novanglus," and which began appearing in the *Boston Gazette* in January, 1775, Adams strenuously denied that any Whig or patriot ever dreamed of independence, while at the same time allowing for the possibility of separation. Outlining the political and legal foundations of the patriot cause, he applied the contract theory of government to each colony and declared that the sovereignty of the king was restricted to a matter of personal allegiance. He also declared that parliamentary authority over the Colonies was limited to the right to regulate their trade—and that only with the Colonies' consent. The following extracts from the "Novanglus" essays illustrate some of the fundamental concepts on which the first government of the United States was constructed.

"Novanglus," 1775

GOVERNMENT BY CONTRACT

A manifest design in the prince, to annul the contract on his part, will annul it on the part of the people. A settled plan to deprive the people of all the benefits, blessings, and ends of the contract, to subvert the fundamentals of the constitution, to deprive them of all share in making and executing laws, will justify a revolution.

THE MEANING OF REBELLION

We are not exciting a rebellion. Opposition, nay, open avowed resistance by arms, against usurpation and lawless violence, is not rebellion by the law of God or the land. Resistance to lawful authority makes rebellion.

ORIGIN OF LAW IN NEW ENGLAND

How, then, do we New Englandmen derive our laws? I say, not from parliament, not from common law, but from the law of nature, and the compact made with the king in our charters. Our ancestors were entitled to the common law of England when they emigrated, that is just so much of it as they pleased to adopt, and no more. They were not bound or obliged to submit to it, unless they chose it.

NATURE OF ALLEGIANCE

Indeed, we owe no allegiance to any crown at all. We owe allegiance to the person of his majesty, King George III, whom God preserve. But allegiance is due universally, both from Britons and Americans to the person of the King, not to his crown; to his natural, not his politic capacity. . . .

Our charter was granted by King William and Queen Mary, three years after the revolution; and the oaths of allegiance are established by a law of the province. So that our allegiance to his majesty is not due by virtue of any act of a British parliament, but by our own charter and province laws. It ought to be remembered that there was a revolution here, as well as in England, and that we, as well as the people of England, made an original, express contract with King William.

ESSEX INSTITUTE

Broadside with extract from minutes of the Massachusetts provincial congress acknowledges "wise and able Exertions" of Adams and his colleagues in the First Continental Congress and reappoints them.

NATURE OF ENGLISH RIGHTS AND LIBERTIES

English liberties are but certain rights of nature, reserved to the citizen by the English constitution, which rights cleaved to our ancestors when they crossed the Atlantic, and would have inhered in them if, instead of coming to New England, had they gone to Otaheite or Patagonia, even although they had taken no patent or charter from the king at all. These rights did not adhere to them the less, for their purchasing patents and charters, in which the king expressly stipulates with them, that they and their posterity should forever enjoy all those rights and liberties.

MEANING OF EMPIRE

If Aristotle, Livy, and Harrington knew what a republic was, the British constitution is much more like a republic than an empire. They define a republic to be a *government of laws, and not of men.* If this definition be just, the British constitution is nothing more nor less than a republic, in which the king is first magistrate. This office being hereditary, and being possessed of such ample and splendid prerogatives, is no objection to the government's being a republic, as long as it is bound by fixed laws, which the people have a voice in making, and a right to defend. An empire is a despotism, and an emperor a despot, bound by no law or limitation but his own will; it is a stretch of tyranny beyond absolute monarchy. For, although the will of an absolute monarch is law, yet his edicts must be registered by parliaments. Even this formality is not necessary in an empire. There the maxim is *quod principi placuit legis habet vigorem* [what is pleasing to the ruler has the force of law], even without having that will and pleasure recorded. There are but three empires now in Europe, the German or Holy Roman, the Russian, and the Ottoman.

There is another sense, indeed, in which the word *empire* is used, in which it may be applied to the government of Geneva, or any other republic, as well as to monarchy or despotism. In this sense it is synonymous with *government, rule,* or *dominion.* In this sense we are within the dominion, rule, or government of the King of Great Britain.

The question should be, whether we are a part of the kingdom of Great Britain. This is the only language known in English laws. We are not then a part of the

British kingdom, realm, or state; and therefore the supreme power of the kingdom, realm, or state is not, upon these principles, the supreme power of us. That "supreme power over America is vested in the estates in parliament," is an affront to us; for there is not an acre of American land represented there; there are no American estates in parliament.

AUTHORITY OF PARLIAMENT

Our patriots have never determined or desired to be independent states, if a voluntary cession of a right to regulate their trade can make them dependent even on parliament; though they are clear in theory that, by the common law and the English constitution, parliament has no authority over them. None of the patriots of this province, of the present age, have ever denied that parliament has a right, from our voluntary cession, to make laws which shall bend the colonies, so far as their commerce extends....

That there are any who pant after "independence," (meaning by this word a new plan of government over all America, unconnected with the crown of England, or meaning by it an exemption from the power of parliament to regulate trade,) is as great a slander upon the province as ever was committed to writing. The patriots of the province desire nothing new; they wish only to keep their old privileges. They were, for one hundred and fifty years, allowed to tax themselves, and govern their internal affairs as they thought best. Parliament governed their trade as they thought fit. This plan they wish may continue forever. But it is honestly confessed, rather than become subject to the absolute authority of parliament in all cases of taxation and internal polity, they will be driven to throw off that of regulating trade.

Trade card (above) of the Boston patriot Paul Revere, and portrait by John Singleton Copley showing him as the fine silversmith he was

On April 19, 1775, open warfare finally erupted at Lexington and Concord. John Adams recorded later in his *Autobiography* that he was convinced, after inspecting the situation, that reconciliation was no longer possible.

Autobiography, 1802–7
A few days after this Event I rode to Cambridge where I saw General Ward, General Heath, General Joseph Warren, and the New England Army. There was great Confusion and much distress: Artillery, Arms, Cloathing

Details from two famous engravings by Amos Doolittle showing battles of Concord (top) and Lexington; right, above, The Yanky Chace, *Americans routing mounted redcoats*

were wanting and a sufficient Supply of Provisions not easily obtained. Neither the officers nor Men however wanted Spirits or Resolution. I rode from thence to Lexington and along the Scene of Action for many miles and enquired of the Inhabitants, the Circumstances. These were not calculated to diminish my Ardour in the Cause. They on the Contrary convinced me that the Die was cast, the Rubicon passed, and as Lord Mansfield expressed it in Parliament, if We did not defend ourselves they would kill Us. On my Return home I was seized with a fever, attended with allarming Symptoms: but the time was come to repair to Philadelphia to Congress, which was to meet on the fifth [actually the tenth] of May. . . .

Congress assembled and proceeded to Business, and the Members appeared to me to be of one Mind, and that mind after my own heart. I dreaded the danger of disunion and divisions among Us, and much more among the People. It appeared to me, that all Petitions, Remonstrances and Negotiations, for the future would be fruitless and only occasion a Loss of time and give Opportunity to the Ennemy to sow divisions among the States and the People. My heart bled for the poor People of Boston, imprisoned within the Walls of their City by a British Army, and We knew not to what Plunder or Massacres or Cruelties they might be exposed. I thought the first Step ought to be, to recommend to the People of every State in the Union, to Seize on all the Crown Officers, and hold them with civility, Humanity and Generosity, as Hostages for the Security of the People of Boston and to be exchanged for them as soon as the British Army would release them. That We ought to recommend to the People of all the States to institute Governments for themselves, under their own Authority, and that, without loss of Time. That We ought to declare the Colonies, free, Sovereign and independent States, and then to inform Great Britain We were willing to enter into Negotiations with them for the redress of all Grievances, and a restoration of Harmony between the two Countries, upon permanent Principles. All this I thought might be done before We entered into any Connections, Alliances or Negotiations with forreign Powers. I was also for informing Great Britain very frankly that hitherto we were free but if the War should be continued, We

were determined to seek Alliances with France, Spain and any other Power of Europe, that would contract with Us. That We ought immediately to adopt the Army in Cambridge as a Continental Army, to Appoint a General and all other Officers, take upon ourselves the Pay, Subsistence, Cloathing, Armour and Munitions of the Troops. This is a concise Sketch of the Plan, which I thought the only reasonable one, and from Conversation with the Members of Congress, I was then convinced, and have been ever since convinced, that it was the General Sense, at least of a considerable Majority of that Body. This System of Measures I publicly and privately avowed, without Reserve.

Shortly after Congress reassembled, John Adams reported to his friend John Gill on the state of public opinion in the City of Brotherly Love.

Philadelphia, 10 June, 1775.
I find that the general sense abroad is, to prepare for a vigorous defensive War, but at the same time to keep open the Door of reconciliation; to hold the Sword in one Hand and the olive Branch in the other; to proceed with warlike measures and conciliatory measures *pari passu* [at the same pace]....

In my opinion, powder and artillery are the most efficacious, sure, and infallible conciliatory measures we can adopt.

On the very day that the Second Continental Congress convened in Philadelphia, Ethan Allen took Fort Ticonderoga on Lake Champlain. In the meantime the British, still in possession of Boston, were preparing further military operations. From Massachusetts calls for assistance poured in to Congress. The most immediate and urgent necessity was to create an army and to appoint a commander in chief. On or about June 14, 1775, John Adams took action.

Autobiography, 1802–7
Apprehending daily that We should he[a]r very distressing News from Boston, I walked with Mr. Samuel Adams in the State house Yard, for a little Exercise and fresh Air, before the hour of Congress, and there represented to him the various dangers that surrounded Us. He agreed to them all, but said what shall We do? I answered

Adams proposed George Washington as the Commander in Chief of the Army (above), and wrote to Abigail on June 18, 1775, that he was sending his letter via the "brave and amiable General Washington."

him, that he knew I had taken great pains to get our Colleagues to agree upon some plan that We might be unanimous: but he knew that they would pledge themselves to nothing: but I was determined to take a Step, which should compel them and all the other Members of Congress, to declare themselves for or against something. I am determined this Morning to make a direct Motion that Congress should adopt the Army before Boston and appoint Colonel Washington Commander of it. Mr. Adams seemed to think very seriously of it, but said Nothing. — Accordingly When congress had assembled I rose in my place and in as short a Speech as the Subject would admit, represented the State of the Colonies, the Uncertainty in the Minds of the People, their great Expectations and Anxiety, the distresses of the Army, the danger of its dissolution, the difficulty of collecting another, and the probability that the British Army would take Advantage of our delays, march out of Boston and spread desolation as far as they could go. I concluded with a Motion in form that Congress would Adopt the Army at Cambridge and appoint a General, that though this was not the proper time to nominate a General, yet as I had reason to believe this was a point of the greatest difficulty, I had no hesitation to declare that I had but one Gentleman in my Mind for that important command, and that was a Gentleman from Virginia who was among Us and very well known to all of Us, a Gentleman whose Skill and Experience as an Officer, whose independent fortune, great Talents and excellent universal Character, would command the Approbation of all America, and unite the cordial Exertions of all the Colonies better than any other Person in the Union. Mr. Washington, who happened to sit near the Door, as soon as he heard me allude to him, from his Usual Modesty darted into the Library Room. Mr. Hancock, who was our President, which gave me an Opportunity to observe his Countenance, while I was speaking on the State of the Colonies, the Army at Cambridge and the Ennemy, heard me with visible pleasure, but when I came to describe Washington for the Commander, I never remarked a more sudden and sinking Change of Countenance. Mortification and resentment were expressed as forcibly as his Face could exhibit them. Mr. Samuel Adams Seconded the Motion, and that did not soften the Presidents Phisiognomy at all.

George Washington was duly elected Commander in Chief of the Continental Forces. John Adams was particularly impressed by the magnanimity of his character on this occasion, as he wrote to his friend Elbridge Gerry.

Philadelphia, 18 June 1775.

There is something charming to me in the conduct of Washington. A gentleman of one of the first fortunes upon the continent, leaving his delicious retirement, his family and his friends, sacrificing his ease and hazarding all in the cause of his country! His views are noble and disinterested. He declared, when he accepted the mighty trust, that he would lay before us an exact account of his expenses, and not accept a shilling for pay.

An agitated letter from his wife, Abigail, soon brought Adams news of the Battle of Bunker Hill, which was fought before Washington could take command at Boston.

Sunday June 18 1775

The Day; perhaps the decisive Day is come on which the fate of America depends. My bursting Heart must find vent at my pen. I have just heard that our dear Friend Dr. [Joseph] Warren is no more but fell gloriously fighting for his Country—saying better to die honourably in the field than ignominiously hang upon the Gallows. Great is our Loss. He has distinguished himself in every engagement, by his courage and fortitude, by animating the Soldiers and leading them on by his own example. A particuliar account of these dreadful, but I hope Glorious Days will be transmitted you, no doubt in the exactest manner.

The race is not to the swift, nor the battle to the strong, but the God of Israel is he that giveth strength and power unto his people. Trust in him at all times, ye people pour out your hearts before him. God is a refuge for us.— Charlstown is laid in ashes. The Battle began upon our intrenchments upon Bunkers Hill, a Saturday morning about 3 o clock and has not ceased yet and tis now 3 o'clock Sabbeth afternoon.

Tis expected they will come out over the Neck to night, and a dreadful Battle must ensue. Almighty God cover the heads of our Country men, and be a shield to our Dear Friends. How [many ha]ve fallen we know not—the

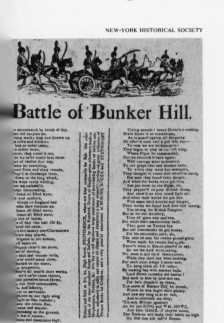

NEW-YORK HISTORICAL SOCIETY

Broadside printed at Providence in 1775 about the Battle of Bunker Hill

constant roar of the cannon is so [distre]ssing that we can not Eat, Drink or Sleep. May we be supported and sustaind in the dreadful conflict. I shall tarry here till tis thought unsafe by my Friends, and then I have secured myself a retreat at your Brothers who has kindly offerd me part of his house. I cannot compose myself to write any further at present.

John Quincy Adams, in his eighth year, watched with his mother the destruction of Charlestown from the top of Penn's Hill in Braintree. Many years later—by then an ex-President of seventy-eight—he recorded his own memories of this unforgettable sight in a draft of a letter to an English friend.

Detail of rare 1775 manuscript map depicts key zones of confrontation.

March 1846

My mother, with her children lived in unintermitted danger of being consumed with them all in a conflagration kindled by a torch in the same hands which on the 17th. of June lighted the fires in Charlestown. I saw with my own eyes those fires, and heard Britannia's thunders in the Battle of Bunker's hill and witnessed the tears of my mother and mingled with them my own, at the fall of Warren a dear friend of my father, and a beloved Physician to me. He had been our family physician and surgeon, and had saved my fore finger from amputation under a very bad fracture.

John Adams soon perceived that independence was going to be a major stumbling block to many influential members of Congress, as he wrote to James Warren, a close friend and a prominent figure in Massachusetts politics.

Phyladelphia, [July] 6th, 1775
Secret and Confidential, as the Saying is.

The Congress is not yet so much alarmed as it ought to be. . . .

You will see a strange Oscillation between love and hatred, between War and Peace—Preparations for War and Negociations for Peace. We must have a Petition to the King and a delicate Proposal of Negociation, etc. This Negociation I dread like Death: But it must be proposed. We cant avoid it. Discord and total Disunion would be the certain Effect of a resolute Refusal to petition and negociate. My Hopes are that Ministry will be afraid of Negociation as well as We and therefore refuse it. If they agree to it, We shall have Occasion for all our Wit Vigilance and Virtue to avoid being deceived, wheedled threatened or bribed out of our Freedom. If we Strenuously insist upon our Liberties, as I hope and am pretty sure We shall however, a Negotiation, if agreed to, will terminate in Nothing, it will effect nothing. We may possibly gain Time and Powder and Arms.

Three days later, over John Adams's strenuous opposition, the conservatives in Congress, led by the influential John Dickinson, author of the justly renowned *Letters from a Farmer in Pennsylvania* (1768), passed the Olive Branch Petition, which the king is reported never to have read.

Autobiography, 1802–7

The Quaker and Proprietary Interests in Pennsilvania now addressed themselves to Mr. Dickinson, who as well as his Wife were Quakers, and in various Ways stimulated him to oppose my designs and the Independence of the Country: and they succeeded so well that although they could not finally prevent any one of my Measures from being carried into compleat Execution, they made him and his Cousin Charles Thompson, and many others of their Friends, my Ennemies from that time to this 2 April 1805.... Mr. Charles Thompson, who was then rather inclined [to] our Side of the Question, told me, that the Quakers had intimidated Mr. Dickinsons Mother, and his Wife, who were continually distressing him with their remonstrances. His Mother said to him "Johnny you will be hanged, your Estate will be forfeited and confiscated, you will leave your Excellent Wife a Widow and your charming Children Orphans, Beggars and infamous." From my Soul I pitied Mr. Dickinson. I made his case my own. If my Mother and my Wife had expressed such Sentiments to me, I was certain, that if they did not wholly unman me and make me an Apostate, they would make me the most miserable Man alive. I was very happy that my Mother and my Wife and my Brothers, My Wifes Father and Mother, and Grandfather Col. John Quincy and his Lady, Mr. Norton Quincy, Dr. Tufts, Mr. Cranch and all her near Relations as well as mine, had uniformly been of my Mind, so that I always enjoyed perfect Peace at home.

The late Magnalimous and Heroic Gen. JOSEPH WARREN, Slain fighting in the Cause of LIBERTY, at BUNKER-HILL.

Let's view brave WARREN in yon azure skies ;
May ev'ry mind with this lov'd object rise.
No more our ORATOR exerts his breath,
Seiz'd by the cruel messenger of death.
What can his dear AMERICANS return ?
But drop a tear upon his happy urn :
Thou tomb shalt safe retain thy sacred trust,
'Till life divine re-animate his dust.

Woodcut of Adams's great friend General Joseph Warren, who lost his life "fighting in the Cause of Liberty"

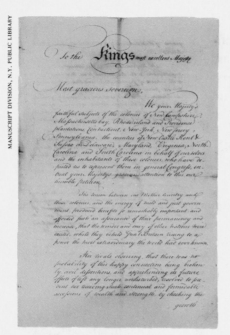

First page and signatures on the document named by Adams the Olive Branch Petition, final effort of Americans to avoid war with England

... The Proprietary Gentlemen, Israel Pemberton and other principal Quakers, now united with Mr. Dickinson, addressed themselves with great Art and Assiduity to all the Members of Congress whom they could influence, even to some of the Delegates of Massachusetts.... I became the dread and terror and Abhorrence of the Party. But all this I held in great contempt.... When the Party had prepared the Members of Congress, for their purpose, and indeed had made no small impression on three of my own Colleagues, Mr. Dickinson made or procured to be made a Motion for a second Petition to the King to be sent by Mr. Richard Penn, who was then bound on a Voyage to England. The Motion was introduced and supported by long Speeches. I was opposed to it, of course; and made an Opposition to it, in as long a Speech as I commonly made, not having ever been remarkable for very long Harrangues, in Answer to all the Arguments which had been urged. When I satt down, Mr. John Sullivan arose, and began to argue on the same side with me, in a strain of Wit, Reasoning and fluency which allthough he was always fluent, exceeded every Thing I had ever heard from him before. I was much delighted and Mr. Dickinson very much terrified at what he said and began to tremble for his Cause. At this moment I was called out to the State house Yard, very much to my regret, to some one who had business with me. I took my hat and went out of the Door of Congress Hall: Mr. Dickinson observed me and darted out after me. He broke out upon me in a most abrupt and extraordinary manner. In as violent a passion as he was capable of feeling, and with an Air, Countenance and Gestures as rough and haughty as if I had been a School Boy and he the Master, he vociferated out, "What is the Reason Mr. Adams, that you New Englandmen oppose our Measures of Reconciliation. There now is Sullivan in a long Harrangue following you, in a determined Opposition to our Petition to the King. Look Ye! If you dont concur with Us, in our pacific System, I, and a Number of Us, will break off, from you in New England, and We will carry on the Opposition by ourselves in our own Way." I own I was shocked with this Magisterial Salutation. I knew of no Pretensions Mr. Dickinson had, to dictate to me more that I had to catechise him. I was however as it happened, at that moment, in a very happy temper, and I answered him very coolly.

"Mr. Dickenson, there are many Things that I can very chearfully sacrifice to Harmony and even to Unanimity: but I am not to be threatened into an express Adoption or Approbation of Measures which my Judgment reprobates. Congress must judge, and if they pronounce against me, I must submit, as if they determine against You, You ought to acquiesce."—These were the last Words which ever passed between Mr. Dickinson and me in private. We continued to debate in Congress upon all questions publickly, with all our usual Candor and good humour. But the Friendship and Acquaintance was lost forever by an unfortunate Accident, which must now be explained.

The unfortunate accident was the interception and subsequent publication by the British of a confidential letter John Adams wrote to James Warren, in which he referred to Mr. Dickinson in irreverent terms. Although "hawk" remains a term for a person of pro-war sentiment, "buzzard" has been replaced by "dove."

Philadelphia, July 24th, 1775

Dear Sir,—In Confidence. I am determined to write freely to you this time. A certain great Fortune and piddling Genius, whose Fame has been trumpeted so loudly, has given a silly Cast to our whole Doings. We are between Hawk and Buzzard.

Mr. Dickinson was clearly offended on learning of this manner of expression, as John Adams was quick to observe in an entry in his *Diary.*

1775 Sept. 16. Saturday.

Walking to the Statehouse this Morning, I met Mr. Dickinson, on Foot in Chesnut Street. We met, and passed near enough to touch Elbows. He passed without moving his Hat, or Head or Hand. I bowed and pulled off my Hat. He passed hautily by. The Cause of his Offence, is the Letter no doubt which Gage has printed in Drapers Paper.

I shall for the future pass him, in the same manner. But I was determined to make my Bow, that I might know his Temper.

We are not to be upon speaking Terms, nor bowing Terms, for the time to come.

While public sentiment was warming toward the idea of separation from Great Britain, political leaders were becoming aware of the inadequacies of the colonial governments in the face of developing war. However inadequate a confederacy might be as a final form of national government, John Adams considered that such a grouping of independent governments now was the best way to win the war and insure the independence of the Colonies from the mother country.

Autobiography, 1802–7

On Fryday June 2. 1775 . . . the President laid before Congress a Letter from the Provincial Convention of Massachusetts Bay dated May 16. which was read, setting forth the difficulties they labour under, for want of a regular form of Government, and as they and the other Colonies are now compelled to raise an Army to defend themselves from the Butcheries and devastations of their implacable Enemies, which renders it still more necessary to have a regular established Government, requesting the Congress to favour them with explicit Advice respecting the taking up and exercising the Powers of civil Government, and declaring their readiness to submit to such a general Plan as the Congress may direct for the Colonies, or make it their great Study to establish such a form of Government there, as shall not only promote their Advantage but the Union and Interest of all America.

This Subject had engaged much of my Attention before I left Massachusetts, and had been frequently the Subject of Conversation between me and many of my Friends Dr. Winthrop, Dr. Cooper, Colonel Otis, the two Warrens, Major Hawley and others besides my Colleagues in Congress and lay with great Weight upon my Mind as the most difficult and dangerous Business that We had to do, (for from the Beginning I always expected We should have more difficulty and danger, in our Attempts to govern ourselves and in our Negotiations and connections with foreign Powers, than from all the Fleets and Armies of Great Britain). It lay therefore with great Weight upon my mind: and when this Letter was read, I embraced the Opportunity to open myself in Congress, and most earnestly to intreat the serious Attention of all the Members and of all the Continent to the measures which the times demanded. For my Part I thought there was great Wisdom in the Adage when the Sword is drawn throw away the Scabbard. Whether We threw it away voluntarily or not, it was useless now and would be useless forever. The Pride of Britain, flushed with late Tryumphs and Conquests, their infinite Contempt of all the Power of America, with an insolent, arbitrary Scotch Faction with a Bute and Mansfield at their head for a Ministry, We might depend upon it, would force Us to call forth every Energy and resource of the Country, to seek the friendship of Englands Enemies, and We had no rational hope but from the *Ratio Ultima Regum et Rerum publicarum* [final justification of kings and republics]. These Efforts could not be made without Government, and as I supposed no Man would think of consolidating this vast Continent under one national Government, We should probably after the Example of the Greeks, the Dutch and the Swiss, form a Confederacy of States, each of which must have a seperate Government. That the Case of Massachusetts was the most urgent, but that it could not be long before every other Colony must follow her Example. That with a View to this Subject I had looked into the Ancient and modern Confederacies for Examples: but they all appeared to me to have been huddled up in a hurry by a few Chiefs. But We had a People of more Intelligence, Curiosity and Enterprize, who must be all consulted, and We must reallize the Theories of the Wisest Writers and invite the People, to erect the whole Building with their own hands upon the broadest foundation. That this could be done only by Conventions of Representatives chosen by the People in the several Colonies, in the most exact proportions. That it was my Opinion, that Congress ought now to recommend to the People of every Colony to call such Conventions immediately and set up Governments of their own, under their own Authority: for the People were the Source of all Authority and Original of all Power. These were new, strange and terrible Doctrines, to the greatest Part of the Members, but not a very small Number heard them with apparent Pleasure, and none more than Mr. John Rutledge of South Carolina and Mr. John Sullivan of New Hampshire.

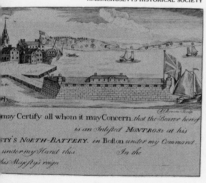

Revere's engraving on a certificate shows the North Battery, Christ's Church, and Charleston across water.

The resolution that was finally passed by Congress with respect to Massachusetts kept the door open for the reestablishment of royal authority. John Adams nevertheless thought it was a step in the right direction.

John Dickinson

Autobiography, 1802–7

On Fryday June 9th. 1775. The report of the Committee on the Letter from the Convention of Massachusetts Bay being again read, the Congress came into the following Resolution:

Resolved, That no Obedience being due to the Act of Parliament, for altering the Charter of the Colony of Massachusetts Bay, nor to a Governor or Lieutenant Governor who will not observe the directions of, but endeavour to subvert that Charter, the Governor and Lieutenant Governor of that Colony are to be considered as absent and their Offices vacant; and as there is no Council there and the Inconveniences arising from the Suspension of the Powers of Government are intollerable, especially at a time when General Gage hath actually levyed War, and is carrying on Hostilities against his Majestys peaceable and loyal Subjects of that Colony; that in order to conform as near as may be to the Spirit and Substance of the Charter, it be recommended to the provincial Convention to write Letters to the Inhabitants of the several Places, which are intituled to representation in Assembly, requesting them to chuse such Representatives, and that the Assembly when chosen, do elect Councillors; and that such Assembly or Council exercise the Powers of Government, untill a Governor of his Majestys Appointment will consent to govern the Colony according to its Charter.

Ordered That the President transmit a Copy of the Above to the Convention of Massachusetts Bay.

Although this Advice was in a great degree conformable, to the New York and Pensilvania System, or in other Words to the System of Mr. Dickinson and Mr. Duane, I thought it an Acquisition, for it was a Precedent of Advice to the seperate States to institute Governments, and I doubted not We should soon have more Occasions to follow this Example.

Congress soon felt impelled to approve resolutions recommending to New Hampshire, South Carolina, and Virginia that they "establish such form of Government, as in their Judgement will best produce the happiness of the People, and most effectually secure Peace and good Order in the Province, during the Continuance of the present dispute between Great Britain and the Colonies." Regarding the particular form or plan of government he would recommend, John Adams was adamant only in excluding a unicameral legislature; otherwise, as one distinguished scholar has pointed out, "His mind was fairly wriggling with plans." When in November, 1775, the resolution with respect to South Carolina was under consideration, Adams attempted to make the idea of independence more explicit.

Autobiography, 1802–7

I laboured afresh to expunge the Word Colony and Colonies, and insert the Words States and State, and the Word Dispute to make Way for that of War, and the Word Colonies for the Word America or States. But the Child was not yet weaned. — I laboured also to get the Resolution enlarged and extended into a Recommendation to the People of all the States to institute Governments, and this Occasioned more Interrogations from one part and another of the House. What Plan of Government would you recommend? &c. Here it would have been the most natural to have made a Motion that Congress should appoint a Committee to prepare a Plan of Government, to be reported to Congress and there discussed Paragraph by Paragraph, and that which should be adopted, should be recommended to all the States: but I dared not make such a Motion, because I knew that if such a Plan was adopted it would be if not permanent, yet of long duration; and it would be extreamly difficult to get rid of it. And I knew that every one of my friends, and all those who were the most zealous for assuming Government, had at that time no Idea of any other Government but a Contemptible Legislature in one assembly, with Committees for Executive Magistrates and Judges. These Questions therefore I answered by Sporting off hand, a variety of short Sketches of Plans, which might be adopted by the Conventions, and as this Subject was brought into View in some Way or other, almost every day and these Interrogations were frequently repeated, I had in my head and at my Tongues End, as many Projects of Government as Mr. Burke says the Abby Seieyes had in his Pidgeon holes, not however constructed at such Length nor laboured with his metaphysical Refinements. I took care however always to bear my Testimony against every plan of an unballanced Government.

Autobiography, 1802–7

Mr. John Rutledge and Mr. Sullivan had frequent Conversations with me upon this subject. Mr. Rutledge asked me my Opinion of a proper form of Government for a State. I answered him that any form, that our People would consent to institute would be better than none. Even if they placed all Power in a House of Representatives, and they should appoint Governors and Judges but I hoped they would be wiser, and preserve the English Constitution in its Spirit and Substance, as far as the Circumstances of this Country required or would Admit. That no hereditary Powers ever had existed in America, nor would they or ought they to be introduced or proposed. But that I hoped the three Branches of a Legislature would be preserved, an Executive, independent of the Senate or Council and the House and above all things the Independence of the Judges. Mr. Sullivan was fully agreed with me in the necessity of instituting Governments and he seconded me very handsomely in supporting the Argument in Congress. Mr. Samuel Adams was with Us in the Opinion of the Necessity and was industrious in Conversation with the Members out of Doors; but he very rarely spoke much in Congress, and he was perfectly unsettled in any Plan to be recommended to a State, always inclining to the most democratical forms, and even to a single Sovereign Assembly; untill his Constituents, afterwards in Boston compelled him to vote for three branches. Mr. Cushing was also for one Sovereign Assembly, and Mr. Paine were silent and reserved upon the Subject at least to me.

Not long after this Mr. John Rutledge returned to South Carolina, and Mr. Sullivan went with General Washington to Cambridge: so that I lost two of my able Coadjutors. But We soon found the Benefit of their Co-operations at a distance.

As the two developing sentiments gathered strength—one for independence and the other for provincial governments capable of waging war and dealing with independence—there appeared on the scene two pamphlets, one by Thomas Paine and the other by John Adams, which were to prove to be the catalysts that precipitated future developments. The appearance of Paine's *Common Sense* in January, 1776, probably did more to crystallize colonial opinion in favor of independence than anything else. John Adams, who came to feel that Paine's life was just as corrupt as the pernicious political doctrines he preached, felt compelled to rebut those precepts in his own publications on government. The following retrospective passage, which evaluates Paine's contribution to the Revolution lower than would many, undoubtedly reflects the anger of subsequent political strife as well as a basic difference in viewpoint.

Autobiography, 1802–7

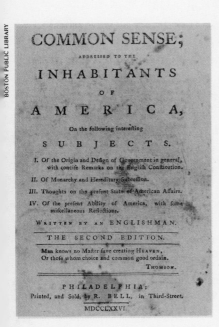

John Adams's copy of Common Sense

In the Course of this Winter appeared a Phenomenon in Philadelphia, *a Star of Disaster...*, I mean Thomas Paine. He came from England, and got into such company as would converse with him, and ran about picking up what Information he could, concerning our Affairs, and finding the great Question was concerning Independence, he gleaned from those he saw the common place Arguments concerning Independence: such as the Necessity of Independence, at some time or other, the peculiar fitness at this time: the Justice of it: the Provocation to it: the necessity of it: our Ability to maintain it &c. &c. Dr. Rush put him upon Writing on the Subject, furnished him with the Arguments which had been urged in Congress an hundred times, and gave him his title of common Sense. In the latter part of Winter, or early in the Spring he came out, with his Pamphlet. The Arguments in favour of Independence I liked very well: but one third of the Book was filled with Arguments from the old Testiment, to prove the Unlawfulness of Monarchy, and another Third, in planning a form of Government, for the seperate States in One Assembly, and for the United States, in a Congress. His Arguments from the old Testiment, were ridiculous, but whether they proceeded from honest Ignorance, or foolish Supersti[ti]on on one hand, or from willfull Sophistry and knavish Hypocricy on the other I know not. The other third part relative to a form of Government I considered as flowing from simple Ignorance, and a mere desire to please the democratic Party in Philadelphia, at whose head were Mr. Matlock, Mr. Cannon and Dr. Young. I regretted however, to see so foolish a plan recommended to the People of the United States, who were all waiting only for the Countenance of Congress, to institute their State Governments. I dreaded the Effect so popular a pamphlet might have, among the People, and determined to do all in my Power, to counter Act the Effect of it. My continued Occupations in Congress, allowed me no time to write any thing of any Length: but I found moments to write a small pamphlet which Mr. Richard Henry Lee, to whom I shewed it, liked so well that he insisted on my permitting him to publish it: He accordingly got Mr. Dunlap to print it, under the Tittle of Thoughts on Government in a Letter from a Gentleman to his Friend.

The first version of John Adams's pamphlet *Thoughts on Government* was very possibly written as a letter to a friend in late March, 1776. The first edition, excerpts of which are given here, was certainly printed anonymously before April 20, 1776, after the author had grown tired of copying it by hand over and over again for friends. It was written at a time when John Adams believed that "where annual elections end, there slavery begins" and that a separate council should mediate between the executive power and legislative assembly. On these formal matters he was to change his mind; but the passage of time only confirmed his belief in the separation of powers, a bicameral legislature, and a strong executive as the indispensable means for the preservation of personal liberty in a republic.

Thoughts on Government, 1776

We ought to consider what is the end of government, before we determine which is the best form. Upon this point all speculative politicians will agree, that the happiness of society is the end of government, as all divines and moral philosophers will agree that the happiness of the individual is the end of man. From this principle it will follow, that the form of government, which communicates ease, comfort, security, or, in one word, happiness, to the greatest number of persons, and in the greatest degree, is the best....

Fear is the foundation of most governments; but it is so sordid and brutal a passion, and renders men in whose breasts it predominates so stupid and miserable, that Americans will not be likely to approve of any political institution which is founded on it.

Honor is truly sacred, but holds a lower rank in the scale of moral excellence than virtue. Indeed, the former is but a part of the latter, and consequently has not equal pretensions to support a frame of government productive of human happiness.

The foundation of every government is some principle or passion in the minds of the people. The noblest principles and most generous affections in our nature, then, have the fairest chance to support the noblest and most generous models of government.

A man must be indifferent to the sneers of modern Englishmen, to mention in their company the names of Sidney, Harrington, Locke, Milton, Nedham, Neville, Burnet, and Hoadly. No small fortitude is necessary to confess that one has read them. The wretched condition of this country, however, for ten or fifteen years past, has frequently reminded me of their principles and reasonings. They will convince any candid mind, that there is no good government but what is republican. That the only valuable part of the British constitution is so; because the very definition of a republic is "an empire of laws, and not of men." That, as a republic is the best of governments, so that particular arrangement of the powers of society, or, in other words, that form of government which is best contrived to secure an impartial and exact execution of the laws, is the best of republics.

Of republics there is an inexhaustible variety, because the possible combinations of the powers of society are capable of innumerable variations.

As good government is an empire of laws, how shall your laws be made? In a large society, inhabiting an extensive country, it is impossible that the whole should assemble to make laws. The first necessary step, then, is to depute power from the many to a few of the most wise and good. But by what rules shall you choose your representatives? Agree upon the number and qualifications of persons who shall have the benefit of choosing, or annex this privilege to the inhabitants of a certain extent of ground.

The principle difficulty lies, and the greatest care should be employed, in constituting this representative assembly. It should be in miniature an exact portrait of the people at large. It should think, feel, reason, and act like them. That it may be the interest of this assembly to do strict justice at all times, it should be an equal representation, or, in other words, equal interests among the people should have equal interests in it. Great care should be taken to effect this, and to prevent unfair, partial, and corrupt elections. Such regulations, however, may be better made in times of greater tranquillity than the present; and they will spring up themselves naturally when all the powers of government come to be in the hands of the people's friends. At present, it will be safest to proceed in all established modes to which the people have been familiarized by habit.

A representation of the people in one assembly being obtained, a question arises, whether all the powers of government, legislative, executive, and judicial, shall be left in this body? I think a people cannot be long free, nor ever happy, whose government is in one assembly. My reasons for this opinion are as follow:—

1. A single assembly is liable to all the vices, follies, and frailties of an individual; subject to fits of humor, starts of passion, flights of enthusiasm, partialities, or prejudice, and consequently productive of hasty results and absurd judgments. And all these errors ought to be corrected and defects supplied by some controlling power.

2. A single assembly is apt to be avaricious, and in time will not scruple to exempt itself from burdens, which it will lay, without compunction, on its constituents.

3. A single assembly is apt to grow ambitious, and after a time will not hesitate to vote itself perpetual. This was one fault of the Long Parliament; but more remarkably of Holland, whose assembly first voted themselves from annual to septennial, then for life, and after a course of years, that all vacancies happening by death or otherwise, should be filled by themselves, without any application to constituents at all.

4. A representative assembly, although extremely well qualified, and absolutely necessary, as a branch of the legislative, is unfit to exercise the executive power, for want of two essential properties, secrecy and despatch.

5. A representative assembly is still less qualified for the judicial power, because it is too numerous, too slow, and too little skilled in the laws.

6. Because a single assembly, possessed of all the powers of government, would make arbitrary laws for their own interest, execute all laws arbitrarily for their own interest, and adjudge all controversies in their own favor.

But shall the whole power of legislation rest in one assembly? Most of the foregoing reasons apply equally to prove that the legislative power ought to be more complex; to which we may add, that if the legislative power is wholly in one assembly, and the executive in another, or in a single person, these two powers will oppose and encroach upon each other, until the contest

Common Sense BY THOMAS PAINE, 1928 EDITION

Thomas Paine

shall end in war, and the whole power, legislative and executive, be usurped by the strongest.

The judicial power, in such case, could not mediate, or hold the balance between the two contending powers, because the legislative would undermine it. And this shows the necessity, too, of giving the executive power a negative upon the legislative, otherwise this will be continually encroaching upon that.

To avoid these dangers, let a distinct assembly be constituted as a mediator between the two extreme branches of the legislature, that which represents the people, and that which is vested with the executive power.

Let the representative assembly then elect by ballot, from among themselves or their constituents, or both, a distinct assembly, which, for the sake of perspicuity, we will call a council. It may consist of any number you please, say twenty or thirty, and should have a free and independent exercise of its judgment, and consequently a negative voice in the legislature.

These two bodies, thus constituted, and made integral parts of the legislature, let them unite, and by joint ballot choose a governor, who, after being stripped of most of those badges of domination, called prerogatives, should have a free and independent exercise of his judgment, and be made also an integral part of the legislature. This, I know, is liable to objections; and, if you please, you may make him only president of the council, as in Connecticut. But as the governor is to be invested with the executive power, with consent of council, I think he ought to have a negative upon the legislative. If he is annually elective, as he ought to be, he will always have so much reverence and affection for the people, their representatives and counsellors, that, although you give him an independent exercise of his judgment, he will seldom use it in opposition to the two houses, except in cases the public utility of which would be conspicuous; and some such cases would happen.

In the present exigency of American affairs, when, by an act of Parliament, we are put out of the royal protection, and consequently discharged from our allegiance, and it has become necessary to assume government for our immediate security, the governor, lieutenant-governor, secretary, treasurer, commissary, attorney-general, should be chosen by joint ballot of both houses. And these and all other elections, especially of representatives and counsellors, should be annual, there not being in the whole circle of the sciences a maxim more infallible than this, "where annual elections end, there slavery begins."

These great men, in this respect, should be, once a year,

"Like bubbles on the sea of matter borne,

They rise, they break, and to that sea return."

This will teach them the great political virtues of humility, patience, moderation, without which every man in power becomes a ravenous beast of prey.

This mode of constituting the great offices of state will answer very well for the present; but if by experiment it should be found inconvenient, the legislature may, at its leisure, devise other methods of creating them, by elections of the people at large, as in Connecticut, or it may enlarge the term for which they shall be chosen to seven years, or three years, or for life, or make any other alterations which the society shall find productive of its ease, its safety, its freedom, or, in one word, its happiness....

The dignity and stability of government in all its branches, the morals of the people, and every blessing of society depends so much upon an upright and skilful administration of justice that the judicial power ought to be distinct from both the legislative and executive, and independent upon both, that so it may be a check upon both, as both should be checks upon that. The judges, therefore, should be always men of learning and experience in the laws, of exemplary morals, great patience, calmness, coolness, and attention. Their minds should not be distracted with jarring interests; they should not be dependent upon any man, or body of men. To these ends, they should hold estates for life in their offices; or, in other words, their commissions should be during good behavior, and their salaries ascertained and established by law. For misbehavior, the grand inquest of the colony, the house of representatives, should impeach them before the governor and council, where they should have time and opportunity to make their defence; but, if convicted, should be removed from their offices, and subjected to such other punishment as shall be thought proper.

A militia law, requiring all men, or with very few exceptions besides cases of conscience, to be provided with arms and ammunition, to be trained at certain seasons; and requiring counties, towns or other small districts, to be provided with public stocks of ammunition and intrenching utensils, and with some settled plans for transporting provisions after the militia, when marched to defend their country against sudden invasions; and requiring certain districts to be provided with field-pieces, companies of matrosses, and perhaps some regiments of light-horse, is always a wise institution, and, in the present circumstances of our country, indispensable.

Laws for the liberal education of youth, especially of the lower class of people, are so extremely wise and useful, that, to a humane and generous mind, no expense for this purpose would be thought extravagant.

The very mention of sumptuary laws will excite a smile. Whether our countrymen have wisdom and virtue enough to submit to them, I know not; but the happiness of the people might be greatly promoted by them, and a revenue saved sufficient to carry on this war forever. Frugality is a great revenue, besides curing us of vanities, levities, and fopperies, which are real antidotes to all great, manly, and warlike virtues. . . .

A constitution founded on these principles introduces knowledge among the people, and inspires them with a conscious dignity becoming freemen; a general emulation takes place, which causes good humor, sociability, good manners, and good morals to be general. . . .

If the colonies should assume governments separately, they should be left entirely to their own choice of the forms; and if a continental constitution should be formed, it should be a congress, containing a fair and adequate representation of the colonies, and its authority should sacredly be confined to these cases, namely, war, trade, disputes between colony and colony, the post-office, and the unappropriated lands of the crown, as they used to be called.

These colonies, under such forms of government, and in such a union, would be unconquerable by all the monarchies of Europe.

You and I, my dear friend, have been sent into life

at a time when the greatest lawgivers of antiquity would have wished to live. How few of the human race have ever enjoyed an opportunity of making an election of government, more than of air, soil, or climate, for themselves or their children! When, before the present epocha, had three millions of people full power and a fair opportunity to form and establish the wisest and happiest government that human wisdom can contrive? I hope you will avail yourself and your country of that extensive learning and indefatigable industry which you possess, to assist her in the formation of the happiest governments and the best character of a great people. For myself, I must beg you to keep my name out of sight; for this feeble attempt, if it should be known to be mine, would oblige me to apply to myself those lines of the immortal John Milton, in one of his sonnets:—

> "I did but prompt the age to quit their clogs
> By the known rules of ancient liberty,
> When straight a barbarous noise environs me
> Of owls and cuckoos, asses, apes, and dogs."

In his *Thoughts on Government*, John Adams claimed that freedom was dependent upon the right form of republican government and that republican government was the only good government upon which every blessing of society depended. Thomas Paine, in his *Common Sense*, admitted that "Society in every state is a blessing," but claimed that "Government, even in its best state, is but a necessary evil; in its worst, an intolerable one." This fundamental philosophical disagreement—between those who view government as indispensible to personal liberty because of its capacity to establish law and order and those who regard government as the enemy of freedom and the instrument of tyranny and oppression—continues today. Adams took particular issue with Paine's view that the sovereignty of the people should be vested in a unicameral legislature.

Autobiography, 1802–7

The Gentlemen of New York availed themselves of the Ideas in this Morsell in the formation of the Constitution of that State. And Mr. Lee sent it to the Convention of Virginia when they met to form their Government and it went to North Carolina, New Jersey and other States. Matlock, Cannon, Young and Paine had influence enough however, to get their plan adopted in substance in Georgia and Vermont as well as Pennsilvania. These three

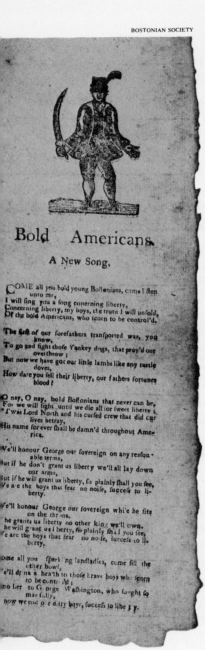

Bold Americans.

A New Song,

COME all you bold young Bostonians, come I sten
unto me,
I will sing you a song concerning liberty,
Concerning liberty, my boys, the truth I will unfold,
Of the bold Americans, who scorn to be control'd.

The first of our forefathers transported was, you
know,
To go and fight those Yankey dogs, that prey'd our
overthrow ;
But now we have got our little lambs like any turtle
doves,
How dare you sell their liberty, our fathers fortunes
blood ?

O nay, O nay, bold Bostonians that never can be,
For we will fight until we die all for sweet liberty ;
I was Lord North and his cursed crew that did our
lives betray,
His name forever shall be damn'd throughout Ame-
rica,

We'll honour George our sovereign on any reasonable terms,
But if he don't grant us liberty we'll all lay down
our arms,
But if he will grant us liberty, so plainly shall you see,
We are the boys that fear no noise, success to liberty.

We'll honour George our sovereign while he sits
on the throne,
he grants us liberty no other king we'll own,
he will grant us liberty, so plainly shall you see,
We are the boys that fear no noise, success to liberty.

come all you sparkling landladies, come fill the
other bowl,
We'll drink a health to those brave boys who scorn
to be control'd ;
no Let to George Washington, who fought so
manfully,
now we end our ditty boys, success to liberty.

*An eighteenth-century broadside
paid tribute to the* Bold Americans.

States have since found them, such Systems of Anarchy, if that Expression is not a contradiction in terms, that they have altered them and made them more conformable to my plan.—Paine soon after the Appearance of my Pamphlet hurried away to my Lodgings and spent an Evening with me. His Business was to reprehend me for publishing my Pamphlet. Said he was afraid it would do hurt, and that it was repugnant to the plan he had proposed in his Common Sense. I told him it was true it was repugnant and for that reason, I had written it and consented to the publication of it: for I was as much afraid of his Work [as] he was of mine. His plan was so democratical, without any restraint or even an Attempt at any Equilibrium or Counterpoise, that it must produce confusion and every Evil Work. I told him further, that his Reasoning from the Old Testament was ridiculous, and I could hardly think him sincere. At this he laughed, and said he had taken his Ideas in that part from Milton: and then expressed a Contempt of the Old Testament and indeed of the Bible at large, which surprized me. He saw that I did not relish this, and soon check'd himself, with these Words "However I have some thoughts of publishing my Thoughts on Religion, but I believe it will be best to postpone it, to the latter part of Life." This Conversation passed in good humour, without any harshness on either Side: but I perceived in him a conceit of himself, and a daring Impudence, which have been developed more and more to this day.... The third part of Common Sense which relates wholly to the Question of Independence, was clearly written and contained a tollerable Summary of the Arguments which I had been repeating again and again in Congress for nine months. But I am bold to say there is not a Fact nor a Reason stated in it, which had not been frequently urged in Congress. The Temper and Wishes of the People, supplied every thing at that time: and the Phrases, suitable for an Emigrant from New Gate, or one who had chiefly associated with such Company, such as "The Royal Brute of England," "The Blood upon his Soul," and a few others of equal delicacy, had as much Weight with the People as his Arguments. It has been a general Opinion, that this Pamphlet was of great Importance in the Revolution. I doubted it at the time and have doubted it to this day.

In May of 1776, John Adams successfully argued in Congress for the adoption of a general resolution that anticipated independence. The main debate took place on May 15, and it concerned the preamble to the resolution, the language of which, drafted by John Adams, went much further in the direction of independence than did the resolution itself.

Arms of King George III, removed from the Old State House in 1775

Autobiography, 1802–7

On Wednesday May 15. 1776 reported the following which was agreed to

Whereas his Britannic Majesty, in conjunction with the Lords and Commons of Great Britain, has, by a late Act of Parliament, excluded the Inhabitants of these united Colonies from the Protection of his Crown; and whereas no Answer whatever to the humble Petitions of the Colonies for redress of Grievances and reconciliation with Great Britain has been or is likely to be given, but the whole force of that Kingdom aided by foreign Mercenaries is to be exerted for the destruction of the good People of these Colonies; and whereas it appears absolutely irreconcileable to reason, and good Conscience, for the People of these Colonies now to take the Oaths and Affirmations necessary for the support of any Government under the Crown of Great Britain, and it is necessary that the Exercise of every kind of Authority under the said Crown should be totally suppressed, and all the Powers of Government exerted under the Authority of the People of the Colonies, for the preservation of internal peace, Virtue and good order, as well as for the defence of their Lives, Liberties and Properties against the hostile Invasions and cruel depredations of their Ennemies; therefore

Resolved That it be recommended to the respective Assemblies and Conventions of the United Colonies, where no Government sufficient to the Exigencies of their affairs hath been hitherto established, to adopt such Government as shall in the Opinion of the Representatives of the People best conduce to the happiness and Safety of their Constituents in particular and America in General.

Ordered that the said Preamble, with the Resolution passed the 10th. instant, be published.—Mr. Duane called it, to me, a Machine for the fabrication of independence. I said, smiling, I thought it was independence itself: but We must have it with more formality yet.

Congress, in addition to creating an army and promoting the establishment of independent local governments, appointed early in June, 1775, a committee to prepare a plan of confederation on the national level. But the Articles of Confederation, which were approved by Congress in November, 1777, but not ratified by the states until March, 1781, were soon to prove inadequate to the successful functioning of a national government. Years later one member of Congress, Henry Marchant, reminded Adams of a prophecy he had uttered in Congress respecting the future of the confederation.

[1789]

You wish me to give you a particular account of the *prophetic declaration* made on the floor of Congress, just as the former confederation was concluded.

When my friend has all his feelings wound up upon an important subject and vent must be given, he has a manner of expression so peculiar to himself, and so striking to the hearers, that the impression, as from a stroke of lightning, is left behind, while the flash and sound, the mode of expression, is lost or forgotten. His words I will not engage to recollect with exactness.

The articles of confederation being completed, the members by rotation were called to place their signatures to them. This being concluded, a pause and perfect calm succeeded. He sat and appeared full of thought. He rose. "Mr. President." His cane slipped through his thumb and forefinger, with a quick tap upon the floor; his eyes rolled upwards; his brows were raised to their full arch.

"This business, Sir, that has taken up so much of our time seems to be finished. But, Sir, I now, upon this floor, venture to predict that before ten years, this confederation, like a rope of sand, will be found inadequate to the purpose, and its dissolution will take place. Heaven grant that wisdom and experience may then avert what we have most to fear!"

I never knew a greater solemnity upon the minds of the members. . . . Congress was adjourned.

John Adams was always proud of his efforts in founding the American Navy and the Corps of Marines, and later as President, he tried to build them into the nation's first instrument of defense. In October, 1775, a committee was appointed to determine what measures should be taken to intercept two British vessels on their way to Canada laden with military supplies. From this committee grew the Naval Committee, which procured ships, issued orders for the deployment of the fleet, and drew up the rules and regulations governing the first navy, often referred to as Adams's rules because he had drafted them. In his *Autobiography* Adams often combined excerpts from the *Journals* of the Continental Congress with his own commentary.

Autobiography, 1802–7

On Thursday October 5. 1775.... Sundry Letters from London were laid before Congress and read, and a motion was made, that it be resolved that a Committee of three be appointed to prepare a Plan for intercepting two Vessells which are on their Way to Canada, laden with Arms and Powder, and that the Committee proceed on this Business immediately. The Secretary has omitted to insert the Names of this Committee on the Journals. But as my Memory has recorded them, they were Mr. Deane, Mr. Langdon and myself, three Members who had expressed much Zeal, in favour of the Motion. As a considerable part of my time, in the Course of my profession, had been spent upon the Sea coast of Massachusetts, in Attending the Courts and Law Suits at Plymouth, Barnstable, Marthas Vineyard, to the Southward and in the Counties of Essex, York and Cumberland to the Eastward, I had conversed much with the Gentlemen, who conducted our Cod and Whale Fisheries, as well as the other Navigation of the Country, and had heard much of the Activity, Enterprize, Patience, Perseverance, and daring Intrepidity of our Seamen, I had formed a confident Opinion that if they were once let loose upon the Ocean, they would contribute greatly to the relief of our Wants as well as to the distress of the Ennemy. I became therefore at once, an Ardent Advocate for this motion, which We carried, not without great difficulty. The Opposition to it was very loud and vehement. Some of my own Colleagues, appeared greatly allarmed at it: and Mr. Edward Rutledge never displayed so much Eloquence as against it. He never appeared to me to discover so much Information and Sagacity, which convinced me that he had been instructed out of Doors, by some of the most knowing Merchants and Statesmen in Philadelphia. It would require too much time and space to give this debate at large, if any memory could Attempt it. Mine cannot. It was however represented as the most wild, visionary mad project that ever had been imagined. It was an Infant, taking a mad Bull

The Pine-tree flag of the young American Navy; detail of cartouche on a French map published in 1776

by his horns. And what was more profound and remote, it was said it would ruin the Character, and corrupt the morals of all our Seamen. It would make them selfish, piratical, mercenary, bent wholly upon plunder, &c. &c. &c. These formidable Arguments and this terrible Rhetoric, were answered by Us by the best Reasons We could alledge, and the great Advantages of distressing the Ennemy, supplying ourselves, and beginning a System of maritime and naval Opperations, were represented in colours as glowing and animating. The Vote was carried, the Committee went out, and returned very soon, brought in the Report, in these Words, The Committee appointed to prepare a plan for intercepting the two Vessells bound to Canada, brought in a Report which was taken into Consideration; whereupon

Resolved, That a Letter be sent to General Washington to inform him that Congress having received certain Intelligence of the Sailing of two north Country built Briggs, of no force, from England, on the eleventh of August last, loaded with Arms, Powder and other Stores for Quebec, without Convoy, which, it being of importance to intercept, desire that he apply to the Council of Massachusetts Bay for the two armed Vessells in their service, and dispatch the same, with a sufficient number of People, Stores &c. particularly a number of Oars, in order, if possible to intercept the two Briggs and their Cargoes, and secure the same for the Use of the Continent; also any other Transports; laden with Ammunition, Cloathing, or other Stores, for the Use of the Ministerial Army or Navy in America, and secure them in the most convenient places for the purpose abovementioned; that he give the Commander or Commanders such Instructions as are necessary, as also proper Encouragement to the marines and Seamen, that shall be sent on this Enterprize, which Instructions are to be delivered to the Commander or Commanders sealed up, with orders not to open the same, untill out of sight of Land on Account of Secrecy.

That a Letter be written to the said honourable Council, to put the said Vessells under the Generals Command....

Resolved That a swift sailing Vessell to carry ten Carriage Guns, and a proportionable Number of Swivells, with Eighty Men, be fitted with all possible dispatch, for a Cruize of three months, and that the Commander be instructed to cruize eastward, for intercepting such Transports as may be laden with warlike Stores, and other Supplies for our Ennemies, and for such other purposes as the Congress shall direct.

On the 10th of November 1775 Congress resolved that two Battalions of Marines be raised, consisting of one Colonel, two Lieutenant Colonels, two Majors, and other Officers as usual in other regiments; that they consist of an equal Number of privates with other Battalions; that particular care be taken, that no Person be appointed to Officers, or inlisted into said Battalion[s], but such as are good Seamen or so acquainted with maritime Affairs, as to be able to serve to Advantage by Sea when required: that they be inlisted and commissioned to serve for and during the present War between Great Britain and the Colonies, unless dismissed by order of Congress; that they be distinguished by the names of the first and second Battalions of American Marines, and that they be considered as part of the number which the Continental Army before Boston is ordered to consist of. Ordered that a Copy of the above, be transmitted to the General.

On the 17th of November 1775. A Letter from Gen. Washington, inclosing a Letter and Journal of Colonel Arnold, and sundry papers being received, the same were read, whereupon

Resolved that a Committee of seven be appointed to take into Consideration so much of the Generals Letter, as relates to the disposal of such Vessells and Cargoes belonging to the Ennemy, as shall fall into the hands of, or be taken by the Inhabitants of the United Colonies. The Members chosen Mr. Wythe, Mr. E. Rutledge, Mr. J. Adams, Mr. W. Livingston, Dr. Franklin, Mr. Wilson and Mr. Johnson.

Thursday. November 23. 1775. The Committee for fitting out armed Vessells laid before Congress, a draught of Rules for the Government of the American Navy and Articles to be signed by the Officers and Men employed in that Service, which were read and ordered to lie on the Table for the Perusal of the Members.

Governor Stephen Hopkins

John Adams enjoyed his work on the Naval Committee more than anything else he did in Congress.

Autobiography, 1802–7

The pleasantest part of my Labours for the four Years I spent in Congress from 1774 to 1777 was in this naval Committee. Mr. Lee, Mr. Gadsden, were sensible Men, and very chearful: But Governor Hopkins of Rhode Island, above seventy Years of Age kept us all alive. Upon Business his Experience and Judgment were very Usefull. But when the Business of the Evening was over, he kept Us in Conversation till Eleven and sometimes twelve O Clock. His Custom was to drink nothing all day nor till Eight O Clock, in the Evening, and then his Beveredge was Jamaica Spirit and Water. It gave him Wit, Humour, Anecdotes, Science and Learning. He had read Greek, Roman and British History: and was familiar with English Poetry particularly Pope, [Thomson] and Milton. And the flow of his Soul made all his reading our own, and seemed to bring to recollection in all of Us all We had ever read. I could neither eat nor drink in those days. The other Gentlemen were very temperate. Hopkins never drank to excess, but all he drank was immediately not only converted into Wit, Sense, Knowledge and good humour, but inspired Us all with similar qualities.

Engraving of the death of General Montgomery at Quebec in 1775

In October, 1775, John Adams was appointed Chief Justice of Massachusetts, an office he was to resign in February, 1777, without ever having been able to serve in it. In December, 1775, he left Congress to take up his judicial duties in Massachusetts, only to find that he was elected once again to represent Massachusetts in Congress. Meantime, the gloom cast by the failure of Montgomery and Arnold to capture Quebec that winter was partially dispelled by the British evacuation of Boston in March, 1776. Washington was now able to shift military operations to New York, while John Adams labored in Congress to open the ports for trade with foreign nations.

Autobiography, 1802–7

Saturday Feb. 17 1776....

This Measure of Opening the Ports, &c. laboured exceedingly, because it was considered as a bold step to Independence. Indeed I urged it expressly with that View and as connected with the Institutions of Government in all the States and a Declaration of National Independence. The Party against me had Art and Influence as yet, to evade, retard and delay every Motion that We made.

John Hancock, President of Congress at this time, had appointed Benjamin Harrison as Chairman of the Committee of the Whole when Congress resumed its business. Adams had little personal respect for either of these two gentlemen, particularly as they seemed to court John Dickinson's party of conciliation.

Autobiography, 1802–7

Fryday March 15. 1776. . . .

This is the first Appearance of Mr. Harrison as Chairman of the Committee of the whole. . . .

Although Harrison was another Sir John Falstaff, excepting in his Larcenies and Robberies, his Conversation disgusting to every Man of Delicacy or decorum, Obscæne, profane, impious, perpetually ridiculing the Bible, calling it the Worst Book in the World, yet as I saw he was to be often nominated with Us in Business, I took no notice of his Vices or Follies, but treated him and Mr. Hancock too with uniform politeness.

April 3. 1776 great Things were done. The Naval System made great Progress.

April 4. 1776. We did great Things again.

Agreable to the order of the Day, the Congress resolved itself into a Committee of the whole to take into Consideration the Trade of the United Colonies, and after some time spent thereon, the President resumed the Chair and Mr. Harrison reported that the Committee had taken into Consideration the matters referred to them and had come to sundry Resolutions, which he was ordered to deliver in. The Resolutions agreed to by the Committee of the whole Congress being read, Ordered to lie on the Table.

April 5. 1776. Good Fryday.

April 6. 1776. Congress resumed the consideration of the Report, from the Committee of the whole, and the same being twice read, and debated by paragraphs, was agreed to. These Resolutions are on the Journal, and

Paul Revere's engraving of John Hancock for an early magazine

amount to something. They opened the Ports and sett our Commerce at Liberty: But they were far short of what had been moved by Members from Massachusetts, Maryland and Virginia. There is one Resolution I will not omit.

Resolved that no Slaves be imported into any of the thirteen Colonies.

By May, 1776, the colonies that had either established independent governments or at least repealed their instructions against independence to their delegates in Congress had grown so numerous that John Adams was able to exclaim: "Every Post and every Day rolls in upon Us Independence like a Torrent." By early June he was writing to William Cushing that he saw the consummation of all his efforts.

Philadelphia, 9 June 1776.
Objects of the most stupendous magnitude, and measures in which the lives and liberties of millions yet unborn are intimately interested, are now before us. We are in the very midst of a revolution, the most complete, unexpected, and remarkable, of any in the history of nations. A few important subjects must be despatched before I can return to my family. Every colony must be induced to institute a perfect government. All the colonies must confederate together in some solemn band of union. The Congress must declare the colonies free and independent States, and ambassadors must be sent abroad to foreign courts, to solicit their acknowledgment of us, as sovereign States, and to form with them, at least with some of them, commercial treaties of friendship and alliance. When these things are once completed, I shall think that I have answered the end of my creation, and sing my *nunc dimittis* [now depart], return to my farm, family, ride circuits, plead law, or judge causes, just which you please.

A resolution of American independence was introduced by Richard Henry Lee and seconded by John Adams on June 7, 1776. The conservative elements managed to postpone debate on the resolution to July 1. Meanwhile on June 11, a committee was appointed to prepare an appropriate declaration on independence should the Lee resolution be adopted. On June 12, John Adams sent this advice to his friend and fellow representative in Congress, Francis Dana.

12 June, 1776.

Be silent and patient, and time will bring forth, after the usual groans, throes, and pains upon such occasions, a fine child, a fine, vigorous, healthy boy, I presume. God bless him and make him a great, wise, virtuous, pious, rich and powerful Man!

The resolution on independence was approved on July 2, 1776, by a vote of twelve to none (the delegates of each colony voting as one and New York abstaining), but only after a prolonged debate in which John Adams had the climactic part.

Autobiography, 1802–7

I am not able to recollect, whether it was on this, or some preceeding day, that the greatest and most solemn debate was had on the question of Independence. The Subject had been in Contemplation for more than a Year and frequent discussions had been had concerning it. At one time and another, all the Arguments for it and against it had been exhausted and were become familiar. I expected no more would be said in public but that the question would be put and decided. Mr. Dickinson however was determined to bear his Testimony against it with more formality. He had prepared himself apparently with great Labour and ardent Zeal, and in a Speech of great Length, and all his Eloquence, he combined together all that had before been written in Pamphlets and News papers and all that had from time to time been said in Congress by himself and others. He conducted the debate, not only with great Ingenuity and Eloquence, but with equal Politeness and Candour: and was answered in the same Spirit.

No Member rose to answer him: and after waiting some time, in hopes that some one less obnoxious than myself, who had been all along for a Year before, and still was represented and believed to be the Author of all the Mischief, I determined to speak.

It has been said by some of our Historians, that I began by an Invocation to the God of Eloquence. This is a Misrepresentation. Nothing so puerile as this fell from me. I began by saying that this was the first time of my Life that I had ever wished for the Talents and Eloquence of the ancient Orators of Greece and Rome, for I was very sure that none of them ever had before him a question of more Importance to his Country and to the World. They would probably upon less Occasions than this have begun by solemn Invocations to their Divinities for Assistance but the Question before me appeared so simple, that I had confidence enough in the plain Understanding and common Sense that had been given me, to believe that I could answer to the Satisfaction of the House all the Arguments which had been produced, notwithstanding the Abilities which had been displayed and the Eloquence with which they had been enforced. Mr. Dickinson, some years afterwards published his Speech. I had made no Preparation beforehand and never committed any minutes of mine to writing. But if I had a Copy of Mr. Dickinsons before me I would now after Nine and twenty Years have elapsed, endeavour to recollect mine.

Before the final Question was put, the new Delegates from New Jersey came in, and Mr. Stockton, Dr. Witherspoon and Mr. Hopkinson, very respectable Characters, expressed a great desire to hear the Arguments. All was Silence: No one would speak: all Eyes were turned upon me. Mr. Edward Rutledge came to me and said laughing, Nobody will speak but you, upon this Subject. You have all the Topicks so ready, that you must satisfy the Gentlemen from New Jersey. I answered him laughing, that it had so much the Air of exhibiting like an Actor or Gladiator for the Entertainment of the Audience, that I was ashamed to repeat what I had said twenty times before, and I thought nothing new could be advanced by me. The New Jersey Gentlemen however still insisting on hearing at least a Recapitulation of the Arguments and no other Gentleman being willing to speak, I summed up the Reasons, Objections and Answers, in as concise a manner as I could, till at length the Jersey Gentlemen said they were fully satisfied and ready for the Question, which was then put and determined in the Affirmative.

John Trumbull's pencil sketch of his first idea for a painting of the Declaration of Independence

Years later John Adams described in his *Autobiography* and in a letter to Timothy Pickering how the committee appointed to prepare the Declaration of Independence came to draft it.

Autobiography, 1802-7

Not long after this the three greatest Measures of all, were carried. Three Committees were appointed, One for preparing a Declaration of Independence, another for reporting a Plan of a Treaty to be proposed to France, and a third to digest a System of Articles of Confederation to be proposed to the States.—I was appointed on the Committee of Independence, and on that for preparing the form of a Treaty with France: on the Committee of Confederation Mr. Samuel Adams was appointed. The Committee of Independence, were Thomas Jefferson, John Adams, Benjamin Franklin, Roger Sherman and Robert R. Livingston. Mr. Jefferson had been now about a Year a Member of Congress, but had attended his Duty in the House but a very small part of the time and when there had never spoken in public: and during the whole Time I satt with him in Congress, I never heard him utter three Sentences together. The most of a Speech he ever made in my hearing was a gross insult on Religion, in one or two Sentences, for which I gave him immediately the Reprehension, which he richly merited. It will naturally be enquired, how it happened that he was appointed on a Committee of such importance. There were more reasons than one. Mr. Jefferson had the Reputation of a masterly Pen. He had been chosen a Delegate in Virginia, in consequence of a very handsome public Paper which he had written for the House of Burgesses, which had given him the Character of a fine Writer. Another reason was that Mr. Richard Henry Lee was not beloved by the most of his Colleagues from Virginia and Mr. Jefferson was sett up to rival and supplant him. This could be done only by the Pen, for Mr. Jefferson could stand no competition with him or any one else in Elocution and public debate.

6 August, 1822.

The committee met, discussed the subject, and then appointed Mr. Jefferson and me to make the draught, I suppose because we were the two first on the list.

The sub-committee met. Jefferson proposed to me to make the draught. I said "I will not."

"You should do it."

"Oh! no."

"Why will you not? You ought to do it."

"I will not."

"Why?"

"Reasons enough."

"What can be your reasons?"

Engraving after Pine and Savage's painting The Congress Voting Independence, July 4th, 1776, *said to be most accurate view of chamber*

"Reason first—You are a Virginian, and a Virginian ought to appear at the head of this business. Reason second—I am obnoxious, suspected, and unpopular. You are very much otherwise. Reason third—You can write ten times better than I can."

"Well," said Jefferson, "if you are decided, I will do as well as I can."

"Very well. When you have drawn it up, we will have a meeting."

A meeting was accordingly had, and conned the paper over. I was delighted with its high tone and the flights of oratory with which it abounded, especially that concerning negro slavery, which, though I knew his Southern brethren would never suffer to pass in Congress, I certainly never would oppose. There were other expressions which I would not have inserted, if I had drawn it up, particularly that which called the King tyrant. I thought this too personal; for I never believed George to be a tyrant in disposition and in nature; I always believed him to be deceived by his courtiers on both sides of the Atlantic, and in his official capacity only, cruel. I thought the expression too passionate, and too much like scolding, for so grave and solemn a document; but as Franklin and Sherman were to inspect it afterwards, I thought it would not become me to strike it out. I consented to report it, and do not now remember that I made or suggested a single alteration.

We reported it to the committee of five. It was read, and I do not remember that Franklin or Sherman criticized any thing. We were all in haste. Congress was impatient, and the instrument was reported, as I believe, in Jefferson's handwriting, as he first drew it. Congress cut off about a quarter of it, as I expected they would; but they obliterated some of the best of it, and left all that was exceptionable, if any thing in it was. I have long wondered that the original draught has not been published. I suppose the reason is, the vehement philippic against negro slavery.

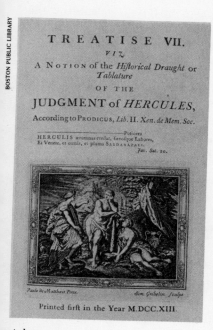

Adams suggested this engraving from a title page for the Great Seal, later admitted it "is too complicated."

The amended Declaration of Independence, approved by the delegates on July 4, again with New York abstaining, was first celebrated on July 8, 1776, the day it was proclaimed and published. Adams described the festivities in a letter to Samuel Chase.

Earliest known drawing of Liberty Bell from an 1839 anti-slavery tract

Philadelphia, 9 July, 1776.

You will see by this Post, that the river is passed, and the bridge cut away. The Declaration was yesterday published and proclaimed from that awful stage in the State-house yard; by whom, do you think? By the Committee of Safety, the Committee of Inspection, and a great crowd of People. Three cheers rended the welkin. The battalions paraded on the Common, and gave us the *feu de joie*, notwithstanding the scarcity of Powder. The bells rang all day and almost all night. Even the Chimers chimed away.

Independence, so newly won, seemed suddenly threatened on September 2, 1776, when immediately following the setback of the Battle of Long Island, John Sullivan, the former staunch supporter of John Adams in Congress and now a captured general on parole from General Sir William Howe, brought word to Congress that the British Commander in Chief had full powers to compromise the dispute between Great Britain and America. He further reported that the general's brother, Admiral Lord Howe, wished to treat of such matters, though he could not recognize the authority of Congress as such. John Adams's reaction to this development, as reported in a letter by Benjamin Rush, was negative.

Philadelphia, April 13, 1790

When General Sullivan brought Lord Howe's proposition to Congress for a conference, in September 1776, Mr. Adams said privately to me "that he wished the first ball that had been fired on the 27th of August had gone through his head." On the floor of Congress he called the General "a decoy duck."

In spite of his opposition to taking notice of this British initiative, Congress on September 6, 1776, appointed John Adams, together with Benjamin Franklin and Edward Rutledge, to go on a diplomatic mission as a representative "of the free, independent States of America" to confer with Lord Howe "to know whether he has any authority to treat with persons authorized by Congress for that purpose, in behalf of America, and what that authority is, and to hear such propositions as he shall think fit to make respecting the same." John Adams speculated in a letter to his wife as to why he was chosen for this, his first diplomatic assignment, and later in his *Autobiography,* he described some of the entertaining and dramatic details of the fruitless mission. It has been necessary to transpose some passages in order to place developments in chronological order.

Autobiography, 1802–7

Philadelphia, Fryday September 6, 1776. I can think of but one Reason for their putting me, upon this Embassy, and that is this. An Idea has crept into many minds here, that his Lordship is such another Mr. Hutchinson: and they may possibly think, that a Man who has been accustomed to Penetrate into the mazy Windings of Hutchinsons heart, and the serpentine Wiles of his head, may be tolerably qualified to converse with his Lordship.

Monday September 9, 1776. Resolved, that in all Continental Commissions, and other Instruments where heretofore the Words, "United Colonies," have been used, the Stile be altered for the future to the United States.

The Board of War brought in a report, which was read.

On this day, Mr. Franklin, Mr. Edward Rutledge and Mr. John Adams proceeded on their Journey to Lord Howe on Staten Island, the two former in Chairs and the last on Horseback; the first night We lodged at an Inn, in New Brunswick. On the Road and at all the public Houses, We saw such Numbers of Officers and Soldiers, straggling and loytering, as gave me at least, but a poor Opinion of the Discipline of our forces and excited as much indignation as anxiety. Such thoughtless dissipation at a time so critical, was not calculated to inspire very sanguine hopes or give great Courage to Ambassadors: I was nevertheless determined that it should not dishearten me. I saw that We must and had no doubt but We should be chastised into order in time.

The Taverns were so full We could with difficulty obtain Entertainment. At Brunswick, but one bed could be procured for Dr. Franklin and me, in a Chamber little larger than the bed, without a Chimney and with only one small Window. The Window was open, and I, who was an invalid and afraid of the Air in the night [blowing upon me], shut it close. Oh! says Franklin dont shut the Window. We shall be suffocated. I answered I was afraid of the Evening Air. Dr. Franklin replied, the Air within this Chamber will soon be, and indeed is now worse than that without Doors: come! open the Window and come to bed, and I will convince you: I believe you are not acquainted with my Theory of Colds. Opening the Window and leaping into Bed, I said I had read his Letters to

The Declaration of Independence as it was first printed in July, 1776

A 1776 broadside of John Adams's
plan for a military establishment

Dr. Cooper in which he had advanced, that Nobody ever
got cold by going into a cold Church, or any other cold
Air: but the Theory was so little consistent with my experience, that I thought it a Paradox: However I had so
much curiosity to hear his reasons, that I would run the
risque of a cold. The Doctor then began an harrangue,
upon Air and cold and Respiration and Perspiration, with
which I was so much amused that I soon fell asleep, and
left him and his Philosophy together. . . .

The next Morning We proceeded on our Journey.

Lord How had sent over an Officer as an Hostage for
our Security. I said to Dr. Franklin, it would be childish
in Us to depend upon such a Pledge and insisted on taking
him over with Us, and keeping our Surety on the same
side of the Water with Us. My Colleagues exulted in the
Proposition and agreed to it instantly. We told the Officer,
if he held himself under our direction he must go back
with Us. He bowed Assent, and We all embarked in his
Lordships Barge. As We approached the Shore his Lordship, observing Us, came down to the Waters Edge to
receive Us, and looking at the Officer, he said, Gentlemen, you make me a very high Compliment, and you may
depend upon it, I will consider it as the most sacred of
Things. We walked up to the House between Lines of
Guards of Grenadiers, looking as fierce as ten furies, and
making all the Grimaces and Gestures and motions of
their Musquets with Bayonets fixed, which I suppose
military Ettiquette requires but which We neither understood nor regarded.

The House had been the Habitation of military Guards,
and was as dirty as a stable: but his Lordship had prepared a large handsome Room, by spreading a Carpet
of Moss and green Spriggs from Bushes and Shrubbs in
the Neighbourhood, till he had made it not only wholesome but romantically elegant, and he entertained Us
with good Claret, good Bread, cold Ham, Tongues and
Mutton. . . .

Lord How was profuse in his Expressions of Gratitude
to the State of Massachusetts, for erecting a marble
Monument in Westminster Abbey to his Elder Brother
Lord How who was killed in America in the last French
War, saying "he esteemed that Honour to his Family,
above all Things in this World. That such was his grati-

tude and affection to this Country, on that Account, that he felt for America, as for a Brother, and if America should fall, he should feel and lament it, like the Loss of a Brother." Dr. Franklin, with an easy Air and a collected Countenance, a Bow, a Smile and all that Naivetee which sometimes appeared in his Conversation and is often observed in his Writings, replied "My Lord, We will do our Utmost Endeavours, to save your Lordship that mortification." His Lordship appeared to feel this, with more Sensibility, than I could expect: but he only returned "I suppose you will endeavour to give Us employment in Europe." To this Observation, not a Word nor a look from which he could draw any Inference, escaped any of the Committee....

The Billop House on Staten Island, where the committee met Howe

Tho' he could not treat with Us as a Committee of Congress, yet, as his Powers enabled him to confer and consult with any private Gentlemen of Influence in the Colonies, on the means of restoring Peace, between the two Countries, he was glad of this Opportunity of conferring with Us, on that Subject, if We thought ourselves at Liberty to enter into a Conference with him in that Character. We observed to his Lordship, that, as our Business was to hear, he might consider Us, in what Light he pleased, and communicate to Us, any propositions he might be authorised to make, for the purpose mentioned; but that We could consider Ourselves in no other Character than that, in which We were placed, by order of Congress....

British cartoon, with play on names, of a conference between the Howe brothers, HOW to get Rich

When his Lordship observed to Us, that he could not confer with Us as Members of Congress, or public Characters, but only as private Persons and British Subjects, Mr. John Adams answered somewhat quickly, "Your Lordship may consider me, in what light you please; and indeed I should be willing to consider myself, for a few moments, in any Character which would be agreable to your Lordship, *except that of a British Subject.*" His Lordship at these Words turn'd to Dr. Franklin and Mr. Rutledge and said "Mr. Adams is a decided Character:" with so much gravity and solemnity: that I now believe it meant more, than either of my Colleagues or myself understood at the time....

His Lordship then entered into a discourse of considerable

Length, which contained no explicit proposition of Peace, except one, namely, That the Colonies should return to their Allegiance and Obedience to the Government of Great Britain. The rest consisted principally of Assurances, that there was an exceeding good disposition in the King and his Ministers, to make that Government easy to Us, with intimations, that, in case of our Submission, they would cause the Offensive Acts of Parliament to be revised, and the Instructions to Ministers to be reconsidered; that so, if any just causes of complaint were found in the Acts, or any Errors in Government were perceived to have crept into the Instructions, they might be amended or withdrawn.

We gave it, as our Opinion to his Lordship, that a return to the domination of Great Britain, was not now to be expected. We mentioned the repeated humble petitions of the Colonies to the King and Parliament, which had been treated with Contempt, and answered only by additional Injuries; the Unexampled Patience We had shewn, under their tyrannical Government, and that it was not till the late Act of Parliament, which denounced War against Us, and put Us out of the Kings Protection, that We declared our Independence; that this declaration had been called for, by the People of the Colonies in general; that every colony had approved of it, when made, and all now considered themselves as independent States, and were settling or had settled their Governments accordingly; so that it was not in the Power of Congress to agree for them, that they should return to their former dependent State; that there was no doubt of their Inclination for peace, and their Willingness to enter into a treaty with Britain, that might be advantageous to both Countries; that, though his Lordship had at present, no power to treat with them as independent States, he might, if there was the same good disposition in Britain, much sooner obtain fresh Powers from thence, for that purpose, than powers could be obtained by Congress, from the several Colonies to consent to a Submission.

His Lordship then saying, that he was sorry to find, that no Accommodation was like to take place, put an End to the Conference.

In our report to Congress We supposed that the Commissioners, Lord and General Howe, had by their Com-

Declaration issued by the brothers Howe, Staten Island, July 14, 1776, offering pardons to those colonists who returned to "their Duty"

John Adams's letter to Abigail on July 3, 1776, predicts that "The Second Day of July 1776, will be the most memorable Epocha, in the History of America." As it turned out, country celebrated the fourth.

mission Power to [except] from Pardon all that they should think proper. But I was informed in England, afterwards, that a Number were expressly excepted by Name from Pardon, by the privy Council, and that John Adams was one of them, and that this List of Exceptions was given as an Instruction to the two Howes, with their Commission. When I was afterwards a Minister Plenipotentiary, at the Court of St. James's The King and the Ministry, were often insulted, ridiculed and reproached in the Newspapers, for having conducted with so much folly as to be reduced to the humiliating Necessity of receiving as an Ambassador a Man who stood recorded by the privy Council as a Rebell expressly excepted from Pardon. If this is true it will acount for his Lordships gloomy denunciation of me, as "a decided Character." — Some years afterwards, when I resided in England as a public Minister, his Lordship recollected and alluded to this Conversation with great politeness and much good humour. Att the Ball, on the Queens Birthnight, I was at a Loss for the Seats assigned to the foreign Ambassadors and their Ladies. Fortunately meeting Lord How at the Door I asked his Lordship, where were the Ambassadors Seats. His Lordship with his usual politeness, and an unusual Smile of good humour, pointed to the Seats, and manifestly alluding to the Conversation on Staten Island said, "Aye! Now, We must turn you away among the foreigners."

Independence was saved by the failure of the conference on Staten Island. John Adams's thoughts on the independence of the United States were summed up in two letters to his wife, both written on July 3, 1776. In these letters he may be pardoned for supposing that future generations of Americans would celebrate the independence of their country on the second of July, the day Congress approved the resolution of independence, instead of the fourth, the day on which Congress voted to approve the revised text of the Declaration of Independence, the document as we know it today.

Philadelphia July 3. 1776
When I look back to the Year 1761, and recollect the Argument concerning Writs of Assistance, in the Superiour Court, which I have hitherto considered as the Commencement of the Controversy, between Great Britain and America, and run through the whole Period from

When John was still in Philadelphia, Abigail wrote to tell him of the probable loss of a child she was carrying, poignantly signed "Yours, Yours." The baby was stillborn.

that Time to this, and recollect the series of political Events, the Chain of Causes and Effects, I am surprized at the Suddenness, as well as Greatness of this Revolution. Britain has been fill'd with Folly, and America with Wisdom, at least this is my Judgment. — Time must determine. It is the Will of Heaven, that the two Countries should be sundered forever. It may be the Will of Heaven that America shall suffer Calamities still more wasting and Distresses yet more dreadfull. If this is to be the Case, it will have this good Effect, at least: it will inspire Us with many Virtues, which We have not, and correct many Errors, Follies, and Vices, which threaten to disturb, dishonour, and destroy Us. — The Furnace of Affliction produces Refinement, in States as well as Individuals. And the new Governments we are assuming, in every Part, will require a Purification from our Vices, and an Augmentation of our Virtues or they will be no Blessings. The People will have unbounded Power. And the People are extreamly addicted to Corruption and Venality, as well as the Great. — I am not without Apprehensions from this Quarter. But I must submit all my Hopes and Fears, to an overruling Providence, in which, unfashionable as the Faith may be, I firmly believe.

Philadelphia July 3d. 1776

But the Day is past. The Second Day of July 1776, will be the most memorable Epocha, in the History of America. — I am apt to believe that it will be celebrated, by succeeding Generations, as the great anniversary Festival. It ought to be commemorated, as the Day of Deliverance by solemn Acts of Devotion to God Almighty. It ought to be solemnized with Pomp and Parade, with Shews, Games, Sports, Guns, Bells, Bonfires and Illuminations from one End of this Continent to the other from this Time forward forever more.

You will think me transported with Enthusiasm but I am not. — I am well aware of the Toil and Blood and Treasure, that it will cost Us to maintain this Declaration, and support and defend these States. — Yet through all the Gloom I can see the Rays of ravishing Light and Glory. I can see that the End is more than worth all the Means. And that Posterity will tryumph in that Days Transaction, even altho We should rue it, which I trust in God We shall not.

Rector of the Parish of
Chaplain to the Brig

If you preserve this
you, to procure the
you will find it fa
the Statesman, the
torian and the Pl
Something of the P
I am with much

Mr. J. Q. Adams